Praise for *Presidential Leadership in Crisis* (?)

"Having dealt with crisis in the White House or two on my own, I appreciate Ken Walsh's informative review of how presidents respond to something nearly inevitable in their tenures: dealing with all the things that disrupt and challenge the normal course of business. Crisis and dealing with it might be a new normal for presidents, but it requires the best and smartest efforts of our nation's chief executive."
—**Mike McCurry**, White House Press Secretary (1995–98) and Director/Professor, Center for Public Theology, Wesley Theological Seminary

"Ken Walsh nails it again as an award winning journalist and an astute student of presidents and the presidency. Ken provides valuable presidential leadership lessons especially in times of crisis."
—**Kenneth M. Duberstein**, White House Chief of Staff (1988–89)

"For those who write about politics, direct experience matters, and so does a knowledge of history. Ken Walsh has an unusual amount of both, which is why he has been able to offer such an insightful account of crises that American presidents from Lincoln to Trump have faced. Incoming presidents would do well to read this book before they take office."
—**William A. Galston**, Senior Fellow, The Brookings Institution

"It has been said that only the 'big things' (war and peace, economic downturns, terrorist attacks) go directly to the president. Lesser matters are handled at lower levels. In this highly readable book, Ken Walsh, one of the nation's shrewdest observers of presidents and the presidency, takes readers on a tour of how fourteen presidents resolved crises that came their way and how a fifteenth, Donald Trump—who regards crises as the norm rather than the exception—has incorporated them into his management style. Anyone interested in how power is exercised will come away enriched by tales Walsh tells of both success and failure at the highest level of the American government."
—**Alvin S. Felzenberg**, author of *The Leaders We Deserved (and Some We Didn't): Rethinking the Presidential Rating Game* and *A Man and His Presidents: The Political Biography of William F. Buckley, Jr.*

PRESIDENTIAL LEADERSHIP IN CRISIS

Crises pose a challenge to leaders beyond any other tests they confront. In this comprehensive and timely book, veteran journalist Kenneth T. Walsh offers a probing look at how presidents from Franklin D. Roosevelt to Donald Trump dealt with crises they faced. Including domestic as well as international issues and assassination attempts, this book stands apart from other accounts of presidents in crisis. Walsh is in search of lessons we can learn, and his findings focus on the presidential attributes and skills that matter most in trying times. This expertly crafted, elegantly written book is appropriate for a variety of college courses and will find its way onto the reading lists of ambitious politicians and interested citizens alike.

Kenneth T. Walsh is a contributor and White House and political analyst for *U.S. News & World Report*. He has covered the White House since 1986, including the presidencies of Ronald Reagan, George H.W. Bush, Bill Clinton, George W. Bush, Barack Obama and Donald Trump. He is also an adjunct professorial lecturer at American University in Washington, D.C.

ALSO BY KENNETH T. WALSH

Ultimate Insiders: White House Photographers and How They Shape History (2018)

Celebrity in Chief: A History of the Presidents and the Culture of Stardom (2015; 2017)

Prisoners of the White House: The Isolation of America's Presidents and the Crisis of Leadership (2013)

Family of Freedom: Presidents and African Americans in the White House (2011)

From Mount Vernon to Crawford: A History of the Presidents and Their Retreats (2005)

Air Force One: A History of the Presidents and Their Planes (2003)

Ronald Reagan: Biography (1997)

Feeding the Beast: The White House Versus the Press (1996)

PRESIDENTIAL LEADERSHIP IN CRISIS

DEFINING MOMENTS OF THE MODERN PRESIDENTS FROM FRANKLIN ROOSEVELT TO DONALD TRUMP

KENNETH T. WALSH

NEW YORK AND LONDON

First published 2020
by Routledge
52 Vanderbilt Avenue, New York, NY 10017

and by Routledge
2 Park Square, Milton Park, Abingdon, Oxon, OX14 4RN

Routledge is an imprint of the Taylor & Francis Group, an informa business

© 2020 Taylor & Francis

The right of Kenneth T. Walsh to be identified as author of this work has been asserted by him in accordance with sections 77 and 78 of the Copyright, Designs and Patents Act 1988.

All rights reserved. No part of this book may be reprinted or reproduced or utilised in any form or by any electronic, mechanical, or other means, now known or hereafter invented, including photocopying and recording, or in any information storage or retrieval system, without permission in writing from the publishers.

Trademark notice: Product or corporate names may be trademarks or registered trademarks, and are used only for identification and explanation without intent to infringe.

Library of Congress Cataloging-in-Publication Data
Names: Walsh, Kenneth T., author.
Title: Presidential leadership in crisis : defining moments of the modern presidents from Franklin Roosevelt to Donald Trump / Kenneth T. Walsh.
Description: New York, NY : Routledge, 2020. | Includes bibliographical references and index.
Identifiers: LCCN 2019043742
Subjects: LCSH: Presidents—United States—History—20th century. | Presidents—United States—History—21st century. | Political leadership—United States. | Crisis management—United States.
Classification: LCC E176.1 .W2858 2020 | DDC 973.09/9—dc23
LC record available at https://lccn.loc.gov/2019043742

ISBN: 978-0-367-42950-8 (hbk)
ISBN: 978-0-367-42949-2 (pbk)
ISBN: 978-1-003-00034-1 (ebk)

Typeset in Galliard
by Apex CoVantage, LLC

For Barclay and Gloria

CONTENTS

About the Author xi
Preface xiii
Acknowledgments xv

Introduction		1
Chapter One	Abraham Lincoln: The Nation's Worst Crisis	7
Chapter Two	Franklin D. Roosevelt: The Great Depression	17
Chapter Three	Harry Truman: The Battle with Douglas MacArthur	35
Chapter Four	Dwight Eisenhower: The U-2 Mission	49
Chapter Five	John F. Kennedy: The Cuban Missile Crisis	59
Chapter Six	Lyndon B. Johnson: The War in Vietnam and Re-election	75
Chapter Seven	Richard M. Nixon: The Watergate Scandal and National Disgrace	85
Chapter Eight	Gerald R. Ford: The Pardon	99
Chapter Nine	Jimmy Carter: The Iranian Hostage Crisis	107
Chapter Ten	Ronald Reagan: A Matter of Life and Death	119

Chapter Eleven	George H.W. Bush: The Persian Gulf War	133
Chapter Twelve	Bill Clinton: Impeachment and Scandal	149
Chapter Thirteen	George W. Bush: 9/11 and the Global War on Terror	161
Chapter Fourteen	Barack Obama: Ending the "Great Recession"	173
Chapter Fifteen	Donald Trump: A New Era of Perpetual Crisis	189
Epilogue		217
Selected Readings		*231*
Index		*237*

ABOUT THE AUTHOR

Kenneth T. Walsh is a contributor and longtime White House and political analyst for *U.S. News & World Report*. He covered the White House for three decades starting in 1986, including the presidencies of Ronald Reagan, George H.W. Bush, Bill Clinton, George W. Bush, Barack Obama and Donald Trump. He is one of the longest-serving White House correspondents in history. This is his ninth book about the U.S. presidency. His other titles include *Air Force One: A History of the Presidents and Their Planes, Celebrity in Chief: A History of the Presidents and the Culture of Stardom* and *Ultimate Insiders: White House Photographers and How They Shape History*. Walsh is former president of the White House Correspondents' Association, and he has won the most prestigious awards for White House coverage. He frequently serves as an analyst on television and radio, and gives many speeches around the country and abroad. He is an adjunct professorial lecturer at American University in Washington, D.C. He and his wife, Barclay Walsh, live in Bethesda, Maryland, and Shady Side, Maryland. They have two children, Jean and Chris.

Preface

The customary historical analysis of presidents in crisis focuses only on international affairs and matters of war and peace. But the modern presidents are expected to navigate through many other types of emergency situations—a fact this book recognizes by discussing a diverse array of crises that presidents must deal with today.

I have developed specific standards for assessing presidential leadership in crisis based on several factors: research for this book, earlier research for my eight other books on the presidency, my experience as White House correspondent for *U.S. News & World Report* since 1986, and the excellent work done by other historians on the presidency.

I hope this book will help the general public as well as students and teachers of history and politics to better comprehend what it's like for presidents to make momentous decisions under great pressure and with enormous stakes. I would be gratified if my analysis also contributes to public understanding of the techniques that tend to work and those that tend to fail under crisis conditions.

And I hope this book will deepen public understanding of each of the modern presidents as individuals and illuminate the leadership skills of each one.

Kenneth T. Walsh
Bethesda, Maryland

Acknowledgments

There are many people I'd like to thank for their assistance and support in writing this book.

At the top of the list are the staff members at the presidential libraries—facilities that have become invaluable to scholars and anyone interested in presidential history.

Also, thanks to a host of individuals who have helped to shape my thinking about presidents in crisis. They include, of course, the first five presidents whom I covered since I began as a White House correspondent in 1986: Ronald Reagan, George H.W. Bush, Bill Clinton, George W. Bush and Barack Obama. I interviewed all of them repeatedly and got to know them well. Among the others I'd like to thank are brilliant scholars and former presidential and political strategists who offered many insights over a period of three decades and, in many cases, specifically for this book, such as David Axelrod, Howard Baker, Ross Baker, Dan Bartlett, Cornell Belcher, Doug Brinkley, Bob Dallek, Dave Demarest, Frank Donatelli, Ken Duberstein, Rahm Emanuel, Al Felzenberg, Marlin Fitzwater, Don Foley, Bill Galston, Geoff Garin, David Gergen, Ed Gillespie, Stan Greenberg, Steve Hadley, Jane Hall, Karen Hughes, Bill Kristol, Joe Lockhart, Frank Luntz, Kevin Madden, Mary Matalin, Mike McCurry, Bill McInturff, Mack McLarty, Leon Panetta, Dana Perino, Roman Popadiuk, Colin Powell, Karl Rove, Bob Rubin, Brent Scowcroft, Leonard Steinhorn, Larry Summers and Sheila Tate.

Thanks also to my colleagues and competitors in journalism. I learned much from them.

Thanks to Jennifer Knerr, my long-time editor at Routledge, for her wise counsel and encouragement.

Most of all, I would like to express my appreciation to Barclay Walsh, my wife and life partner, for her help in preparing this book. Barclay is a professional researcher of great talent. Her fact-finding skills were invaluable, as was her assistance in editing the manuscript, locating photographs and providing unstinting support for the project from the beginning. Barclay improved this book in many ways, and I will always be grateful.

Introduction

All modern U.S. presidents have faced at least one major crisis during their terms in office. These were sudden events or a series of defining moments that required decisions of the utmost importance—made under great pressure—and that had far-reaching consequences for the world, the nation, and the presidents themselves.

Crisis management has become a key part of the modern presidency, central to the job and a reflection of our turbulent, dangerous times. And the public has very high expectations for the presidents during such episodes. The presidents who measure up and navigate a major crisis to a positive outcome are often hailed as heroes or historically important figures. Those who fail to meet public expectations and rise to the occasion often see their approval ratings plummet, their credibility shattered and their political standing shredded.

I have found that five qualities are most important in presidential crisis management:

- Taking action.
- Adapting to changing circumstances.
- Balancing principle with what works.
- Persevering.
- An instinct for achieving success—the most important quality of all.

But it's important to realize that leadership in a crisis can't be boiled down to a single set of standards. As retired Gen. Stanley McChrystal has said,

> We tend to . . . assume leadership follows a specific, replicable formula. The truth is, it doesn't work that way. Leadership is not just one individual dictating action and achieving results, but rather a process that involves leaders and followers working in a system that is very dependent on situation and context.[1]

Each president must lead during his or her own time and under circumstances that often change dramatically. My goal is to show that some qualities are most helpful to leaders in crisis, with the understanding that no set of standards applies to every president at every defining moment.

There are four types of crisis I will examine in this book: national security, economic, political and personal.

In each case, my goal is to describe the strengths and weaknesses of each president and illuminate the leadership traits that tend to be most effective when the nation's top official is dealing with an emergency.

THE STAKES for a president in a crisis often are very high. A Chief Executive's decisions can cost lives, damage the country and jeopardize an administration's popularity if the crisis is handled badly, or enhance a president's popularity and increase his influence if the crisis is handled well.

I focus on all 14 of the modern presidents—from Franklin D. Roosevelt to Donald Trump—and examine one crisis for each of them, except for Trump, who is given more attention on a wider front. His presidency is still so new that his crisis management skills haven't been thoroughly examined in a historical context, which I undertake in this book for the first time. As the Trump era proceeds and the 2020 presidential campaign moves into high gear, I give special attention to how Trump is shattering presidential norms day after day as he lurches from one crisis to another, many of his own making.

I have also included an analysis of Abraham Lincoln's leadership under crisis conditions. Lincoln was not a modern president—he served in office more than 150 years ago, prior to the rise of the United States as a superpower, and prior to the emergence of the communications culture that pervades the nation today. But Lincoln's ability to handle the worst crisis in American history—the Civil War—provides enduring lessons in leadership for all his successors.

In all cases, my goal is to show how presidential leadership succeeds or fails under extreme circumstances and how such leadership, or lack of it, can define an era. Just as important, I aim to illuminate the presidents as individuals and provide insights into their character, values, talents, judgment and ability to grow in office as seen through the prism of crisis management.

THERE HAS always been a duality in the American character—a tension between what Lincoln called the "better angels" of our nature and the dark side. The United States is diverse in so many ways that different forces take over the country's psyche and politics at different times and raise varied expectations for each president. In recent years, the country has gone from the administrative competence, calm decency and liberalism of Barack Obama to the chaotic style, blustery arrogance and quasi-conservatism of Donald Trump. One can scarcely imagine two more different people serving in the Oval Office. The fact that each man was elected within a four-year span shows how Americans change their minds about what kind of leadership they want, depending on conditions in the nation and the circumstances in their own lives.

THERE WERE, of course, many crises from which to choose. I have selected some episodes that have been examined frequently by other historians because these situations were so consequential. I also selected crises that were pivotal but have not received enough attention in the past.

National security remains a bedrock concern central to the success or failure of any presidency. Other make-or-break situations include preserving the health of the economy, resolving a political crisis and overcoming a personal crisis such as a scandal or an assassination attempt. These crucibles can be just as important as national security episodes in determining a president's effectiveness and political survival, in shaping a president's reputation, deciding a leader's place in history, and revealing the strengths and weaknesses of these leaders as individuals. This book shows the amazing depth and breadth of decisions that face any modern president.

In the current era of a showman-as-president, moments of truth have taken on an even broader definition. This is because Donald Trump is upending so many traditions and norms in Washington and international relations. He has been intent on disrupting the status quo and forcing the nation to consider new standards for assessing whether he has been a success, a failure or, like most presidents, something in between.

AMERICANS TEND to want strong, decisive action from a president in a crisis. Historian Julian Zelizer of Princeton says great presidents build things.

> They push grand legislation; they help the nation to reach difficult agreements; they push members of their party to go beyond their political comfort level, and they put forth bold ideas that transform the way we think of problems.[2]

Historian Doris Kearns Goodwin adds that several traits are commonly recognized by historians as vital to leadership, both during a crisis and in less turbulent times: "humility, acknowledging errors, shouldering blame and learning from mistakes, empathy, resilience, collaboration, connecting with people and controlling unproductive emotions."[3]

Historian Robert Dallek says the standards he uses to evaluate presidents in crisis are vision, pragmatism, tactical politics, charisma (in today's era of instant communication), credibility and trust.[4]

"Americans want assurance that there is someone in charge and that the president has a plan," historian Al Felzenberg told me. " . . . and that he assures them they will be safe and that the nation will pull out of it . . . and he will pull us through it . . . It's important for the president to be calm and collected." Otherwise, the president could make things worse by panicking people or increasing their fears about the future.[5]

Felzenberg points to Roosevelt's initial response to the Depression when he took over as president in March 1933 and moved forward dramatically during his first 100 days in office. FDR's famous inaugural speech noted that the nation had nothing to fear but fear itself—an important point to make in those desperate times. To communicate directly with the country, Roosevelt use periodic "fireside chats"—folky radio speeches that were broadcast live directly into American homes—as if he were talking to middle-class neighbors in their living rooms. It was very reassuring.

"We have seen people who inject fear" during times of duress, Felzenberg said, referring to Donald Trump, but FDR offered hope. In another contrast to Trump, Ronald Reagan also offered hope. Building on these qualities, both Roosevelt and Reagan, the Democrat and the Republican, became excellent crisis managers and leaders. These are historical lessons worth remembering.

Notes

1. Interview with Stanley McChrystal conducted by Portfolio/Penguin, October 23, 2018, mcchrystalgroup.com.
2. Julian Zelizer, "The Trump Shutdown Is Fitting," CNN, December 22, 2018, cnn.com/2018/12/22/opinions/trump-shutdown-is-fitting-zelizer/index/html?
3. James B. Stewart, "Why Trump's Unusual Leadership Style Isn't Working in the White House," *The New York Times*, January 10, 2019, nytimes.com/2019/01/10/business/trump-staff-turnover-leadership-html
4. Author's interview with Robert Dallek, January 17, 2019.
5. Author's interview with Al Felzenberg, December 7, 2018.

CHAPTER ONE
ABRAHAM LINCOLN
THE NATION'S WORST CRISIS

Abraham Lincoln met with Gen. George McClellan in October 1862 after the battle of Antietam. Recognizing the need for bold military action, Lincoln urged McClellan to be more aggressive in pursuing the Confederacy's Army of Northern Virginia. McClellan balked and Lincoln eventually fired him—an example of Lincoln's strength, resolve and flexibility during trying times. (Library of Congress)

Although this book focuses on the 14 modern presidents, one additional commander in chief must be included in the analysis—Abraham Lincoln. He managed the worst crisis in U.S. history and is generally regarded by historians as among the best U.S. presidents and probably the greatest of them all.[1]

Of course, Lincoln was not a truly "modern" president. He was in office long before the era of the mass media that dominate today's politics and culture. And it's doubtful that he could even be elected today: his homely appearance, high-minded rhetoric and insistence on explaining issues in depth would not be widely appealing in a world where good looks, sustained personal attacks and over-simplification are central to national life, especially when it comes to elections and governing. He also served before the United States became a world leader, which vastly complicated the modern president's job and may not have been a good fit for a man so steeped in domestic affairs.

But many of Lincoln's leadership skills have stood the test of time, and his success in managing the nation's ultimate crisis can still be instructive. He was, of course, president during the Civil War, which threatened the very existence of the Union and became a test of the nation's fundamental values, notably its commitment to ending slavery and promoting social justice. His ability to end this calamity makes his crisis-management abilities of enduring importance.

What helped him succeed was, most of all, his vision: he was devoted to principle in setting goals but was flexible in finding the means to achieve those goals. He showed perseverance despite adversity. He demonstrated empathy even to his opponents. And he had the ability to explain his ideas in ways that the public could understand—in other words, he was a skilled communicator for his era, mid-nineteenth-century America. Lincoln summarized his approach to crisis management in a message to Congress on December 1, 1862, as the Civil War raged:

> The dogmas of the quiet past are inadequate to the stormy present. The occasion is piled high with difficulty, and we must rise—with the occasion. As our case is new, so we must think anew, and act anew. We must disenthrall ourselves, and then we shall save our country.[2]

Michael Burlingame, professor emeritus of history at Connecticut College, wrote

> His great achievement, historians tell us, was his ability to energize and mobilize the nation by appealing to its best ideals while acting

"with malice towards none" in the pursuit of a more perfect, more just, and more enduring Union . . . No President in American history ever faced a greater crisis and no President ever accomplished as much.[3]

He succeeded in preserving the Union and ending slavery—his two overriding goals. "Because he understood that victory in both great causes depended upon purposeful and visionary presidential leadership as well as the exercise of politically acceptable means, he left as his legacy a United States that was both whole and free," Burlingame noted.[4]

Historian Jean Edward Smith wrote,

> When Gen. P.G.T. de Beauregard fired on Fort Sumter in April 1861 [the act that officially started the Civil War], Lincoln was as green as any recruit. The United States regular Army numbered only 16,000 men, and a third of the officer corps, including a disproportionate number of high-ranking officers, were from the South. Lincoln was not necessarily left with the dregs of the service, but he had to fashion an army almost from scratch.[5]

After the fall of Fort Sumter to the rebels, Smith noted that Lincoln faced the ultimate American crisis when the governments of 11 Southern states tried to secede in 1861. "[O]ne man, Abraham Lincoln, stood in the way. It was his wise use of the war powers . . . that preserved the Union," Smith noted.[6]

Lincoln at first deferred to his generals, but he became a rigorous student of military history and tactics, and he eventually emerged as a self-taught commander in chief. Relatively early in the conflict, he concluded that the Union Army's senior officers didn't have the will or the skills to destroy the rebellion. As a result, Lincoln took a more direct military role as the war dragged on. He was disappointed with one senior commander after another, including Nathaniel P. Banks, Benjamin Butler and Lew Wallace, and he replaced them. He complained that General George McClellan, his most important commander and the man with whom Lincoln was probably the most disappointed, had the "slows" and was unwilling to commit his army to unrelenting pressure against the Southerners.[7] Lincoln gave McClellan a chance to lead, fired him, re-hired him and then fired him again.

"Not until the president discovered Ulysses S. Grant, and not until Grant came to Washington as general in chief in early 1864, did Lincoln have a leader ready to end the rebellion by destroying the Confederacy's ability to resist," observed historian Smith.[8]

Following the president's lead, Grant told Gen. George Meade, one of his subordinates, in April 1864, "Lee's army will be your objective point. Wherever Lee goes, there you will go also."[9] This was precisely what Lincoln wanted. The president realized he had finally found a fighting commander, a general who would relentlessly pursue the Confederate armies and destroy them rather than simply occupy enemy territory or disrupt their supply lines. Grant wanted to absolutely crush the Confederate military, and he proceeded inexorably to do so.

HISTORIAN DORIS KEARNS GOODWIN said, "Lincoln surrounded himself with people, including his rivals, who had strong egos and high ambitions; who felt free to question his authority; and who were unafraid to argue with him."[10] Among them were Treasury Secretary Salmon Chase and Secretary of War Edwin Stanton. This exposed the president to many diverse viewpoints and gave him many options from which to choose. Goodwin added,

> But you have to remember, the idea is not just to put your rivals in power—the point is that you must choose the best and most able people in the country, for the good of the country. Lincoln came to power when the nation was in peril, and he had the intelligence, and the self-confidence, to know that he needed the best people by his side, people who were leaders in their own right and who were very aware of their own strengths. That's an important insight, whether you're the leader of a country or the CEO of a company.[11]

Lincoln shared credit with members of his team when there were successes, and he shared responsibility when there were mistakes by others, which made his advisers and supporters very loyal to him. This is alien to Donald Trump, who regularly takes all the credit for successes and blames others—not himself—for mistakes.

The most effective presidents were able to connect to the public through the media of the times, whether that's through radio as with Franklin D. Roosevelt, or television as with John F. Kennedy and Ronald Reagan, and Twitter with Donald Trump. In Lincoln's case, he used carefully crafted speeches that were widely publicized in the newspapers and impressed Americans with their clarity and vision.

LINCOLN'S RESOLVE and perseverance went far beyond helping him cope with the vicissitudes of the war. These traits also helped him deal with a profound personal loss while he was president. He and his wife, Mary Todd Lincoln, suffered immense pain when their beloved 11-year-old son Willie died of a severe fever on February 20, 1862.

Mary Todd's grief was so intense that she tried to communicate with Willie in the afterlife by participating in seances or spirit circles run by self-styled mediums. The president didn't believe in such supernatural contacts, but he went along with it because they seemed in a small way to relieve his wife's emotional pain.

But his personal and political woes caused Lincoln to regularly descend into what his friends called melancholy throughout his presidency—today we would call it depression.

All this trauma makes the level-headed, steady leadership displayed by President Lincoln in fulfilling his duties and prosecuting the war all the more impressive.

IN THE END, Lincoln's approach led to success. With Grant in charge of military operations and with new successes in the field, Lincoln was re-elected in November 1864. The president told a visitor to the White House in early 1865, "Grant has the bear by the hind leg" and was proceeding to bring about the final destruction of the Confederacy.[12]

The Confederates evacuated Richmond, their capital, on April 2. Two days later Lincoln walked through the streets of Richmond with an escort of only ten sailors, while thousands of former slaves pressed close to see the man they considered their savior. A week later, the rebel Army of Northern Virginia under the fabled General Robert E. Lee surrendered at Appomattox.[13]

Finding a Moral Cause

When the Civil War erupted, Lincoln at first argued that the struggle was about preserving the Union and not about slavery. He avoided issuing an anti-slavery proclamation immediately despite being urged to do so by abolitionists and radical Republicans. But he came to believe that ending slavery was a profound moral cause—adding to his sense of vision—and on September 22, 1862, Lincoln issued a preliminary Emancipation Proclamation. This set a date for the freedom of more than 3 million black slaves in the United States and redefined the Civil War as a fight against bondage.[14]

On January 1, 1863, Lincoln issued the final Emancipation Proclamation, which declared "that all persons held as slaves" within the rebel states "are, and henceforward shall be free." The proclamation also called for the recruitment and establishment of black military units among the Union forces.

About 180,000 African Americans eventually served in the Union army during the Civil War, and another 18,000 served in the navy.

After the proclamation was issued, any nation supporting the Confederacy was considered to be favoring slavery, Burlingame wrote, adding:

> It became impossible for anti-slavery nations such as Great Britain and France, who had been friendly to the Confederacy, to get involved on behalf of the South. The proclamation also unified and strengthened Lincoln's party, the Republicans, helping them stay in power for the next two decades.[15]

The proclamation was a presidential order, not a law passed by Congress. After this bold stroke, Lincoln pushed for an anti-slavery amendment to the U.S. Constitution to make sure it would be permanent. With the passage of the 13th Amendment in 1865, slavery was eliminated throughout the country, although African Americans would face another century of discrimination before they gained equal rights under federal law.

"As the most activist president in history, Lincoln transformed the President's role as commander in chief and as chief executive into a powerful new position, making the President supreme over both Congress and the courts," Burlingame said.

> His activism began almost immediately with Fort Sumter when he called out state militias, expanded the army and navy, spent $2 million without congressional appropriation, blockaded Southern ports, closed post offices to treasonable correspondences, suspended the writ of habeas corpus in several locations, ordered the arrest and military detention of suspected traitors, and issued the Emancipation Proclamation on New Year's Day 1863.[16]

Lincoln strained and broke the legal norms of his day, arguing that the Civil War justified his taking extraordinary powers in order to save the Union. He led the fight against the South without a declaration of war. He thwarted opposition by the Supreme Court, arguing that the president was the final arbiter of the Constitution, especially in wartime. Lincoln said it made no sense "to lose the nation and yet preserve the Constitution." He adopted a theory of "unilateral action," arguing that he was elected by the people to determine when an emergency existed that justified his assuming extraordinary powers, not subordinate to Congress or the courts. He said the Civil War was such a crisis.[17]

Presidential use of executive authority eroded during the four decades after Lincoln's assassination in 1865, as Congress and the courts reasserted their own authority. But during his term, he preserved the Union and ended slavery, two permanent accomplishments of historic importance.

"What Lincoln had, it seems to me, was an extraordinary amount of emotional intelligence," Goodwin said.

> He was able to acknowledge his errors and learn from his mistakes to a remarkable degree. He was careful to put past hurts behind him and never allowed wounds to fester . . . . In times of crisis, things become possible that wouldn't be possible in ordinary times. The way the U.S. government is set up, with so many checks and balances, means that it almost takes a deep crisis to move forward. So there are only certain moments in history when great change can take place. FDR had this opportunity in the Depression. Lincoln did during the Civil War.[18]

This view was echoed in 2008 when Rahm Emanuel, President Barack Obama's White House chief of staff, said the financial meltdown of that year was a crisis that should not "go to waste."[19]

Historian Richard Norton Smith argued that,

> . . . Lincoln's zeal for recognition was being diluted—some would say purified—through his involvement with the anti-slavery movement. Over time he morphed into that rarest of creatures, the political animal who dignifies ambition while rising above the grubby pursuit of office. As president, Lincoln embodied what Theodore Roosevelt's

biographer Kathleen Dalton has called "the American spirit of self-improvement, change, and growth."[20]

This is the test—rising to the occasion in a crisis—that faced every one of the 14 modern presidents, and remains the ultimate measurement of presidential leadership.

Precis

Lincoln took action as required. He adapted to changing circumstances in leading the Union through the most traumatic and devastating period in U.S. history. He balanced principle with pragmatism, such as when he delayed issuing the Emancipation Proclamation until the North won impressively on the battlefield. He persevered. He won the war and ended slavery, two colossal achievements.

Notes

1. Michael Burlingame "Abraham Lincoln: Impact and Legacy," millercenter.org/president/lincoln/impact-and-legacy, downloaded March 25, 2019.
2. Abraham Lincoln's Annual Message to Congress—Concluding Remarks, December 1, 1862, abrahamlincolnonline.org/lincoln/speeches/congress.htm.
3. Burlingame, ibid.
4. Burlingame, ibid.
5. Jean Edward Smith "Crisis Manager," *New York Times*, October 17, 2008, p. BR20, nytimes.com/2008/10/19/books/review/Smith-trial-by-war.
6. Smith, ibid.
7. Rick Beard, "A Terminal Case of the 'Slows,'" *New York Times*, November 5, 2012, opinionator.blogs.nytimes.com/2012/11/05/a-terminal-case-of-the-slows/.
8. Smith, *New York Times*, ibid.
9. Smith, ibid.
10. Diane Coutu, "Leadership Lessons from Abraham Lincoln," *Harvard Business Review*, April 2009, hbr.org/2009/04/leadership-lessons-from-abraham-lincoln.
11. Ibid.
12. Smith, ibid.
13. Smith, ibid.
14. "This Day in History," September 22, 1862, history.com/this-day-in history/lincoln-issues-emancipation-proclamation, November 24, 2009.
15. Burlingame, ibid.

16. Burlingame, ibid.
17. Burlingame, ibid.
18. Coutu, ibid.
19. Gerald F. Seib, "In Crisis Opportunity for Obama," *Wall Street Journal*, November 21, 2008, wsj.com/articles/SB122721278056345271.
20. Richard Norton Smith, "The Magnificent Lion," Interview contained in Brian Lamb, Susan Swain and C-SPAN, *The Presidents: Noted Historians Rank America's Best—and Worst—Chief Executives.* New York: Public Affairs, 2019, pp. 8–9.

Chapter Two
Franklin D. Roosevelt
The Great Depression

Franklin D. Roosevelt described his "New Deal" program for revitalizing the economy and ameliorating the Great Depression on many occasions, such as during this Topeka, Kansas campaign stop on September 14, 1932. His optimism was infectious. (Franklin D. Roosevelt Presidential Library and Museum)

It was a desperate time, and Americans were eager for a new leader who would restore hope. On November 8, 1932, they chose him in Democrat Franklin D. Roosevelt, who won a landslide victory in the presidential election. He captured 42 of the 48 states in crushing Republican incumbent Herbert Hoover.

The Depression was spreading economic misery everywhere. One out of every three workers, or 15 million people, had lost their jobs. Banks were failing, Wall Street had collapsed, and malnutrition and even starvation were becoming real problems. Foreclosures on homes and farms were common. Millions of Americans in all walks of life were looking to their new leader for answers as he prepared to take over on March 4, 1933. To that end, voters also gave him a House controlled by fellow Democrats by a margin of nearly three-to-one and a Senate controlled by Democrats by two-to-one, conveying enormous political power.

But during the four-month period between his election and his inauguration, FDR refused to say what he would do to save the economy. He didn't want to commit himself until the last moment in case things changed or he found better options. And he didn't want to be associated with his discredited predecessor. He waited until Hoover was out of office to announce the details of his agenda so he could start fresh.

FDR was not sure what would work, so he tried many programs that he thought had potential—the pragmatic, flexible approach that was needed. He got his ideas from many places, notably what historians have called his "brain trust," consisting of long-time advisers, scholars he admired, and labor and business leaders, and everyday people whom he encountered and whose stories he was eager to hear. His wife, Eleanor, served as his indispensable "eyes and ears" on her many fact-finding trips to assess the condition of the country. He also relied on his intuition about what the country wanted and needed.

Roosevelt was never an average citizen. He had been raised in a privileged household as part of America's aristocracy of wealth, far removed from everyday American life as experienced by the poor, the working class and the middle class. But he had one trait that stood out—empathy.

This was the result in large part of his enduring the pain, limitations and setbacks caused by polio, which paralyzed his legs in 1921, when he was 39 years old. Despite his best efforts, he was unable to recover the use of his legs, but the experience gave him a deep understanding of people who were down on their luck, who struggled against adversity and needed help.

Eleanor said her husband learned "the greatest of all lessons—infinite patience and never-ending persistence" from his disability. He seemed "more aware of the feelings of people" and drew on reservoirs of "strength and courage he had not had before," she said. He made a point of getting to know local citizens both around his family estate in Hyde Park, New York and at his rural retreat in Warm Springs, Georgia, such as farmers, mailmen, delivery boys, tenants, shop owners, and people with land for sale. His goal was to learn what their lives were like.[1]

He once told a friend in Georgia:

> Down here at Warm Springs I can't generalize the way a politician's supposed to. A national problem strikes me as simply people needing help. What people? Where? What kind of help? . . . The national farm problem? What about Ed Doyle up there on Pine Mountain? The bank? Well, what sort of trouble does Uncle Henry Kimbrough have with his little bank over there in Chipley?[2]

He noticed that his electric bill at the small Warm Springs cottage was four times higher than at his big house in Hyde Park. This made him determined to find ways to make electricity more affordable in rural areas, and he said his "little cottage at Warm Springs, Georgia was the birthplace of the Rural Electrification Administration."[3]

He also maintained a leadership trait that is essential to any president's success in a crisis—optimism. Through his many years in public life he had mastered the stagecraft of the positive outlook with his broad smile, soothing voice and sunny disposition, always on display. He radiated confidence that he would set things right, and most Americans believed him. This was essential to his success.

His courage in dealing with an assassination attempt in a Miami park on February 15, 1933, the month before his inauguration, showed his mettle. Giuseppe Zangara, an unemployed brick layer, fired a gun six times at FDR after the president-elect delivered a speech from the back seat of an open touring car. Five people were hit, but Roosevelt was not hurt. Chicago Mayor Anton Cermak, shot in the stomach as he was standing next to Roosevelt's vehicle, eventually died of his wound.[4]

"All reports of Roosevelt's response to the shooting emphasized his composure and even his disdain at his brush with death," reports historian Robert Dallek. An aide said he was "easy, confident, poised, to all appearance unmoved." And the public appreciated his grace under fire. Dallek writes:

> Franklin viewed the assassination attempt as a blessing in disguise—a postelection rallying event carrying him into the presidency on a wave of sympathy and approval that he believed would greatly serve his initial presidential actions in the coming struggle with the Great Depression.[5]

AS SOON AS he took over on March 4, 1933, Roosevelt began an unprecedented series of federal actions to reduce the effect of the economic calamity on everyday Americans. Much of what he did was experimental. But he persevered. In the end, FDR didn't end the Depression, but he created an invaluable safety net to help those in need, especially the unemployed and the elderly, and he helped to give Americans the optimism they needed to endure.

Some left-of-center legislators and activists were pushing the new president to assert his power even more expansively than he did. He probably could have won public approval for officially declaring a national emergency and ruling by decree, as if it were wartime. Even Eleanor Roosevelt suggested to him that the country might benefit from a benevolent dictator "who could force through reforms." But FDR rejected the idea. He believed representative government was sacrosanct and that he could lead the country out of the crisis without damaging its democratic institutions or wielding dictatorial powers.[6]

Still, working with a compliant Congress, Roosevelt exerted federal authority more aggressively than had ever been done during peacetime, and he moved with amazing speed to implement what he called "the New Deal." Action is what he offered and action is what the country wanted. "It was enough to know that something was happening that had not happened before," wrote FDR adviser and former Columbia professor Raymond Moley. "The American people wanted their government to do something, anything, so long as it acted with assurance and vigor."[7]

The First Hundred Days concept was based on the three months during which the newly elected Congress, controlled by fellow Democrats, was in special session to pass Roosevelt's New Deal laws from March 9 to June 17, 1933. What happened during those hundred days included a vast array of new laws and also many unilateral executive actions.

ROOSEVELT IS REMEMBERED TODAY as the iconic leader who greatly expanded the federal government's spending, power and role in American life. He didn't start off that way—another insight into his adaptability.

Initially, Roosevelt was relatively conservative compared to what he would become later, when he and Congress created the Securities and Exchange Commission in 1934, the Social Security aid-to-the-elderly system in 1935 and many other programs later in his presidency. Initially, he attempted unsuccessfully to balance the budget. He persuaded Congress to pass legislation reducing military veterans' benefits, including pensions, and cutting the salaries of government workers, including his own and the pay of members of Congress.

Adds Dallek:

> He relished his emerging role on the world stage, and approached the presidency with the excitement of a born leader who was about to make a lasting mark on the country's political history. To be sure, the challenge would test his skills as a politician, but he appreciated the chance to lead a transformational administration with the cunning a successful leader needed to use if he were to buoy the economy and put institutions in place that would make America more humane and less vulnerable to future economic downturns.[8]

From the start, he focused on cultivating his image as a creative, strong and sensitive individual; important leadership traits to project during a crisis. He refused to attend the customary ball on the night of his inauguration. He thought this would show insensitivity to the plight of Americans suffering from the Depression. He also wanted to avoid an event that might call attention to his disability from polio. He thought it best to keep his paralyzed legs hidden from the public as much as possible so as not to show vulnerability or weakness. So he let the partying go on but didn't attend the ball himself.

The news photographers and reporters who covered him at the White House went along with this gambit by not focusing on FDR's paralysis. They were offered regular access to him and a friendly personal relationship in exchange for overlooking his disability. Today this would be seen as a cover-up or conspiracy to protect the president, which it was. But it passed muster with the journalists at the time.

The morning of his swearing-in, he attended a prayer service at St. John's Episcopal Church in Washington, to demonstrate humility and impress the millions of religious Americans with his spirituality.[9]

Roosevelt also realized the importance of favorable news coverage on a day-to-day basis, and from the start he treated White House reporters to big doses of charm. The evening after his inauguration, he invited a few reporters to the White House, had them ushered into the Red Room, and introduced himself to each journalist with a smile. "Roosevelt was in a good mood," recalled Raymond Clapper of the *Washington News*. "No atmosphere of tension." His motive was not only to start getting to know his press corps but also to shape their coverage. The new president pleasantly suggested that they call his declaration of a banking "shutdown" or "moratorium" a "modified bank holiday" or a "partial holiday." His language sounded less ominous, and these were the terms that most of the reporters used.[10]

He also showed a deft sense of public relations in other ways. Attempting to add a sweetener to his austerity programs, he issued a three-sentence message to Congress asking that 3.2 beer be legalized. This was a partial change from the 18th Amendment, which began prohibition in 1918 and aimed at stopping the sale of alcoholic beverages. The House and Senate quickly passed legislation to legalize the beer and this proved to be a brilliant public relations move that put Roosevelt on the side of everyday people. Beer parties were held all over the country shortly after the beer measure passed, and author Studs Terkel wrote of the reaction in his hometown of Chicago: "Something was happening immediately! Bars were opening overnight, with every other beer on the house! In the midst of the Depression it was a note of hope that something would be better."[11]

As historian Dallek points out, Roosevelt choreographed "every detail of his first days in Washington." To disguise his disability from polio, he stationed a car at the city's Union Station when he got off the train on March 2, two days before his inauguration, and he immediately got into the vehicle so spectators, reporters and photographers wouldn't see that his legs were paralyzed and he couldn't walk without help. He and his family stayed at the Mayflower Hotel on Connecticut

Avenue rather than the traditional and more posh Willard Hotel closer to the White House, in deference to all the people suffering from the Depression.[12]

Former Supreme Court Justice Oliver Wendell Holmes said Roosevelt had "a second-class intellect but a first-class temperament." It was meant as a compliment. FDR was convivial, cheerful, considerate and confident. He didn't agonize over decisions. All this was impressive after four years of the dour, distant and uncertain Herbert Hoover as president.[13]

He enjoyed being the nation's celebrity in chief. He loved being in the spotlight and associating with the famous people of Hollywood. He once told the actor Orson Welles, "There are only two great actors in America—you are the other one."[14] He knew his pleasant, soothing voice could be a major asset to calm the country, and he used it deftly in his speeches and by giving live radio addresses to the nation called "fireside chats." These radio talks were homespun and soothing, and they reached millions of listeners as the president explained the nation's problems in understandable terms and detailed his objectives, persuading his fellow citizens that he was their champion.

The country needed every bit of FDR's stagecraft and optimism. "When Roosevelt took power on March 4, 1933, many influential Americans doubted the capacity of a democratic government to act decisively to save the country," writes historian Anthony J. Badger. "Machine guns guarded government buildings. The newspapers and his audience responded most enthusiastically to Roosevelt's promises in his inaugural to assume wartime powers if necessary. That sense of emergency certainly made Congress willing to give FDR unprecedented power."[15]

Political scientist William Leuchtenburg says: "Roosevelt came to office at a desperate time, in the fourth year of a worldwide depression that raised the gravest doubts about the future of Western civilization."[16] Sen. Hiram Johnson, a California Republican, said,

> The admirable trait in Roosevelt is that he has the guts to try . . . He does it all with the rarest good nature . . . We have exchanged for a frown in the White House a smile. Where there were hesitation and vacillation, weighing always the personal political consequences, feebleness, timidity, and duplicity, there are now courage and boldness and real action.[17]

FDR knew that, under the crisis conditions that existed, the country and much of the world would be paying close attention to his inaugural address, and he gave a memorable one. He combined a recognition of the ongoing economic calamity with his declaration that the country, under his leadership, eventually would prosper once more. It was just what Americans wanted to hear.

This address, delivered on a cold, gray afternoon, is still praised today as an excellent example of presidential rhetoric during a crisis, achieving an effective balance between recognizing harsh reality and being positive about the future. Speaking before 100,000 persons from the east front of the Capitol, FDR stood coatless and hatless despite the frigid wind. He said "the present situation of our Nation" required him "to speak the truth, the whole truth, frankly and boldly" about the economic calamity and added: "Only a foolish optimist can deny the dark realities of the moment."[18]

But he expressed his own brand of brave and sensible optimism when he predicted that:

> this great Nation will endure as it has endured, will revive and will prosper. So first of all, let me assert my firm belief that the only thing we have to fear is fear itself—nameless, unreasoning, unjustified terror which paralyzes needed efforts to convert retreat into advance.[19]

He blamed greedy business leaders for the Depression—"a generation of self-seekers . . . the money changers" who put their own ability to make profits above the welfare of the nation. But he didn't dwell on finding blame or casting aspersions.

Instead, he promised "action and action now." He understood the public mood and the public will, and he could communicate this very effectively, in contrast to his hapless predecessor.

Roosevelt said the first priority had to be "to put people to work." He proposed doing this by having the government create jobs on an unprecedented scale rather than relying solely on private enterprise, which was collapsing. He pledged strong supervision of banks and "an end to speculation with other people's money." And he promised to stop widespread foreclosures on "small homes and our farms." All of these statements struck chords with the middle class and the working class.

"They have made me the present instrument of their wishes," the new president declared. "In the spirit of the gift I take it."[20]

Historian Dallek observes:

> The public reception to his speech was all that Roosevelt could have wished. In the days immediately after March 4, close to half a million people sent messages of support and thanks for restoring their faith in America . . . Just the promise of action now by a leader brimming with confidence was enough to excite popular approval and expectations of a rising economy.[21]

First, he took unilateral action—announcing a bank "holiday" for four business days starting March 6, a clever, non-threatening way of describing the closing of banks to prevent panicked citizens from immediately withdrawing so much of their money that the financial institutions would fail. At this point, more than half of the banks in the United States had either gone bankrupt or suspended withdrawals, unsettling millions of depositors.[22]

He made clear that the move was only temporary and that depositors would soon have access to their funds. During the hiatus, he ordered federal auditors to inspect the books of the affected financial institutions to determine which ones were solvent and would be allowed to reopen. Congress also approved the Emergency Bank Act authorizing the president to reopen financially secure banks.

These actions sent a message that the new president was a decisive leader who would be very aggressive in dealing with the Depression, as he had promised.

On Sunday, March 12, the day before the bank holiday was supposed to end, FDR gave the first of what he called "fireside chats," starting with a discussion of the banking crisis. Using the increasingly pervasive medium of radio, Roosevelt talked directly to the American people in his avuncular and reassuring way and explained exactly what he was doing and why. The address had precisely the calming effect he was seeking. The fireside chats became a key part of Roosevelt's presidency and he went on to give a total of 30 of them during his 12 years in office.

This radio address turned out to be the start of a revolution in presidential communication. He delivered the fireside chats in a casual, low-key manner with his charming, distinctive voice as if he were chatting with a family in their living room. His aim was to reassure Americans that their lives would improve and the nation would regain its footing.

As part of his preparation, he would imagine what he considered an average family, where the breadwinner was perhaps a house painter, a car mechanic, or a clerk. He said that before each talk, "I tried to picture a mason at work on a new building, a girl behind a counter, a farmer in his field."[23]

Frances Perkins, one of his key advisers who was present at many fireside chats, said,

> He saw them gathered in the little parlor, listening with their neighbors. He was conscious of their faces and hands, their clothes and homes. As he talked, his head would nod and his hands would move in simple natural, comfortable gestures. His face would smile and light up as though he were actually sitting on the front porch or parlor with them. People felt this, and it bound them to him in affection.[24]

He would assess what such people would like to hear from their president, and he crafted his words to be calming. He always attempted to provide understandable explanations for complex issues such as the banking crisis.[25]

In this live radio address to the nation on the evening of Sunday, March 12, Roosevelt said, "I have no expectation of making a hit every time I come to bat. What I seek is the highest possible batting average, not for myself but for the team."[26]

To improve his radio performance, he would insert a "pivot tooth" into his mouth to replace the tooth that had been knocked out with a stick by a playmate 40 years earlier on Campobello Island. As a result, Roosevelt sometimes emitted a slight whistle when he talked. Before his fireside chats he would insert the denture to eliminate the distracting sound.[27]

It was estimated that more than half of American households owned at least one radio and most of the remainder had access to a radio from a neighbor or at a store when they wanted. It was an increasingly popular mass medium for everyday people. FDR quickly recognized its value as a way to unite people and talk to them informally, unfiltered by the newspapers of the time.[28]

Ever since then, presidents have searched for ways to communicate directly with the public and bypass the media just as FDR did. John F. Kennedy and Ronald Reagan did it by mastering television. Barack Obama used various forms of social media and the White House web site. Donald Trump pioneered the use of Twitter. The objective was the same—bond directly with the people.

Roosevelt called Congress into special session beginning on March 9 to deal with the crisis and kept it in session for three months. He sent Congress a bill on March 9 to reform banks in order to stabilize them with support from the federal government. He didn't nationalize the nation's financial institutions and preferred instead to unify Congress by not being too radical. This was a wise move, showing his sensitivity to what was politically possible at this crucial time. After less than 40 minutes of debate, the House passed the president's bank-reform measure and the Senate adopted it that evening, 73–7. Roosevelt quickly signed the measure into law.[29]

On May 12, he won congressional approval for the Agricultural Adjustment Act and he also created a Farm Credit Administration to refinance farm mortgages, which prevented many farmers from losing their homes and livelihoods in part by raising agricultural prices and income.

For Roosevelt, everything was part of a grand strategy of reassurance. "In the first Hundred Days of his administration, Roosevelt famously signed fifteen major bills into law," Dallek says. "But the greatest importance of these measures was less what people believed each would achieve in righting the country's economic balance than in creating a sense of movement that would somehow restore national prosperity."[30]

Roosevelt's guiding principle was to try different methods to ease the Depression, and if one program failed, he tried something else.

The series of social, economic and job-creating bills that he quickly moved to passage greatly increased the authority and activism of the federal government. Among them: the National Recovery Administration, which pushed the federal government deeper into management of the economy than ever before; the Federal Emergency Relief Administration (FERA), which supplied states and localities with federal money to help the jobless; the Civil Works Administration to create jobs during the first winter of FDR's presidency, and the Works Progress Administration, which replaced FERA, pumped money into circulation and concentrated on long-term projects. The Public Works

Administration focused on increasing jobs through heavy construction in such areas as water systems, power plants, and hospitals. The Federal Deposit Insurance Corp. protected bank accounts. The Civilian Conservation Corps provided immediate jobs for unemployed young men. Also approved were the Emergency Banking Act and the Farm Credit Act.

The humorist Will Rogers said, "Congress doesn't pass legislation anymore—they just wave at the bills as they go by." Historian James McGregor Burns wrote, "Never before had a president converted so many promises into so much legislation so quickly."[31]

Roosevelt made clear he would expand the role of the government if he considered this necessary to restore a healthy economy—something he eventually did many times. One harbinger of his expanded government program was the Securities Act of 1933, a hastily assembled piece of legislation designed to end abuses by bankers and Wall Street speculators. It required that any company selling securities to the public disclose its financial condition and register with the federal government. It was later strengthened through additional legislation that created the Securities and Exchange Commission in 1934.

Moley later wrote,

> To look upon the programs as the result of a unified plan was to believe that the accumulation of stuffed snakes, baseball pictures, school flags, old tennis shoes, carpenter's tools, geometry books and chemistry sets in a boy's bedroom could have been put there by an interior decorator.[32]

Key adviser Frances Perkins said FDR's approach was like an artist "who begins his picture without a clear idea of what he intends to paint or how it should be laid out on the canvas, and then, as he paints, his plan evolves out of the materials."[33]

Roosevelt compared himself to football quarterbacks who know the overall team strategy and what the next play will be

> but they cannot tell you what the play after the next play is going to be until the next play is run off. If the play makes 10 yards, the succeeding play will be different from what it would be if they were thrown for a loss.[34]

Another case in point was the Agricultural Adjustment Act (AAA). It set the precedent for increasing the Department of Agriculture's authority to intervene in the farm economy, particularly by paying farmers not to grow certain crops such as wheat, corn, rice and cotton. This amounted to subsidizing farmers in a way that was radical and controversial at the time but has become accepted since then. He established the principle that Washington has a responsibility for farm prices and should pay farmers to create scarcity in order to help the farmers financially.

Roosevelt also pushed to help people facing foreclosure, which inspired undying gratitude among thousands of Americans whose homes were saved by government loans. This was a groundbreaking idea that established the federal government as an agent in fostering home ownership rather than simply a builder of public housing. It is a policy that remains to this day.[35]

And during his first hundred days he laid the groundwork for the creation of the Tennessee Valley Authority, which gave rebirth to an entire region through the federally financed construction of dams and power plants and the creation of soil conservation, reforestation and other projects.

His empathy was pivotal in shaping other important social policies. One summer while he relaxed at his family estate in Hyde Park, New York, he took a drive around the community and came upon a family of elderly siblings, all apparently in their eighties, who were trying to make a living on a modest farm. When he returned after the winter, he learned that one brother had died, possibly freezing to death between the barn and the house on his way back from milking cows. Another brother was in a home for the indigent. A sister was in what was described to FDR as an asylum. Roosevelt was unsettled at this turn of fortune and complained to Moses Smith, who managed his farm. "Moses, this thing can't go on," he said. "I'm going to plan some way or somehow to put over an old-age security so that the poor house in time will actually be done away with." Some FDR associates said this experience personalized his understanding of the living conditions of needy Americans. It also informed his deliberations when he proposed and won enactment of the Social Security system, which became a bedrock of the American economy and a source of financial security for millions of the elderly.[36]

He learned about the need for rural electrification from neighbors at his Warm Springs, Georgia, retreat and rehabilitation center. In a speech nearby on August 11, 1938, Roosevelt talked about his first stay at Warm Springs 14 years earlier. "When the first-of-the-month bill came in for electric light for my little cottage, I found that the charge was 18 cents a kilowatt-hour—about four times as much as I paid in Hyde Park, New York," he said.

> That started my long study of proper public-utility charges for electric current and the whole subject of getting electricity into farm houses. So it can be said that a little cottage at Warm Springs, Georgia, was the birthplace of the Rural Electrification Administration.[37]

Roosevelt inspired thousands of young people to work in Washington, bringing their ideas and energy to government service as never before. Milton Katz, a young government worker who arrived during the Herbert Hoover administration, said of Roosevelt's first few months,

> I can only describe the change as physical, virtually physical. The wind blew through the corridors (and) a lot of old air blew out the windows. You suddenly felt, "By God, the air is fresh, it's moving, life is resuming. April maybe the cruelest month, but now the world is beginning over again."[38]

Perhaps the best example of Roosevelt's crisis management skills and leadership style was the creation of the Civilian Conservation Corps (CCC), which he announced in a message to Congress on March 21. Congress did his bidding and quickly passed a bill creating the CCC, which the president signed on March 31.

Under this program, 250,000 young unmarried men between the ages of 18 and 25 from poor families began to work in the national forests and on other government property planting trees, fighting forest fires, constructing breaks for forest-fire prevention in the West, draining marshlands, building dams and clearing trails. It gave the participants desperately needed money for their families (many sent home nearly all of the $30 each man made per month) and kept them out of trouble.

The genesis of the CCC illustrated FDR's relentless push for action and his refusal to accept excuses for delay. Roosevelt knew that this program should be aimed at giving young men work immediately, so he chose projects that could be started quickly. He realized that big public-works facilities such as dams and massive bridges would take many months to begin and years to complete.

When his advisers raised objections on pragmatic grounds, such as the lack of tents and kitchens for the CCC thousands, FDR ordered his aides to make the program succeed regardless of the obstacles. He wouldn't take no for an answer, a common technique for can-do leaders in any sphere. "He put the dynamite under the people who had to do the job and let them fumble for their own methods," Perkins said.[39]

"The urgency and resourceful problem solving paid off," author Jonathan Alter wrote.

> By April 7, only thirty-four days into the administration, the first corps members were enlisted. By July 1, less than four months after Roosevelt made his outlandish demand, he exceeded his quarter-million goal. Nearly 275,000 young men were enrolled in 1,300 camps across the country, supporting their families and undertaking much-needed projects.[40]

African Americans and Native Americans were included, but no women. During a period of nine years, more than 3 million men were given work by the CCC. And they accomplished an amazing amount, including the planting of 3 billion trees, developing 800 state parks, and protecting 20 million acres from erosion.[41]

FDR's crisis management had a much larger purpose than providing work during those early months of his presidency. He was showing the country for the first time that a strong federal government, directed by an able and inspirational leader, can be the most effective force in the United States to help those in need during a crisis.

His leadership served as a model for all his successors and made him one of the most popular presidents in U.S. history. On March 26, 1933, after he had been in office less than a month, Anne O'Hare McCormick wrote in the *New York Times*:

> Mr. Roosevelt thinks and talks a great deal about government. He has very pronounced ideas on the functions of the Presidency. He believes that the President is literally the leader of the people, particularly in the development of ideas. He believes that at every turning

point of history someone rises up who can enunciate and in a sense personify the new direction of the public mind and will. In his view America has reached such a crossroads. He does not go so far as to speak of himself as the leader of the economic revolution now in progress but there is no doubt that he considers the President of the United States at this juncture the instrument by which profound and necessary change in the American system are to be effected.[42]

Columnist Walter Lippmann wrote,

We were a congeries of disorderly panic-stricken mobs and factions. In the Hundred Days from March to June, we became again an organized nation confident of our power to provide for our own security and to control our own destiny.[43]

Historian Douglas Brinkley said,

Franklin Roosevelt had changed the role of the president from a mere executive to a nearly daily presence in American homes, along with his active family. In both respects, FDR was not just the president. To many people, he was the federal government—omnipresent in ways that none of his predecessors had been. With Franklin Roosevelt, fascination with the presidency grew quickly. For better or for worse, Americans began to look at the history of their nation in terms of the presidents.[44]

These were exactly the perceptions that Roosevelt had been striving to create. He was seen as the man for the moment, an extraordinary leader handling an extraordinary crisis. It was no wonder that the nation elected him president four times, more than anyone else, and that historians consistently rank him among the top three presidents along with George Washington and Abraham Lincoln.

Precis

FDR was a brilliant crisis manager. He took bold action to alleviate the suffering of the Depression. He adapted to changing circumstances. He balanced principle with pragmatism, taking presidential power to new levels but maintaining democratic ideals. He persevered through adversity. And he achieved success in restoring optimism and creating a social safety net to help Americans in their time of need.

Notes

1. Theo Lippman, Jr., *The Squire of Warm Springs: FDR in Georgia 1924–1945*, Chicago: Playboy Press, 1977, pp. 80–81.
2. Lippman, *The Squire of Warm Springs*, p. 140.
3. Lippman, *The Squire of Warm Springs*, p. 143.
4. Giuseppe Zangara: "FDR Escapes Assassination in Miami," history.com.
5. Robert Dallek, *Franklin D. Roosevelt: A Political Life*, New York: Viking, 2017, pp. 131–132.
6. Dallek, *Franklin D. Roosevelt*, pp. 133–134.
7. Jonathan Alter, *The Defining Moment: FDR's Hundred Days and the Triumph of Hope*, New York: Simon & Schuster Paperbacks, 2006, p. 225.
8. Dallek, *Franklin D. Roosevelt*, p. 134.
9. Dallek, *Franklin D. Roosevelt*, p. 136.
10. Alter, *The Defining Moment*, p. 227.
11. Alter, *The Defining Moment*, p. 477.
12. Dallek, *Franklin D. Roosevelt*, pp. 134–135.
13. Alter, *The Defining Moment*, pp. 234–235.
14. Kenneth T. Walsh, *Celebrity in Chief: A History of the Presidents and the Culture of Stardom*, London and New York: Routledge, 2017, p. 33.
15. Anthony J. Badger, *FDR: The First Hundred Days*, New York: Hill and Wang, 2008, p. 169. See also Kenneth T. Walsh, "The First 100 Days: Franklin Roosevelt Pioneered the 100-Day Concept," *U.S. News & World Report*, Feb. 12, 2009, usnews.com/news/history/articles/2009/02/12/the-first-100-days-franklin-roosevelt-pioneered-the-100-day-concept.
16. Kenneth T. Walsh, "The First 100 Days: Franklin Roosevelt Pioneered the 100-Day Concept," *U.S. News & World Report*, February 12, 2009, usnews.com/news/history/articles/2009/02/12/the-first-100-days-franklin-roosevelt-pioneered-the-100-day-concept.
17. Walsh, ibid.
18. Dallek, *Franklin D. Roosevelt*, p. 136.
19. Dallek, *Franklin D. Roosevelt*, p. 136.
20. Dallek, *Franklin D. Roosevelt*, p. 137.
21. Dallek, *Franklin D. Roosevelt*, pp. 137–138.

22. Miller Center Staff at UVA, "FDR's First Fireside Chat: The Banking Crisis," April 12, 2016, millercenter.org/issues-policy/economics/fdr-s-first-fireside-chat-the-banking-crisis.
23. Alter, *The Defining Moment*, pp. 263.
24. Alter, *The Defining Moment*, p. 266.
25. Alter, *The Defining Moment*, p. 266.
26. Dallek, *Franklin D. Roosevelt*, p. 143.
27. Alter, *The Defining Moment*, p. 268.
28. Alter, *The Defining Moment*, pp. 264–265.
29. Dallek, *Franklin D. Roosevelt*, pp. 138–139.
30. Dallek, *Franklin D. Roosevelt*, p. 144.
31. The humorist Will Rogers: Walsh, ibid.
32. Walsh, ibid.
33. Jonathan Alter, *The Defining Moment*, pp. 272–273.
34. Alter, *The Defining Moment*, p. 273.
35. Alter, *The Defining Moment*, p. 284.
36. Moses Smith, oral history, Jan. 15, 1948, available at FDR Library, Hyde Park, N.Y.
37. Richard A. Pence, ed., *The Next Greatest Thing*, Washington, D.C.: National Rural Electric Cooperative Association, 1984, p. 77.
38. Alter, *The Defining Moment*, p. 283.
39. Alter, *The Defining Moment*, p. 293.
40. Alter, *The Defining Moment*, p. 299.
41. Alter, *The Defining Moment*, pp. 295, 299.
42. Walsh, ibid.
43. Quoted in Dallek, *Franklin D. Roosevelt*, p. 165.
44. Douglas Brinkley, "A Brief History of Presidential Rankings," Interview Contained in Brian Lamb, Susan Swain and C-SPAN, *The Presidents: Noted Historians Rank America's Best—and Worst—Chief Executives*, New York: Public Affairs, 2019, pp. 12–13.

Chapter Three
Harry Truman
The Battle with Douglas MacArthur

Harry Truman met with Gen. Douglas MacArthur on Wake Island on October 15, 1950 to coordinate strategy as the Korean war intensified. Truman eventually fired MacArthur for insubordination despite the general's popularity with Americans. (Harry S. Truman Library)

Harry Truman's presidency was filled with crises and controversy. Many of his decisions were historic, such as dropping the atomic bomb on Japan to hasten the end of World War II in the Pacific, his executive order to desegregate the armed forces, and his move to stop North Korea's invasion of South Korea.

But none of his decisions outraged more people and caused him more immediate political harm than his dismissal of five-star Gen. Douglas MacArthur. MacArthur was a hero of World War II in the Pacific who led the American resistance to the Japanese at Bataan, later liberated the Philippines, and, in effect, ruled post-war Japan for several years. During Truman's presidency, MacArthur was commander of U.S. forces throughout Asia, including Korea. In Truman's estimation, the preening and arrogant MacArthur was a would-be American Caesar. Truman eventually considered the general to be guilty of insubordination as he attempted to take control of national-security policy from the president and flout the Constitution, which provides for civilian authority over the military.

THE UNITED STATES withdrew from its post-World War II occupation of the Korean peninsula in 1948 and 1949, leaving the area divided between the communist north and the capitalist south. The Truman administration hoped the pro-American government in Seoul, South Korea, would govern effectively and keep the communist government of North Korea at bay.

But on June 25, 1950, North Korean troops crossed the 38th Parallel, which divided Korea under an agreement among the great powers after World War II. Seeking to take over the south, they began to fight their way deeper and deeper into South Korea. MacArthur was embarrassed that the forces he supervised were doing so poorly, and Truman was worried about imminent defeat. The president believed giving in would encourage communist aggression around the world, including elsewhere in Asia and in Europe, the Middle East and the Mediterranean. "There's no telling what they'll do if we don't put up a fight now," Truman told an aide on June 26, the day after the North Korean attack.[1] Truman approved what he called a "police action" to reverse the tide in Korea, and received immediate United Nations approval.

Truman, following MacArthur's advice, flooded the war zone with U.S. forces and they began making progress. In mid-September, MacArthur ordered a risky amphibious landing at Inchon, behind enemy lines, and it succeeded brilliantly, forcing the north's forces into retreat. On September 29, MacArthur recaptured Seoul and by early October, South Korea was liberated.[2]

Now came a key decision—whether to cross the 38th parallel, invade North Korea and free it from communist control. MacArthur favored a very aggressive approach, but Truman, fearing the onset of World War III in which the Soviet Union and China would confront the United States and its allies in Korea, insisted on a limited and far more cautious strategy.

The president decided that U.S. and South Korean forces could cross the parallel but under strict rules. "MacArthur was told to stop American troops from entering North Korea if Soviet or Chinese forces appeared in the North," historian Robert Dallek notes.

> Moreover, even if U.S. units crossed the parallel, they were not to accompany the South Koreans to the border areas with China or Russia. With the Chinese issuing repeated warnings through their press and foreign embassies that an invasion of North Korea would provoke their intervention, Truman decided to meet General MacArthur in the Pacific on Wake Island on October 14.[3]

Truman's goal was to size up MacArthur face to face as the crisis intensified and to make sure the general understood Truman's desire for a limited war, not an all-out conflict.

The October 14 meeting generated huge amounts of publicity. Some critics said the president appeared to be a supplicant, traveling on a 21-hour flight to see his subordinate instead of having MacArthur fly to meet him in Washington.

Privately, Truman warned MacArthur, "We don't want the Chinese in this war but they're in it. We don't want to do anything to bring Russia in. And you're not going to get the atomic bomb. Now what are we going to be doing?" MacArthur said, "I can handle it. Give me the troops I need and it will be all right." Truman thought he had made his points clear and he flew back home.[4]

Each man initially said positive things about the other but this was only a temporary détente. Each harbored what the other considered dangerous views on how to deal with North Korea and the communists, and it turned out eventually that the differences couldn't be bridged.

The Wake Island conference may have made matters worse because the commander in chief and the general later felt betrayed by the other, based on the cordial comments and mutual commitments they made during their meeting in the middle of the Pacific.

IT WAS NO WONDER that Truman was initially careful. He had come to power suddenly and felt he had a lot to prove, so he was reluctant to take on the elites. As a relatively undistinguished U.S. senator from Missouri and, years before that, a failed haberdasher, he was never a part of the nation's ruling class or social aristocracy, as Franklin D. Roosevelt had been, and was a surprise choice as Roosevelt's vice president in the 1944 election. The Roosevelt–Truman ticket won, but FDR died of a stroke in April 1945, only a few weeks after being inaugurated for the fourth time. Truman was initially off balance, realizing that the weight of the world was on his shoulders. He even asked for the prayers of the reporters who were covering him, but pledged to throw himself into the job and perform his duties to the best of his ability. His task was daunting. World War II was still raging in the Pacific, a new world order needed to be worked out for the future, and Truman had been left out of many FDR's decisions, including his authorization for using the atomic bomb on Japan. But Truman learned quickly, and his candor and pluck impressed many Americans, although many still weren't sure he was up to the job.

ON THE BATTLEFIELD, U.S. troops pushed the Chinese and their North Korean allies back and captured Pyongyang, the North's capital, then began moving north to the Chinese border. This campaign went well at first.

Then disaster struck.

Historian Alonzo Hamby wrote:

> In fact, the Chinese Communists were unremittingly suspicious of American intentions and had planned from the beginning to intervene if North Korean troops were thrown back and might well have done so even if American troops had not moved close to Manchuria . . . In late October, news reports indicated that Chinese troops had moved into the fighting in northern Korea. In Washington, CIA estimates were cautious—they pegged the number of Chinese combatants at 15,000 to 20,000 on November 1, and 30,000 to 40,000 a week later.[5]

By early November, MacArthur was convinced that the Chinese were pouring troops into the fight and he announced publicly that "A new and fresh army now faces us," and he asked for permission to bomb the bridges over the Yalu River, a key point at the Chinese–North Korea border. Truman agreed.[6]

There was an early November lull in fighting with the Chinese—U.S. officials didn't know what to make of it. But American voters weren't happy with the costly and dangerous entanglement. They were concerned about the future of the economy, as inflation rose and people worried about the kind of shortages they experienced in World War II. And many fretted about allegations of communist influence in Washington as spread by Senator Joe McCarthy (R-Wis.). In America's November 7 midterm elections, Truman's Democratic party suffered serious defeats in races for Congress; the Republicans picked up five seats in the Senate and 28 in the House of Representatives.

On November 9, the Joint Chiefs of Staff advised MacArthur privately to be cautious, and told him to avoid provoking China. The chiefs also suggested, rather than ordered, that he stop his offensive operations short of the Yalu River, the border with China. MacArthur responded that such a course would be appeasement to the communists and took a defiant stance by dismissing the joint chiefs' suggestions. They didn't press him to change his military course or his defiant tone.[7]

On November 24, MacArthur began a major offensive, without the clear and full endorsement of the Joint Chiefs of Staff. He declared that it would result in a quick victory and he planned to bring American troops "home by Christmas."[8]

MacArthur also made a key tactical mistake. He split his army in two, on opposite sides of a mountain range. It was a huge blunder, allowing each wing of his troops to be attacked separately. The Chinese—with a force estimated at up to 300,000 troops—came roaring back into battle across the Yalu River into North Korea and MacArthur's army was pushed back into South Korea.

In a November 28 cable, MacArthur admitted to his superiors, the Joint Chiefs of Staff at the Pentagon, that he faced "an entirely new war" because the enemy opposition was stronger than he had anticipated, and he would need massive reinforcements.[9]

He asked permission to request help from Chinese nationalist forces in Taiwan, the mortal enemies of the regime in Beijing. He wanted approval to bomb Chinese bases in Manchuria and to allow American fighter jets to follow Chinese combat aircraft across the Yalu to destroy them over mainland China. Truman and his advisers were worried that such escalations would generate a wider war with China, and possibly bring the Soviet Union into the conflict. Truman rejected MacArthur's requests, and MacArthur told the press that he was operating under "an enormous handicap without precedent in history."[10]

MacArthur demanded the use of the atomic bomb, and Truman seethed. He told MacArthur, again, that he wasn't going to use the atomic bomb in Korea, but MacArthur continued to ask for it.[11]

The fighting was very heavy, and MacArthur publicly urged an all-out war against China, defying Truman's desire for peace talks and a limit to the Korean conflict.[12]

As the allied forces were reeling, President Truman told the country in a speech carried on radio and television on December 15, 1950, "Our homes, our Nation, all the things we believe in are in great danger." He said he was declaring a state of national emergency and warned that Americans would have to accept cuts in civilian production, higher taxes and reduced nonmilitary spending. Truman added: "The American people have always met danger with courage and determination. I am confident we will do that now, and with God's help we shall keep our freedom."[13]

Despite his dramatic rhetoric, Truman still favored only limited war in Korea and wanted a negotiated settlement. He was willing to settle for a mixed result as long as it wasn't a clear, embarrassing defeat for the United States and the U.N.

But the allies were facing one reverse after another. On December 22, 1950, the Chinese massed for an attack on Seoul, the South Korean capital, and they took the city after it was abandoned by U.N. forces on January 3, 1951.[14] And Truman's support was fading with the American public.

MacArthur continued to urge an aggressive use of U.S. military power far beyond what Truman was willing to accept as part of the president's endorsement of "limited war" in Korea. MacArthur urged the bombing of China, the use of nationalist Chinese forces from Taiwan in the conflict, and the possible use of nuclear weapons. MacArthur was, in effect, insisting on the authority to wage the war in his own way with unlimited resources, to turn the tide against China.[15]

The president had a different concept. "Truman thought the Cold War could be won without an all-out war with the Soviet Union, but MacArthur did not believe that was possible," historian H.W. Brands said.

> MacArthur essentially believed that World War III had begun and the U.S. had to wage it. He believed there was no substitute for victory . . . World War II, however, was the last war that Americans have been able to fight all out. The reason is that the dangers of escalation outweigh the benefits of victory.[16]

The reality is that nuclear weapons have changed warfare. Going all out—going nuclear—is simply too catastrophic to contemplate.

At the end of December, MacArthur advocated a coastal blockade of China, heavy bombing of industrial areas there, and the use of Nationalist forces from Taiwan. On January 13, 1951, Truman rejected these steps in a letter to MacArthur and explained his more modest objectives, noting that it was vital to maintain strong international support for the war (which MacArthur's plan for an all-out effort would have jeopardized). Truman also indicated that the issues were more complicated than MacArthur supposed, notably that it was imperative to prevent an even larger war with the Soviet Union, ostensibly China's ally.

Within the next few weeks, Gen. Matthew Ridgway, the top U.N. field commander, pushed the Chinese north and retook Seoul on March 15. His forces advanced to the 38th Parallel, the border between North and South Korea when the war started. But this positive news didn't improve Truman's political position. Americans were tired of the cycle of setbacks followed by successes followed by more setbacks in a faraway land, with no assurance of a quick and overwhelming victory, and they had grave doubts about Truman's judgment in Korea. Only 21 percent of voters told pollsters he should run for another term in 1952. Only 28 percent approved of his job performance in late March 1951, a dismal number.[17]

MacArthur was embarrassed and angry. He had staked his reputation on greatly expanding the war, and now Ridgway was showing that progress could be made with existing forces.

On March 15, 1951, MacArthur told a journalist that stopping the war at the 38th Parallel was impractical and untenable, and he wanted to move northward, reunify Korea and topple the North Korean communist regime. On March 24, aware that Truman was about to call for a negotiated settlement, MacArthur brazenly declared that U.S. and U.N. forces had just won the war in South Korea, announced that Chinese military capabilities were inferior, and threatened expansion of the war beyond Korea. He even offered to meet with the enemy commander in chief to accept an unconditional surrender.[18]

Truman, hoping to avoid inflaming the situation further, declined to give his own statement about negotiations. The Chinese leaders, however, were offended. They didn't believe they were defeated in Korea and announced that they wouldn't be humiliated by accepting peace talks on MacArthur's terms. A negotiated settlement seemed out of the question at this point, partly because of MacArthur's arrogance and belligerence.

Even though Truman knew that many Americans liked MacArthur's tough approach, the president was approaching the point of no return with his insubordinate general. Reflecting the president's feelings, the Joint Chiefs reminded the wayward MacArthur that he was not to make statements setting new policies without prior approval.

MacArthur got into more trouble. On April 5, 1951, House Republican Minority Leader Joe Martin revealed that MacArthur had agreed with Martin's comments that the legislator made in a letter to the general that called for the establishment of "a second Asiatic front" by the Chinese nationalists from Taiwan. MacArthur, in his response to Martin, called for "maximum counterforce" and said the loss of Asia was very possible, and this would in turn result in the fall of Europe to the communists. "There is no substitute for victory," MacArthur concluded.[19]

"This looks like the last straw. Rank insubordination," Truman wrote in his diary on April 6, referring to MacArthur's response to Martin.[20]

Five days later, on April 10, 1951, after consulting with many people, including Secretary of State Dean Acheson, General Omar Bradley (another World War II hero, like MacArthur), and legislative leaders, Truman relieved MacArthur of his command and replaced him with General Ridgway.

Truman said:

> With deep regret I have concluded that General of the Army Douglas MacArthur is unable to give his wholehearted support to the policies

of the United States Government and of the United Nations in matters pertaining to his official duties.[21]

Within 24 hours of Truman's dismissal of MacArthur, citizens sent more than 5,000 telegrams to the White House in reaction and three-quarters of them backed MacArthur. In the wake of the firing, Truman's approval rating set a negative record not matched before or since—sinking to 22 percent—lower even than Richard Nixon's at the depth of Watergate. In contrast, MacArthur returned home to a hero's welcome, including a ticker-tape parade attended by millions of people in New York City on April 18 and an address to a joint session of Congress. Speaking from the well of the House of Representatives, where presidents deliver their State of the Union addresses, MacArthur showed his flair for drama. "I am closing my 52 years of military service," he said and quoted from the most popular barracks ballad of his time at West Point. "Old soldiers never die; they just fade away," MacArthur said somberly. "And like the old soldier of that ballad, I now close my military career and just fade away—an old soldier who tried to do his duty as God gave him the light to see that duty. Good-by."[22] He received a huge ovation.

MacArthur took these developments as signs of overwhelming public support for a MacArthur candidacy for president the following year. But public and elite opinion gradually turned against the brash general as a man who should not be given the power of the presidency.

This didn't mean that Truman gained in popularity. He was widely excoriated. Some Republicans called for his impeachment. His approval ratings in the polls continued to be poor. After April 1951, Truman's approval rating never rose above 33 percent, and in October 1951, the Gallup research organization found that 56 percent of Americans agreed that Korea was a "useless war."[23]

"The bitter, overheated, partisan debate that had followed MacArthur's dismissal provided yet another lease on life for McCarthyism," the anti-communist witch hunts of Sen. Joseph McCarthy, Hamby wrote.

> The casualty lists from Korea would sustain it for the remainder of Truman's tenure in the White House. To an increasingly passionate opposition, they provided proof positive that Truman and his national security advisers were not dedicated to victory in the struggle against

Communism, that they were in fact soft on Communism, and that they might not be disturbed by Red victories abroad.[24]

Truman wrote in his memoirs that he wasn't upset and was confident he would be vindicated later. He wondered what Jesus Christ, Moses or Martin Luther would have done if there had been polls about them during their eras. "It isn't polls or public opinion alone of the moment that counts," he wrote a friend. "It is right and wrong, and leadership—men with fortitude, honesty and a belief in the right that make epochs in the history of the world."[25]

Generals George Marshall and Omar Bradley later told a Senate committee in secret testimony that MacArthur's concept of total war would never work, backing Truman's view. And they argued that the United States was at that time not capable of winning another world war.[26]

The general's keynote address at the 1952 Republican National Convention seemed overly narcissistic and politically naive, and even conservatives who admired his military leadership soured on him. The GOP turned to another general, to a more likeable and moderate one, and nominated former Gen. Dwight Eisenhower for president. He went on to win the White House in a landslide.

TRUMAN'S POLITICAL COURAGE and resolve to protect the Constitution are now seen by historians as a sterling example of presidential leadership.

Historian H.W. Brands said Truman had bravely committed "political suicide."[27] And it's true that Truman didn't run for re-election in 1952 partly because of public reaction against his firing of MacArthur. But it's also true that his handling of MacArthur's insubordination stands out today as a powerful case of presidential courage and character.

"If there is one basic element in our Constitution, it is civilian control of the military," Truman wore in his *Memoirs*. " . . . If I allowed him to defy the civil authorities in this manner, I myself would be violating my oath to uphold and defend the Constitution."[28]

Truman's view of MacArthur hardened after he left office. Years later, he told biographer Merle Miller:

> I didn't fire him because he was a dumb son of a bitch, although he was, but that's not against the law for generals. If it was, half to

three-quarters of them would be in jail . . . I fired him because he wouldn't respect the authority of the President.[29]

Truman said MacArthur "wasn't right in his head . . . there was never anybody around him to keep him in line. He didn't have anybody on his staff that wasn't an ass kisser."[30]

Specifically, Truman said he removed MacArthur for three reasons: 1. The general had defied presidential edicts to submit public statements for clearance before issuing them. 2. MacArthur had publicly disagreed with the president's foreign-policy positions. 3. MacArthur had tried to convert a limited war into a full-scale war with China and risked a response from the Soviet Union that could have caused World War III.[31]

Truman told Miller:

> He disobeyed orders, and I was Commander in Chief, and either I was or I wasn't . . . So I acted as Commander in Chief and called him home . . . The thing you have to understand about me is if I've done the right thing and I *know* I've done the right thing, I don't worry over it. There's nothing to worry over. Didn't have a minute's doubt about it, and I knew that's the way history would judge it, too, and I guess you can say looking back on it now, that it has.[32]

Historian H.W. Brands, who has studied Truman's firing of MacArthur, says:

> I think the enduring legacy is that Truman took a great political risk, and he did it immediately to prevent World War III, but also to prove the principle that civilian elected officials are above military officials, however grand and decorated they may be . . . Generals ever since have taken that lesson. With Lyndon Johnson, the generals in Vietnam knew not to take their differences outside of the administration or popular opinion would probably be against them.[33]

OVERALL, Truman handled the MacArthur issue well. Despite the president's grievances against MacArthur, he moved against him cautiously at first and expressed hope that the charismatic general would back off from his outrageous departures from government policies in conducting the Korean war, and his public disparagement of President Truman's foreign-policy ideas.

When he came up against MacArthur, he was taking on a revered figure in America, a man considered a military hero and a charismatic leader. But even though MacArthur was a brilliant military tactician in both World War II and in Korea, he lacked political and diplomatic skills and good judgment in geopolitics. Just as important, MacArthur badly underestimated Truman's strength of character and willingness to act boldly on a matter of principle.

The Cold War ended under President Ronald Reagan in the 1980s because a succession of U.S. commanders in chief, including Reagan, adopted Truman's strategy of exerting firm pressure—economic, diplomatic, military and moral—on the Soviets to back down from their expansionist goals, but stopping short of war. It worked, and much of the grounding in this came from Truman's decision to fire MacArthur and reject the general's bellicose attitudes. "The courage of Truman's decision had never been in question; six decades later, its wisdom was apparent as well," Brands concluded.[34] His decision has stood the test of time as a brilliant example of crisis management and presidential leadership.

Precis

Harry Truman took bold action in his confrontation with General Douglas MacArthur. He adapted to changing circumstances, assessing the degree of MacArthur's insubordination and concluding that the results MacArthur was getting on the battlefield did not justify keeping him in command during the Korean war. Truman balanced principle with pragmatism, giving MacArthur the benefit of the doubt at first and then moving decisively to remove him. He persevered. And Truman succeeded in protecting his constitutional role as commander in chief.

Notes

1. Robert Dallek, *Harry S. Truman*, New York: Times Books, 2008, p. 106.
2. Dallek, *Harry S. Truman*, p. 107.
3. Dallek, *Harry S. Truman*, p. 108.
4. Aida D. Donald, "Harry S. Truman," Interview contained in Brian Lamb, Susan Swain and C-SPAN, *The Presidents: Noted Historians Rank America's Best—and Worst—Chief Executives*, New York: Public Affairs, 2019, pp. 90–91.

5. Alonzo L. Hamby, *Man of the People: A Life of Harry S. Truman*, New York: Oxford University Press, 1995, p. 546.
6. Hamby, pp. 546, 551.
7. Hamby, p. 551.
8. H.W. Brands, *The General vs. the President: MacArthur and Truman at the Brink of Nuclear War*, New York: Anchor Books, 2017, p. 212.
9. Hamby, pp. 551–552.
10. Dallek, p. 113.
11. Donald, p. 91.
12. Bob Drogin, "MacArthur and Truman Face Off in H.W. Brands' new history," *Los Angeles Times*, October 14, 2016.
13. Hamby, p. 553.
14. Hamby, p. 554.
15. Hamby, p. 554.
16. Christopher Klein, "MacArthur vs. Truman: The Showdown That Changed America," history.com, October 13, 2016, history.com/news/macarthur-vs-truman-the-showdown-that-changed-america/10-13-2016.
17. Dallek, p. 117.
18. Hamby, p. 555.
19. Hamby, p. 555.
20. Klein, ibid.
21. Hamby, pp. 555–556.
22. Dallek, p. 121.
23. Hamby, p. 564.
24. Hamby, p. 564.
25. Harry S. Truman, *Memoirs of Harry S. Truman, Volume 2: Years of Trial and Hope*: New York, Doubleday, 1956, pp. 451–452.
26. Klein, ibid.
27. Klein, ibid.
28. Truman, pp. 436–450.
29. Merle Miller, *Plain Speaking: An Oral Biography of Harry S. Truman*, New York: Berkeley Publishing, 1974, pp. 287, 291, 308, 312–313.
30. Miller, ibid.
31. Truman, pp. 443–444.
32. Truman, pp. 310, 306.
33. H.R. Brands quoted in Klein, ibid.
34. Klein, ibid.

Chapter Four
Dwight Eisenhower
The U-2 Mission

Dwight Eisenhower was popular and largely successful as president but his dealing with Soviet leader Nikita Khrushchev during the U-2 spy-plane fiasco in 1960 was a failure that led to escalating superpower tensions. Eisenhower and Khrushchev are shown here at Camp David during happier times in September 1959. (United States Naval Photographic Agency, Eisenhower Presidential Library)

It was one of the low points of Dwight D. Eisenhower's presidency and a particularly tense moment in the Cold War between the United States and the Soviet Union. The shooting down of an American U-2 spy plane by the U.S.S.R. on May 1, 1960, and Eisenhower's subsequent lies about it, probably was the worst debacle of Ike's administration. How he handled it showed his capacity for miscalculation and his willingness to cover up his mistakes, but, on the positive side, it also demonstrated his ability to eventually change course and make the best of a bad situation.

Eisenhower had ordered the U-2 reconnaissance planes built by Lockheed in 1954, and he was very impressed by the aircraft's capabilities. The U-2 could fly at 70,000 feet, about double the altitude of a commercial jet, and it was equipped with spy cameras that could take a clear photo of an object 2.5 feet wide from an altitude of 60,000 feet. The intelligence it gathered turned out to be so important—revealing the location and readiness of Soviet long-range bombers and intercontinental ballistic missiles—that Eisenhower approved a series of missions over Soviet territory. This was illegal and sure to provoke the Kremlin if they found out, which they did almost immediately.

"It was a disastrous decision, perhaps the worst of his presidency," writes historian William I. Hitchcock.[1]

Added Army Gen. Andrew Goodpaster, White House staff secretary and a key adviser to Eisenhower: "The handling of that critical international situation was about as clumsy in my opinion as anything our government has ever done."[2]

ON APRIL 25, Eisenhower, under pressure from his military advisers and the intelligence community, gave the go-ahead for the 24th U-2 spy flight over the U.S.S.R. if it could be launched on or before May 1.[3] Knowing that such missions were provocative and illegal, he didn't want the mission to absorb his time or stir up the Soviets in advance of a planned international summit meeting with Premier Nikita Khrushchev on May 16 and so it was launched more than two weeks in advance, on May 1.

Twenty-three spy flights into the U.S.S.R by U-2 aircraft had occurred with Eisenhower's permission, during the previous four years, and by 1960 they were no secret to the Soviets. Premier Nikita Khrushchev, in fact, had ordered the last one shot down when it crossed his border on April 9. But the Soviets, through their own incompetence and lack of adequate technology, failed to destroy the American plane.

When he was told of another U-2 flight at 5 a.m., on May 1, by his Defense Minister Marshal Rodion Malinovsky, Khrushchev again ordered Malinovsky to shoot it down. This time the Soviets succeeded—and the American pilot Francis Gary Powers was captured.[4]

Powers, a CIA employee, had left before dawn on May 1 and flown his U-2 out of an airfield near Peshawar, Pakistan, on a mission that was to cover 3,788 miles and include a Soviet missile test facility at Tyuratam and other Soviet military sites. Powers was to land at an airstrip in Bodo, Norway. His plane never arrived, and Eisenhower was informed later that day that the aircraft was "overdue and possibly lost." Actually, Powers' U-2 had been badly damaged by a Soviet SA-2 surface-to-air missile, which detonated just behind the American aircraft as it flew over the city of Sverdlovsk. Powers lost control of the plane and ejected as it started to break up. He failed to set off the explosives designed to destroy the aircraft; large parts of it fell to the ground and were found by the Soviets. Powers was captured by farmers and local residents, turned over to the authorities and found himself within a few hours at Lubyanka prison in Moscow.

The next morning, May 2, the U.S. military confirmed that the plane was indeed lost, and Eisenhower returned quickly by helicopter to the White House from the presidential retreat at Camp David. But he decided not to say anything publicly. "President Eisenhower's decision to do nothing led to a chain of poor decisions and outright deceptions during the crisis," writes historian Michael K. Bohn. "Historians believe the resulting calamity extended the Cold War for years."[5]

As it turned out, CIA Director Allen Dulles and other members of the Eisenhower administration had done little to prepare for the loss of a U-2 over the U.S.S.R.—a key lapse in judgment. They thought the Soviets wouldn't even disclose the incident because they would look foolish or inept in failing to prevent or stop it. Eisenhower's advisers also believed that the U-2 was so fragile that it would be totally destroyed if it were hit by a missile or if it crashed, and these advisers concluded that the pilot couldn't survive the destruction of the plane at 70,000 feet. In addition, the pilot had the ability to destroy the plane with a special explosive device if the plane got into trouble, and he could always use a poison pin he carried to kill himself. For these reasons, the Americans thought any U-2 mission would remain secret.[6]

So as soon as they realized Powers' plane had been lost, U.S. officials began fabricating information, distorting and lying to keep the U-2 program under wraps and limit any damage to the credibility of the United States and its president.

First, on May 3, in a statement approved by President Eisenhower, the National Aeronautics and Space Administration (NASA) said the U.S. plane had been on a weather research flight.[7]

On May 5, Khrushchev announced that the shoot-down had occurred but withheld information on the pilot's capture. He wanted to get credit for ruining the American mission—after failing to do so for other overflights in the past—and still have some information in reserve to further embarrass the White House as the Americans spread their lies about the U-2 program. When Khrushchev informed hundreds of Kremlin officials, meeting as the Supreme Soviet, of the shoot-down, the deputies applauded him amid anti-American shouts of "Shame! Shame!"[8]

In response, White House Press Secretary Jim Hagerty told reporters in a prepared statement, "At the direction of the president, a complete inquiry is being made."[9] It was a temporary damage-control measure designed to give the administration more time to get its story straight amid speculation about what had happened to the plane and the pilot. But already questions were being raised about the initial NASA comment that the U-2 had been on a weather mission, which was false.

Next, Dulles and Undersecretary of State Douglas Dillon made up a longer statement claiming, falsely, that the weather-mission pilot had problems with his oxygen equipment and lost consciousness. Then, the plane's autopilot system took over and flew the U-2 into Soviet air space, the U.S. officials said.

On Saturday, May 7, Khrushchev revealed the biggest surprise of all—telling a meeting of the Supreme Soviet that the pilot was alive and had admitted he worked for the CIA. He was in Soviet custody, and the Soviet military had gathered much of the plane's wreckage. Khrushchev even showed spy photographs that Powers had taken.

Ike was furious not only because the Soviets had shot down the spy plane but because the U.S. story was unraveling fast and his credibility was fading.

Secretary of State Christian Herter recommended that the administration contain the damage by acknowledging that a civilian U-2 had overflown the Soviet Union to gather intelligence that might relieve

U.S. concerns about a surprise nuclear attack.[10] This was done with Ike's approval. State Department officials also said the flight was not authorized by top government authorities, which was false, and the president went along with this deception, too. Beforehand, Eisenhower told Herter, "It is worth a try."[11] But the gambit engulfed the administration in even more of a cloud of distortions and miscalculation. The comment about the mission being unauthorized added to perceptions, spread by domestic critics, that Ike was delegating too much responsibility and giving aides too much leeway. Columnist James Reston wrote in the *New York Times* on May 8, "This was a sad and depressed capital tonight. It was depressed and humiliated by the United States' having been caught spying over the Soviet Union and trying to cover up its activities in a series of misleading official announcements."[12]

On Monday, May 9, Eisenhower convened a meeting of his National Security Council at the White House and admitted that the crisis was growing intense, and was now focusing on him. "Well, we're just going to have to take a lot of beating on this—and I'm the one who's going to have to take it," he said. "Of course, one had to expect that the thing would fail at one time or another. But that it had to be such a boo-boo and that we would be caught with our pants down was rather painful."[13]

On May 11, Eisenhower bit the bullet and held a news conference in the Indian Treaty Room of the Executive Office Building next to the White House. In a prepared statement, Ike tried to put the best spin on what had happened. He said the mission was conceived to obtain much-needed intelligence because, "No one wants another Pearl Harbor. This means that we must have knowledge of military forces and preparations around the world, especially those capable of massive surprise attacks." He said intelligence gathering "is a distasteful but vital necessity" that must be done in secret. And he tried to blame the Soviets by saying, "The emphasis given to the flight of an unarmed nonmilitary plane can only reflect a fetish for secrecy"—a hypocritical condemnation of Soviet secrecy even though Ike was insisting that American intelligence-gathering must be kept secret.[14]

Argues historian Hitchcock:

> The May 11 press conference marked an important moment in Ike's presidency and in the history of the cold war. Rather than leave things vague or heap blame on a subordinate or offer a muted apology

and a reassurance that such things would not happen in the future, Eisenhower embraced spying as a professional obligation and threw a cloak of invulnerability around all his subordinates who had worked on the U-2 program. He would not offer a head on a platter. He would not apologize. On the contrary, he would blame the Soviets for their obsessive secrecy and militarism.[15]

While his aides loved Eisenhower for this, and his fans said he showed admirable loyalty and willingness to accept responsibility for mistakes, others weren't so kind. Critics said Eisenhower had papered over his aides' unforgivable failures in judgment, accepted a cover-up, and left superpower relations in tatters. Hitchcock adds:

> Eisenhower chose an honorable path, one that kept his reputation for decency and integrity intact. Yet the price of that noble act was a dramatic worsening of the cold war. It is fair to ask if the price was too high.[16]

Khrushchev saw the American response to the U-2 shoot-down as weak and riddled with falsehoods. "Eisenhower's stand canceled any opportunity for us to get him out of the ticklish situation he was in," Khrushchev wrote later. "He had, so to speak, offered us his back end, and we obliged him by kicking it as hard as we could."[17]

One important result was Khrushchev's terminating the planned May 16 five-power summit meeting in Paris involving the United States, the Soviet Union, Great Britain, France and Germany. And Khrushchev tried to humiliate the Americans as much as possible while doing it.

Upon his arrival on May 14, he called on host Charles de Gaulle at Élysée Palace and rudely handed the French president a written set of prerequisites for his participation in the meeting. The Soviet premier presented three demands: Eisenhower must apologize for the latest U-2 flight; he must ban all future overflights, and he must punish those responsible for the U-2 flyover. De Gaulle made no commitments. Privately, Ike, who was still in the United States, fumed when told of Khrushchev's gambit. He said the Soviets had assigned spies throughout the United States, and other nations engaged in their own spying, and he would be "damned" if he was going to apologize for allowing what so many other countries were doing.[18]

Eisenhower arrived in Paris the following day, May 15, and conferred with his allies and aides. He decided, above all, not to "grovel" to the Soviet leader. No one was sure how Khrushchev would behave, but the Americans expected bluster. They got it.

Among the consequences was cancellation of the international summit meeting scheduled to start on May 16, 1960, in which Eisenhower hoped to win agreements from Moscow on disarmament, nuclear weapons testing and how to deal with potential conflict over who controlled the divided city of Berlin. Eisenhower earlier told defense officials he wanted to "thaw out the rigidity between the two sides or there would be a disaster in the world."[19] The U-2 incident also led to the cancellation of Eisenhower's planned trip to the Soviet Union on June 10. All in all, it caused a serious setback to improved superpower relations and made the Cold War worse.

The immediate collapse of the Paris summit turned out to be another drama that embarrassed Ike.

At 11 a.m. on Monday, May 16, Eisenhower met with Khrushchev along with de Gaulle, United Kingdom Prime Minister Harold Macmillan and West German Chancellor Konrad Adenauer and their advisers in a grand, high-ceilinged room on the second floor of the Élysée. De Gaulle, the host, asked Ike to speak first but Khrushchev rudely stood up and began shouting objections. When the interpreters translated his remarks, de Gaulle looked at Eisenhower, who nodded in agreement that the Soviet leader should have his say. Khrushchev began berating Eisenhower and the United States. De Gaulle said there was "no need" for the Soviet leader "to raise his voice," but the Kremlin leader resumed his denunciations, condemning the U-2 flight, clenching his right fist and shouting, "I have been overflown." After 45 minutes of fury, Khrushchev ended his diatribe by warning that unless Eisenhower apologized, he would not attend any more of the sessions.[20]

Eisenhower had listened quietly but his face was flushed with anger. He controlled himself, however, and in his remarks said he had already stopped overflights of the U.S.S.R. and promised not to allow any more. But he did not apologize and he said this particular U-2 flight on May 1 was not an aggressive act, only a mission designed to gather intelligence.

Khrushchev interrupted again and demanded an apology or he wouldn't remain, whereupon de Gaulle chastised Khrushchev for wasting everyone's time by suddenly issuing an ultimatum about boycotting the rest of the conference. The Soviet premier stormed out of the room, ending his participation and causing the conference to collapse.

The four other leaders formally ended the summit meeting the next day when Khrushchev declined de Gaulle's invitation for him to return, leaving Ike with profound disappointment that his hopes for a thaw in the Cold War had been shattered.

It wasn't until February 1962, 21 months later, that the Soviets traded U-2 pilot Francis Gary Powers for Rudolf Abel, a convicted Soviet spy being held in the United States. At this point, Ike was no longer president, and John F. Kennedy was in command, and he also was to make his share of mistakes in handling Khrushchev.

Eisenhower's political critics at home attacked him vehemently. In fact, the U-2 mess quickly became a major issue of the 1960 presidential campaign. Ike was not running because he was constitutionally prohibited from serving a third term. But his policies were, in effect, on the ballot. Kennedy, a senator from Massachusetts, won the Democratic nomination and the image of "a befuddled, ill-prepared Eisenhower out of his depth in a dangerous world became the leitmotif of Kennedy's campaign"—and the U-2 incident was one of his prime examples, wrote historian Hitchcock. " . . . [T]he Paris fiasco—Khrushchev's sneering, Eisenhower's fumbling, the sense of dashed hopes—irked Americans all across the political spectrum."[21] Kennedy, of course, won the 1960 election.

Concluded Hitchcock:

> Though Eisenhower treated the U-2 affair with nonchalance in his memoirs, the downing of the spy plane had a huge impact on his presidency and on the cold war itself. It shattered his hopes to bring about a thaw in the war, thereby robbing him of a brilliant achievement in his last months in office. It led to a sharp intensification of cold war hostilities. It undermined all of his efforts to establish himself as a man of peace and goodwill in the eyes of the world's peoples. And it provided his domestic political rivals with powerful ammunition to use against him and his handling of the cold war. In retrospect his decision to approve the U-2 overflights in the spring of 1960 was the biggest mistake he ever made.[22]

Khrushchev also made serious errors. Writes author Bohn, former director of the White House Situation Room under President Ronald Reagan:

> The Soviet leader had a chance to handle the incident in a manner that could have helped US–Soviet relations, but instead he felt he had to exploit the shoot-down to strengthen his position within the Soviet leadership. This was his way of offsetting the humiliation wrought by the U-2 technology and the doubts it created among Khrushchev's opponents in the Politburo.

Still, some of Khrushchev's opponents later criticized him for being overly aggressive and engaging in "inexcusable hysterics."[23]

But Eisenhower took most of the blame. "Ike offered a case study for future presidents on how not to handle an unanticipated crisis," Bohn said.

> In rapid order, he elected to do nothing, fabricated a cover-up that changed in detail daily, and set up himself and the country for humiliation by his Cold War opponent. The incident halted the slight thaw then underway in US–Soviet relations and put the two countries on a track to the Cold War's most dangerous time, the Cuban Missile Crisis.[24]

Eisenhower later admitted botching the crisis in a basic way. "The big error," he wrote in his memoirs, "was, of course, the issuance of a premature and erroneous cover story." He also told an interviewer after leaving office that his biggest regret as president was "the lie we told about the U-2. I didn't realize how high a price we were going to pay for that lie."[25]

Bohn concludes, "In the years since, rule number one in crisis management, whether in the White House or during run-of-the mill Washington scandals, has been 'Tell the truth and tell it early.'"[26]

Precis

Dwight Eisenhower failed a big test of his leadership in the U-2 incident. He showed bad judgment in scheduling the ill-timed overflight just before a key superpower summit meeting, which was extremely provocative to the Kremlin. He failed to adapt to changing circumstances when he continued to lie about the incident after the plane was shot down, damaging his credibility at home and abroad. The episode turned into a debacle for the United States and caused a serious setback to superpower relations.

Notes

1. William I. Hitchcock, *The Age of Eisenhower: America and the World in the 1950s*, New York: Simon & Schuster, 2018, p. 456.
2. Hitchcock, p. 463.
3. Michael K. Bohn, *Presidents in Crisis: Tough Decisions inside the White House from Truman to Obama*, New York: Arcade Publishing, 2015, 2016, p. 41.
4. Bohn, pp. 40–41.
5. Bohn, p. 42.
6. Bohn, p. 42.
7. My reporting on the U-2 is based on several accounts, including the version published by Bohn, ibid, pp. 42–44, and Hitchcock, ibid., pp. 462–474.
8. Hitchcock, ibid., p. 463.
9. Bohn, p. 43.
10. Hitchcock, p. 465.
11. Bohn, pp. 42–44.
12. Hitchcock, p. 465.
13. Bohn, p 43.
14. Bohn, p. 44, and Hitchcock, p. 466.
15. Hitchcock, p. 466.
16. Hitchcock, p. 467.
17. Bohn, p. 44.
18. Hitchcock, p. 476.
19. Hitchcock, p. 456.
20. Bohn, pp. 44–45.
21. Hitchcock, p. 472.
22. Hitchcock, p. 469.
23. Bohn, p. 46.
24. Bohn, p. 46.
25. Bohn, pp. 46–47.
26. Bohn, p. 47.

Chapter Five
John F. Kennedy
The Cuban Missile Crisis

John F. Kennedy gave a televised address to the nation and the world from the Oval Office on October 22, 1962 to demonstrate his resolve in dealing with the Soviet Union during the Cuban Missile Crisis. Kennedy's performance throughout this dangerous episode displayed his leadership skills in dramatic fashion. (Cecil Stoughton, White House Photographs, John F. Kennedy Presidential Library and Museum)

The Cuban Missile Crisis in October 1962 was one of the most dangerous international confrontations in history, and President John F. Kennedy handled it with skill and prescience, balancing caution and strength. Historians have used it as a case study for presidential leadership under emergency conditions ever since.

The showdown took the United States and the Soviet Union to the brink of nuclear war, imperiling the lives of hundreds of millions of people. Arthur Schlesinger, Jr., a Kennedy adviser and scholar, later said the Cuban Missile Crisis was "the most dangerous moment in human history."[1] Many other historians have concluded that it was the closest that the world has come to a nuclear conflagration.

From the start, Kennedy took a pragmatic approach and was correctly skeptical of his military advisers' bellicose and trigger-happy attitudes.[2]

Kennedy wisely attempted to give Soviet leader Nikita Khrushchev a face-saving exit from the confrontation even as his military advisers pushed for more confrontation.

And in its peaceful resolution, the crisis showed that human beings can solve even the worst of their problems if they rely on the best that leadership can offer—namely the traits of understanding, good judgment, steadiness and strength. In the end, both Kennedy and Khrushchev showed enough of these characteristics to overcome the vast gulf of distrust between them and the deep ideological differences that separated their countries in order to extricate themselves from the doomsday scenario that faced them. For nearly two weeks, they held the fate of the world in their hands, and, despite some blunders and misjudgments, they performed admirably.[3]

KENNEDY AND KHRUSHCHEV should never have allowed the situation to reach crisis proportions to begin with. And each man should be faulted for taking the world to the brink. But once the crisis started, they pulled back from their mutual machismo and removed their ideological blinders to avoid the ultimate catastrophe.

Kennedy had suffered a serious political setback and a major humiliation with the Bay of Pigs fiasco in April 1961, only a few months after he took office. This was a failed U.S.-backed invasion of Cuba by exiled anti-communists from the island. More than 100 of the 1,400-man invasion force were killed and 1,200 captured.[4] JFK learned from his mistakes and in the Cuban Missile Crisis refused to accept the bellicose solutions of the military brass as he had done with the Bay of Pigs.

There were many pressures on both Kennedy and Khrushchev that led them to the brink. First, there was lasting enmity from President Eisenhower's handling of the U-2 incident in 1960, in which a U.S. U-2 spy plane was destroyed flying over Soviet territory, and the U.S. pilot Francis Gary Powers was captured. This seriously intensified Cold War tensions.

Things got worse during the summer and fall of 1961. The Soviets and their allies the East Germans erected a wall around West Berlin, which was allied with the United States and the West. Kennedy considered a military response but eventually rejected the idea and accepted the wall. But his critics wondered if he was tough enough to deal with Khrushchev and the Kremlin. Khrushchev also mistook Kennedy for a weak leader who could be bullied when they met in Vienna in 1961, not long after JFK took office.

Castro and Khrushchev believed another invasion of Cuba was in the works, and that Kennedy sought revenge for the Bay of Pigs disaster. When the U.S. military held training exercises in the spring of 1962 that tested contingency plans for invading Cuba, Khrushchev considered it especially provocative.[5]

Khrushchev began looking for a way to confront and threaten Kennedy. He decided to install medium-range ballistic missiles in Cuba, a Soviet ally 90 miles from Florida, as a direct response to the medium-range ballistic missiles that the United States and NATO had deployed in Italy and Turkey to threaten the nearby U.S.S.R.

ON OCTOBER 14, 1962, a U-2 reconnaissance plane (the same type of aircraft involved in Eisenhower's U-2 incident), flying at 72,500 feet, revealed the presence of Soviet ballistic missiles in Cuba.

Intelligence officers confirmed the findings and White House National Security Adviser McGeorge Bundy briefed Kennedy at the White House Residence at 8 a.m. on October 16. The president was in his pajamas and robe, and was reading a *New York Times* story headlined "Eisenhower Calls President Weak on Foreign Policy."[6] This line of attack—that Kennedy was weak—was being increasingly used by the Republicans. And it was becoming a political concern at the White House.

Bundy explained that the Soviet medium-range ballistic missile system, known in NATO as the SS-4, had been set up in San Diego de los Banos in western Cuba. The weapons system included a missile that carried a one-megaton nuclear warhead and had a maximum range of

1,292 nautical miles, which threatened much of the U.S. East Coast. Kennedy recalled that Khrushchev had assured him that he would not install such offensive weapons in Cuba. "He can't do this to me," Kennedy complained.[7]

Kennedy immediately understood the gravity of the situation. Such missiles could reach U.S. shores within minutes, threatening millions of Americans with annihilation. Installing these weapons, he knew, was one of the most provocative acts of the Cold War.

At noon on October 16, 1962, Kennedy and his senior advisers gathered in the Cabinet Room and studied aerial photos of the missile site in Cuba. A military aide placed the enlargements on an easel in front of the fireplace, under a Stuart portrait of George Washington, who had dealt with so many crises during the Revolutionary War and during his presidency nearly two centuries earlier. But Kennedy was handling a crisis that was much more dangerous and potentially catastrophic than any that Washington had ever faced. An aide said that JFK, usually quick with a joke to ease the pressure of tense situations, was "very clipped, very tense. I don't recall a time when I saw him more preoccupied and less given to any light touch at all."[8]

Attending the October 16 meeting were senior Kennedy advisers including Bundy, Defense Secretary Robert McNamara, Secretary of State Dean Rusk, Undersecretary of State George Ball, Treasury Secretary Douglas Dillon, Attorney General Robert Kennedy (the president's brother), Gen. Maxwell Taylor, the chairman of the Joint Chiefs of Staff, and Lt. Gen. Marshall Carter, the deputy CIA director.

The advisers discussed the intelligence reports and how alarming they were, and speculated on when the weapons might be operational—considered a key factor because the military officers wanted the missile system taken out before it could be used. They quickly began discussing alternative responses to the Soviet provocation. Kennedy initially seemed to lean toward a punitive air strike to destroy the missiles but he didn't push the idea aggressively and welcomed the subsequent discussion of alternatives.

The choices included an invasion of Cuba, a naval blockade of the communist-run island, or diplomacy.

The crisis went on for 13 days as Kennedy continued a series of secret, tension-filled meetings with his senior advisers to determine what to do.

Secretary of State Rusk had learned about the missiles the night before, on October 15, and after studying the situation and reviewing the options, he told Kennedy and the other advisers on the 16th that it was time for action. "We, all of us, had not really believed the Soviets could carry it this far," Rusk said.

> Now I do think we have to set in motion a chain of events that will eliminate this base. I don't think we can sit still. The questioning becomes whether we do it by sudden, unannounced strike of some sort—or we build up the crisis to the point where the other side has to consider very seriously about giving in, or even the Cubans themselves take some . . . action on this.[9]

Rusk suggested using a back channel to privately tell Cuban leader Fidel Castro that his country was being "victimized" and that the Kremlin was preparing for the "destruction or betrayal" of Cuba. Rusk added that the crisis "could well lead to general war."[10]

At a news conference on September 13, Kennedy had warned of dire consequences if the Soviets installed offensive weapons in Cuba but neither the president nor his senior advisers thought the Soviets would directly challenge him as they now were doing. In fact, Kennedy had been very tough, declaring on September 13 that if Cuba became "an offensive military base of significant capacity for the Soviet Union, then this country will do whatever must be done to protect its own security and that of its allies."[11] This threat weighed heavily on Kennedy throughout the crisis. His credibility was at stake, nationally and internationally. He later said if he hadn't moved to get rid of the missiles, "I would have been impeached."[12]

Kennedy was very concerned about appearances. He didn't want to tip anyone off, especially his likely Republican critics who he felt were ready to pounce on any show of weakness, until he knew what he was going to do. He tried to maintain a public stance of business as usual. On Wednesday, October 17, the second day of the crisis, he flew to Connecticut to campaign for Senate candidate Abraham Ribicoff. On this same day, October 17, JFK's advisers met twice without the president. They discussed a range of options for his consideration with no consensus on what should be done. At the end of the meetings, they came up with five choices: issue an ultimatum to Khrushchev followed by an air strike on the missile sites; launch limited surprise air strikes; make diplomatic threats, coupled with starting a naval blockade in coordination with U.S. allies; stage large-scale air strikes after limited diplomatic preparation, or invade Cuba.[13]

At 11 a.m. on Thursday, October 18, Kennedy met in the Cabinet Room again with his crisis advisers, known inside the White House as "ExComm" (for the Executive Committee of the National Security Council). According to historian Bohn:

> The debate moved in circles, and participants changed positions as others made well-reasoned arguments. Bobby Kennedy raised the moral question of launching a surprise, unilateral action and cited the reviled Japanese attack at Pearl Harbor. All agreed, meanwhile, that the president should take his planned political trip to the Midwest the next day. Likewise, the president stuck to his schedule at 5:00 p.m. when he kept a previously arranged appointment with Soviet foreign minister Andrei Gromyko. The two spoke about the Soviet weapons deployed in Cuba, and the Russian claimed they were strictly defensive. Later revelations, however, proved that Gromyko was fully informed about the ballistic missiles' offensive capabilities.

The president made no mention of the intelligence discoveries in order to safeguard his options for a surprise attack.[14]

"I was dying to confront him with our evidence," Kennedy said of Gromyko, condemning him as "that lying bastard."[15]

On Friday, October 19, the fourth day of the crisis, the president met with the Joint Chiefs of Staff in the Cabinet Room. As they entered, Kennedy gravely shook hands with each of them, four generals and an admiral, each of them wearing decks of ribbons on their chests in testament to their wartime courage and long years of service in the military. Kennedy sat in the middle of the long table with his back to the windows facing the Rose Garden, the same spot where other presidents had presided over meetings to discuss issues both pedestrian and profound. But the Cuban Missile Crisis had taken on a whole new order of magnitude.

Gen. Maxwell Taylor, the chairman of the Joint Chiefs appointed by Kennedy less than three weeks earlier, started the meeting by explaining that the chiefs agreed on the need for bold military action. Before he could continue and before the other military men could chime in, the president interrupted. "Let me just say a little, first, about what the problem is, from my point of view," Kennedy said. He wanted to set the terms of the discussion rather than allow the Pentagon brass to do it. He didn't trust the joint chiefs, considering them too bellicose and simplistic in their thinking, and believed he had to take charge because they viewed him as an immature politician who lacked toughness.[16]

Kennedy said he feared that the confrontation in Cuba could escalate into war with the Soviet Union. He expressed concern that the Soviets might seize West Berlin, isolated inside communist East Germany, if the United States attacked Cuba. "Which leaves me with only one alternative, which is to fire nuclear weapons—a hell of an alternative," Kennedy said.[17]

But Air Force Gen. Curtis LeMay, the gruffest and most bellicose of the chiefs, broke in. Pulling his cigar out of his mouth, LeMay announced, "We don't have any choice except direct military action," and then resumed smoking in a display of machismo.[18]

The president asked, "What do you think the Soviet reply would be?"[19]

LeMay replied, "I don't think they're going to make any reply." As he blew a puff of smoke across the table, LeMay added: "I see no other solution. This blockade and political action, I see leading into war. This is almost as bad as the appeasement at Munich." He was referring to how Western nations led by the United Kingdom had attempted to appease German leader Adolf Hitler in 1938 when Hitler used aggression to expand Germany territory. The appeasement only encouraged Hitler and gave the impression that the UK-led democracies were frightened and weak.[20]

All three of the other chiefs—Admiral George Anderson of the Navy, Gen. Earle Wheeler of the Army and Gen. David Shoup of the Marines (an ad hoc JCS member)—agreed with LeMay in calling for an immediate attack. Kennedy admitted that such a move might be necessary, and he asked when the military leaders would be ready to strike by air if he were to approve it. LeMay said the Air Force could be ready in two days, on Sunday, October 21, but Tuesday, October 23 would be preferable.

Kennedy said a naval blockade had the advantage of giving the Soviet premier maneuvering room without going to war. But Gen. LeMay pugnaciously replied, "I think that a blockade, and political talk, would be considered by a lot of our friends and neutrals as being a pretty weak response to this." The general added imperiously and with considerable condescension: "You're in a pretty bad fix, Mr. President."

Kennedy looked at him coldly and asked, "What did you say?"

LeMay replied defiantly, "You're in a pretty bad fix."

"You're in it with me personally," Kennedy declared.[21]

Kennedy then steered the discussion to the possibility of a naval blockade to prevent Soviet ships from reaching Cuban waters. But nothing was resolved.

After the meeting, Kennedy seethed. "These brass hats have one great advantage in their favor," he told personal assistant David Powers as they walked to the Oval Office. "If we do what they want us to do, none of us will be alive later to tell them that they were wrong." But LeMay's impertinence hardened the young president's resolve to do things in his own careful way.[22]

And the situation was getting worse. While the military leaders and other advisers debated, photo interpreters in Washington discovered additional missile sites, this time in Guanajay and Remedios. And these were more dangerous than the one that had been discovered earlier. They were larger intermediate-range ballistic missile systems with a maximum range of 2,400 nautical miles and one-megaton warhead. They could threaten all major U.S. cities except Seattle. It turned out that the Soviets also were pouring soldiers into Cuba—an estimated 42,000 troops at this time—along with more missiles and other weapons for both offensive and defensive purposes.[23]

After his contentious morning session with the Joint Chiefs on October 19, Kennedy asked his brother Robert and one of his most trusted aides, Ted Sorensen, to try to build a consensus among top government officials in favor of the blockade while he left town to attend a political rally in Cleveland. He hadn't made his final decision yet, but was leaning heavily toward the blockade and didn't want to seem like he was overruling his advisers in any way, especially the military hawks. The ExComm continued deliberating for many hours and the next morning, Saturday, October 20, the members, under pressure from Robert Kennedy and Sorensen, agreed to accept the naval blockade or quarantine, if that's what the president wanted as his final decision. And the wording was important. Most world leaders felt that a blockade was an act of war so the Americans decided to call it the less belligerent "quarantine," arguing that this would not require a congressional declaration of war.

During the weekend, the military made its preparations. Navy officials eased the minds of other advisers by declaring that they were ready to stop ships on the way to Cuba and search their cargo for offensive weapons.

On Saturday, October 20, Robert Kennedy phoned the president at the Blackstone Hotel in Chicago, where he had gone for another political trip, and said there was consensus on the quarantine if that's how the president wanted to proceed.

White House Press Secretary Pierre Salinger lied to reporters, telling them the president had developed a cold and was returning to the White House. This was a cover story. Kennedy didn't want to tip his hand quite yet.

At 2:30 p.m., Kennedy met with his advisers in the Oval Room of the Residence and announced that he was ready to make a final decision on what to do next. "Gentlemen, today we're going to earn our pay," he said.[24] This was to be the decision meeting.

Kennedy asked each of the 12 persons in attendance for his personal recommendation on what to do. Kennedy didn't reveal his own preferences at first but conveyed a general sense of restraint and a desire to make prudent choices.[25]

After each adviser had his say, Kennedy got up from the table and walked onto the Truman Balcony overlooking the expanse of the White House grounds and the Washington Monument beyond. He stood there, alone with his thoughts, for several minutes as everyone in the room sat silently. Robert Kennedy and Sorensen joined the commander in chief on the balcony and then the three of them returned to the room. "I know each of you is hoping I didn't take your advice," Kennedy quipped in an attempt to break the tension. He then announced that he had decided to impose the quarantine.[26] They would aim to start it Wednesday, October 24—in four days.

It was an intermediate move, blending military action with diplomacy and threat. "He wanted this incremental first step not to be his last; he wanted room to take follow-on action," Bohn wrote. "Moreover, the quarantine gave Khrushchev an avenue to back away. In taking this approach, Kennedy set a fine example for presidents who followed."[27]

The planning reached fever pitch. On Sunday, October 21, the sixth day of the crisis, the Defense Department made contingency plans for air strikes in case the president ordered them. Administration officials even made contingency plans to evacuate Kennedy and hundreds of other officials from Washington in case there was a nuclear war. Meanwhile, Kennedy aides drafted the president's speech to the nation that he intended to give Monday night, and other aides prepared an ultimatum to Khrushchev, also to be delivered Monday. Kennedy got heavily involved in the public relations, successfully appealing to the publishers of the *New York Times* and *Washington Post* to hold their speculative stories about the brewing crisis until after his Monday speech.[28]

On Monday, October 22, Kennedy briefed congressional leaders at the White House, and the reaction among several was shock and opposition. Sen. Richard Russell, D-Ga., chairman of the Senate Armed Services Committee, was stunned when Kennedy told the group that some Soviet missiles were operational. Urging an air strike and invasion, Russell said, "We're either a world-class power or we're not." Sen. J. William Fulbright, D-Ark., agreed with Russell and added: "A blockade seems to me the worst alternative."[29]

At 7 p.m. that same day, October 22, Kennedy revealed to the world what was going on. He spoke live on TV and radio, described the deployment of Soviet missiles in Cuba, and declared,

> The cost of freedom is always high—but Americans have always paid it. And one path we shall never choose is the path of surrender or submission. Our goal is not the victory of might but the vindication of right.[30]

He explained that he was imposing a naval blockade around Cuba, which he called a quarantine, and made it clear that the United States was prepared to use military force if necessary to stop the threat. And he blamed the Soviets for the crisis. "I call upon Chairman Khrushchev to halt or eliminate this clandestine, reckless, and provocative threat to world peace," Kennedy said.[31]

The speech set off a frenzy of concern in the United States and in many other countries, including the Soviet Union. Khrushchev sent two confrontational letters to Kennedy on October 23 and 24. But the Soviet leader was uncertain about exactly what to do.[32]

At 10 a.m. on Wednesday, October 24, day nine of the crisis, the Navy imposed the quarantine, and at first it went smoothly. It developed that Khrushchev had ordered Soviet ships headed for Cuba to stop, except for one vessel, the *Aleksandrovsk*, which Khrushchev allowed to enter a Cuban port on October 23, the day before the quarantine started. *Aleksandrovsk* carried 24 medium-range nuclear warheads and 40 tactical nuclear warheads. Sixteen ships carrying missiles and other weapons were ordered to return to the U.S.S.R.

Secretary of State Rusk summed up the reaction of Kennedy and his senior advisers: "We're eyeball to eyeball and the other fellow just blinked."[33]

On Thursday, October 25, Kennedy replied to Khrushchev's messages of October 24. "I repeat my regret that these events should cause a deterioration in our relations," the president wrote. Khrushchev apparently was pleased by Kennedy's reasonable attitude. Also, the administration floated to the *New York Times* and *Washington Post* the idea of swapping the largely outmoded U.S. Jupiter missiles in Turkey for the Soviet weapons in Cuba.[34]

At an 11 a.m. meeting on October 25, Kennedy met with his ExComm advisers in the Cabinet Room and they discussed a variety of topics related to the crisis, including whether to trade the Jupiter missiles in Turkey in exchange for moving or destroying the Soviet SS-4s and SS-5s from Cuba. This question remained unresolved.

Kennedy seemed prepared to escalate if the quarantine didn't work quickly in persuading the Kremlin to remove the missiles. The president said, "So we've only got two ways of removing the weapons. One is to negotiate them out or trade them out. And the other is to go over and just take them out."[35]

On Friday, October 26, Robert Kennedy met secretly with Soviet Ambassador Anatoly Dobrynin and told Dobrynin that the president planned to remove the Jupiter missiles from Turkey once the current situation calmed down. Dobrynin cabled Moscow with this information that evening. The crisis seemed to be easing.[36]

Also on Friday, October 26, Navy destroyer USS *Joseph P. Kennedy* (named after the president's father, a former U.S. ambassador to the Court of St. James) halted the first ship to cross the quarantine line. It was a freighter named *Marcula*. The naval officers found no weapons and allowed the *Marcula* to proceed to Cuba.[37]

But the next day, Saturday, the tension escalated again. Aerial reconnaissance revealed that the Soviets were still constructing the missile sites in Cuba and assembling Il-28 bombers. And the FBI said the Soviets were destroying sensitive documents at the United Nations in New York, presumably because they saw the crisis getting worse.[38]

At 10 a.m., ExComm met to discuss the appropriate response to Khrushchev's letter of Friday. But as the meeting was taking place, a second letter from the Soviet leader arrived. Khrushchev insisted that the United States withdraw its Jupiter medium-range missiles from Turkey in exchange for the Soviets removing their missiles from Cuba. It seemed like a setback because the tone was so abrasive and demanding.[39]

What the Americans didn't know at that point was that Khrushchev, hoping to defuse the crisis, had just prohibited Soviet military leaders in Cuba from using the nuclear weapons, including the tactical nuclear systems.[40]

Then came another setback. On the morning of Saturday, October 27, an Air Force pilot accidentally flew a U-2 spy plane off course in the Arctic and intruded into Soviet air space. The pilot was supposed to be on a mission to detect fallout from a Soviet nuclear test, U.S. officials said, but his errant flight path caused Soviet air defense officials to scramble six interceptors, thinking the U-2 was possibly an advance mission preceding an American attack over the North Pole. The pilot quickly corrected his course and flew safety to Alaska, and this reduced the tension.[41]

But the tension quickly returned when a Soviet SA-2 surface-to-air missile destroyed a U.S. Air Force U-2 plane over eastern Cuba, killing the pilot, Major Rudolf Anderson.[42] Kremlin officials had ordered Soviet forces not to engage U.S. aircraft, but Cuban military officials had fired at low-level U.S. reconnaissance planes that day. Lt. Gen. Stepan Grechko, the commander of Soviet air defense forces in Cuba, jumped to the conclusion that war had begun and, since he was unable to reach his superior, Grechko authorized the launch of two SA-2 missiles at the U-2, downing it and killing Anderson.[43]

Pentagon officials learned of the shootdown at about 2:30 p.m. on Sunday, October 28, and the Joint Chiefs called for air strikes on Cuba on Monday, followed with a ground invasion on Tuesday. At a 4 p.m. meeting, most members of ExComm agreed, but President Kennedy said no. "It isn't the first step that concerns me, but both sides escalating to the fourth or fifth step," he explained.[44] Still, Kennedy agreed to powerful air strikes—1,190 sorties—on Tuesday, and the clock was ticking.[45]

At this point, Kennedy also decided to respond directly to Khrushchev's first letter from Friday, rather than the more bellicose letter of Saturday which demanded the removal of the U.S. Jupiter missiles. Kennedy told Khrushchev in his own letter that he promised not to invade Cuba in exchange for U.N.-observed missile removal from Cuba. This letter was transmitted at 8:05 p.m.[46] But in a directly related move, Kennedy also sent his brother Robert to visit Soviet Ambassador Dobrynin again in a move to reply to Khrushchev's Saturday demand. Robert Kennedy brought a secret offer to remove the Jupiter missiles but warned Dobrynin that any Soviet disclosure of the offer would void it.

Both Kennedy and Khrushchev, despite their lack of information about how far the other leader would go, realized how close they were to war and began pulling back from the brink.

Kennedy, hoping for compromise, ordered any potential attacks on Cuba delayed until Tuesday. But he did authorize the call-up of Air Force reserves needed for a potential Cuban invasion. In Moscow, Khrushchev demonstrated restraint by not reacting harshly to the U-2 straying off course in the Arctic. He said the incident was probably an error by the pilot, not an intentional provocation by the Americans.

But Khrushchev shared Kennedy's concerns about the crisis spinning out of control because of bad judgments or impulsive actions by their subordinates. The premier, referring to the U-2 shootdown that killed the American pilot Rudolf Anderson, noted that "one general had decided it was a good idea to launch an antiaircraft missile," Khrushchev's son said later. "Tomorrow, a different one might decide to launch a ballistic missile—also without asking Moscow's permission."[47]

Khrushchev, after studying Dobrynin's report on his two secret conversations with Robert Kennedy, decided he had won sufficient concessions to declare victory. He had extracted a pledge from Kennedy not to invade Cuba and another promise to remove the Jupiter missiles from Turkey, along the Soviet border. So Khrushchev sent an immediate message to Kennedy agreeing to dismantle and remove the missiles from Cuba with U.N. inspection and supervision.

Kennedy felt he had won the crisis, too. The missiles would be gone, after all, which had been his prime objective.

Bohn wrote,

> With that big stick [U.S. military superiority in the region] at the ready, Kennedy successfully muddled through the crisis, or in other words, acted with incremental steps, with the naval quarantine being

the most important. He also wisely followed a rule from military theorist Carl von Clausewitz: Don't take the first step without thinking about what may be the last. And he took those steps coupled with a healthy dose of realism, a willingness to understand the other fellow's problem and the good sense to compromise. Both leaders made concessions while maintaining an appearance of resolve, and thus became coconspirators. Both men blinked.[48]

These traits—incremental steps, planning for contingencies, realism, understanding the other side and the willingness to compromise—have become commonly accepted by historians and national-security specialists as pivotal in presidential crisis management. And the Cuban Missile Crisis has become a prime example of effective presidential leadership in a very dangerous and delicate situation.

"The point is JFK understood that being president was not a set-piece affair," said historian Robert Dallek. "He evolved, and he grew in that office. That, in many ways, was his greatest strength: Kennedy grew in the office." And he showed it in the Cuban Missile Crisis.[49]

Precis

John F. Kennedy took strong action by ordering a naval blockade of Cuba. He adapted well to changing circumstances in a fast-moving crisis, showing flexibility under extreme pressure. He balanced principle with pragmatism in pressuring the Soviet Union to remove its missiles from the communist-ruled island. He persevered. And, with compromise, he achieved success in getting the missiles out.

Notes

1. Arthur Schlesinger, Jr., "On the Brink: The Cuban Missile Crisis," transcript of forum at John F. Kennedy Library, Oct. 20, 2002, p. 13, jfklibrary.org/events-and-awards/forums/past-forums/transcripts/on-the-brink-the-cuban-missile-crisis. Also, Arthur Schlesinger, Jr., Foreword, Robert F. Kennedy, *Thirteen Days: A Memoir of the Cuban Missile Crisis*, New York: W.W. Norton & Company, 1999, p. 7.
2. Michael K. Bohn, *Presidents in Crisis: Tough Decisions inside the White House from Truman to Obama*, New York, Arcade Publishing, 2015, 2016, p. 50. Also, see Bohn's overall account of the Cuban Missile Crisis, Chapter 3, *Presidents in Crisis*.

3. Author's interview with historian Robert Dallek, September 20, 2018.
4. Bohn, p. 51.
5. Bohn, p. 51.
6. Bohn, p. 52.
7. Barbara Learning, *Jack Kennedy*, New York: W. W. Norton, 2006, p. 401.
8. Quoted in Michael R. Beschloss' essay "The Crisis Years" in Nathaniel May, ed., *Oval Office: Stories of Presidents in Crisis from Washington to Bush*. New York: Thunder's Mouth Press, 2002, p. 114.
9. Beschloss, p. 115.
10. Beschloss, ibid.
11. Transcript of Kennedy News Conference, *Washington Post*, September 14, 1962.
12. Sheldon M. Stern, *Averting 'The Final Failure,'* Stanford, CA: Stanford University Press, 2003, p. 204.
13. Bohn, p. 54.
14. Bohn, p. 55.
15. Kenneth P. O'Donnell and David F. Powers, with Joe McCarthy, *Johnny, We Hardly Knew Ye*, Boston: Little, Brown, 1972, p. 319.
16. Ernest R. May and Philip D. Zelikow, eds., *The Kennedy Tapes*, Cambridge, MA: Harvard University Press, 1997, p. 121. Also see Bohn, pp. 48–49.
17. This account comes from May and Zelikow, p.121. Also see Bohn, pp. 48–49.
18. May and Zelikow, ibid. Also see Bohn, pp. 48–49.
19. Ibid.
20. Ibid.
21. O'Donnell and Powers, p. 276. Also, see Bohn's overall account of the Cuban Missile Crisis, Chapter 3, *Presidents in Crisis*.
22. O'Donnell and Powers, p. 276. Also, see Bohn's overall account of the Cuban Missile Crisis, Chapter 3, *Presidents in Crisis*.
23. Bohn, p. 55.
24. Stern, p. 133.
25. Bohn, p. 57.
26. Bohn, p. 57.
27. Bohn, p. 58.
28. Bohn, p. 58.
29. Michael Dobbs, *One Minute to Midnight*, New York: Alfred Knopf, 2008, p. 41.
30. Quoted in Patti Davis, "The Child in the White House," *Washington Post*, December 18, 2018, p. A19.
31. Bohn, p. 59.
32. "Cuban Missile Crisis," History.com, Jan 4, 2010, https://www.history.com/topics/cold-war/cuban-missile-crisis.
33. O'Donnell and Powers, p. 332.
34. Bohn, pp. 61–62.

35. May and Zelikow, p. 464.
36. Raymond L. Garthoff, *Reflections on the Cuban Missile Crisis*, Washington, DC, Brookings Institution, 1989, p. 18.
37. Bohn, p. 62.
38. Bohn, p. 63.
39. Bohn, p. 64.
40. Bohn, p. 64.
41. Bohn, p. 64.
42. Dobbs, p. 237.
43. Bohn, p. 65.
44. Kennedy, p. 74.
45. Bohn, p. 67.
46. Stern, p. 367.
47. Bohn, p. 66.
48. Bohn, p. 68.
49. Robert Dallek, "John F. Kennedy," Interview Contained in Brian Lamb, Susan Swain and C-SPAN, *The Presidents: Noted Historians Rank America's Best—and Worst—Chief Executives*, New York: Public Affairs, 2019, p. 186.

Chapter Six
Lyndon B. Johnson
The War in Vietnam and Re-election

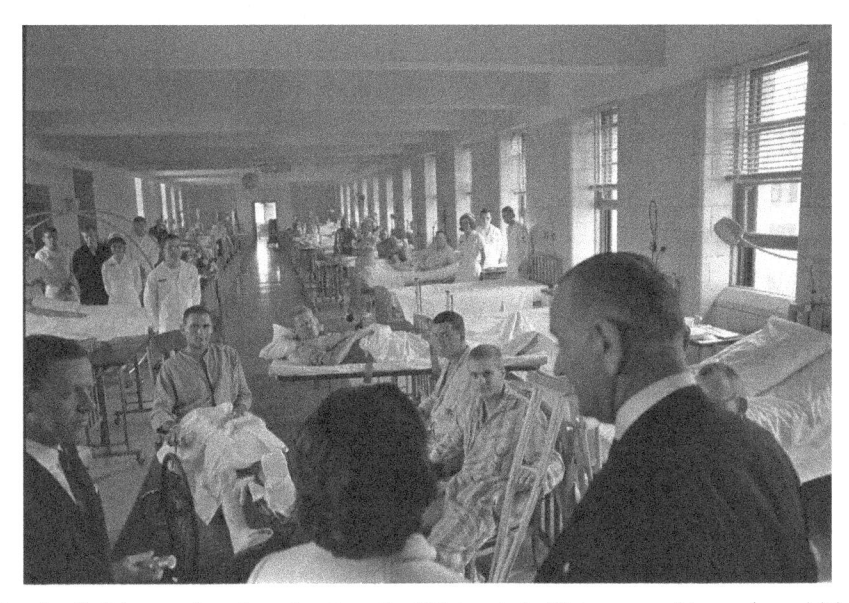

Lyndon B. Johnson often showed support for U.S. troops in Vietnam, and is seen here visiting wounded soldiers at the National Naval Medical Center in Bethesda, Maryland, during October 1965. But he couldn't rally the country behind the war and, facing setbacks in the conflict and with his popularity sagging, declined to run for re-election in 1968. (Yoichi Okamoto, LBJ Library)

Lyndon B. Johnson's shocking decision not to run for re-election in 1968 was one of the most important moments of his crisis-ridden presidency. It illustrated not only the essence of Johnson as a politician who loved to dominate everyone and everything around him, it also underscored his larger-than-life boldness, which pervaded American politics for all five years of his presidency.

LBJ, ever the showman, liked to stay at the center of attention and keep his critics off balance. President Donald Trump has a lot in common with Johnson today on this score.

In the process of deciding not to seek a second full term, Johnson gave up the job he had pursued for so long and that he loved. It was a gut-wrenching decision for him but in the end it was the correct one. He wanted to spare the country at least some of the bitterness caused by his escalation of the Vietnam war and his social activism, an agenda known as the Great Society, that broadened and deepened the power of the federal government. But ending the rancor proved impossible in such a divided country. He was the only commander in chief to be driven from office by war.

Johnson made his stunning announcement on March 31, 1968, and it was one of the biggest surprises of any presidential cycle.

LBJ's problems had been intensifying since the start of the year. In late January and February, communist forces launched a series of surprise attacks across South Vietnam in the Tet offensive. As casualties mounted on all sides—American, South Vietnamese and North Vietnamese, military and civilian—it became clear that LBJ's policies in Vietnam weren't working. The offensive gave the lie to the declarations by Johnson and his military commanders that the war was close to being won. And it quickly became clear that the American leaders had badly underestimated the enemy's strength and determination, and that the war was deadlocked.

"Such as it was, the strategy remained to inflict losses until the enemy gave up," noted historian James R. Arnold. "After four years of American intervention, there were no signs that the enemy's will was wavering. No one could predict when the Communists would desist . . . There was no reassurance that sending more men would change anything."[1]

The irony was that Tet was far more costly for the communists than for the United States or its South Vietnamese allies. But it was a political and public relations nightmare in the United States. "While Tet failed to defeat the U.S. combat soldier, it defeated their generals and their political leaders," Arnold wrote,

> and it reversed the support of the people back home. Before Tet, American leaders sought some form of victory. After Tet, they sought to withdraw gracefully. If a decisive battle is one in which a world power is overthrown by armed combat, then Tet was one of history's rare decisive battles.[2]

Privately, LBJ vacillated and equivocated before making his no-run decision. On the one hand, he loved the power of the presidency, a job he had hoped to attain for many years. But on the other side, he was in deep political trouble and did not want to be humiliated by a defeat in seeking re-nomination or in the general election.

Some of his aides, friends and family members, including his wife, Lady Bird Johnson, suspected that he would announce his retirement during his State of the Union address on January 17, 1968. Mrs. Johnson wanted him to retire because of his deteriorating health. She recalled later that she noticed a line in an early draft of this speech that he would indeed retire, and was delighted at the prospect. But he didn't use the line and gave the State of the Union with no hint of a possible departure. The fact that he was considering retirement was kept secret.[3]

On March 12, Johnson survived a serious challenge in the first-in-the-nation New Hampshire Democratic presidential primary. Sen. Eugene McCarthy, D-Minn., campaigned against the war and received nearly 42 percent of the vote. Johnson was held below 50 percent. This was considered a serious blow to LBJ, who had won the 1964 general election in a landslide. McCarthy ran an under-funded and unexciting campaign, but the results showed the growing strength of the anti-war movement. Four days later, Sen. Robert Kennedy, D-N.Y., entered the race, further jeopardizing Johnson's position because Kennedy was so popular as the political heir to his assassinated brother, President John F. Kennedy.

Polls showed that the public was souring on the war and Johnson himself, and anti-war protests were growing around the country as more and more young men were drafted and U.S. casualties mounted. He was so unpopular that he drew protesters almost everywhere he went, and an angry chant would fill the air: "Hey, hey, LBJ. How many kids did you kill today?" He resorted to giving speeches on conservative college campuses, to veterans' groups and on military bases where he could guarantee at least a cordial welcome for the commander in chief.

All the opposition deeply offended Johnson, who always wanted to be loved by his fellow citizens, just as his idol Franklin D. Roosevelt had been loved.

Privately, even his family was questioning his war policy. At one point, his daughter Lynda returned to the White House after seeing her husband, Chuck Robb, off to his deployment to Vietnam as a Marine combat officer. Lynda, emotionally distraught because her husband was heading into harm's way, asked her father, "Why do we have to be in Vietnam?" She showed her father a letter she had received from a woman whose husband had been killed in Vietnam hours before he was scheduled to come home. "If that happens to Chuck, I will never forgive you," Lynda said. Lady Bird later noted that she had never until this moment seen such pain in her husband's eyes since his mother died.[4]

But LBJ had another overriding concern—fear of failure. He said,

> I knew that if I ran out that I'd be the first American President to ignore our commitments, turn tail and run, and leave our allies in the lurch, after all the commitments Eisenhower had made, and all that SEATO had made, and all that the Congress had made, and all that the Tonkin Gulf said, and all the statements that Kennedy had made, and Bobby Kennedy had made, and that everybody had made. I'd be the first American President to put my tail between my legs and run out because I didn't have the courage to stand up.[5]

At the end of March, Johnson requested time from the three major television networks, ABC, CBS and NBC, to address the nation in prime time. The speech was expected to be an attempt to rally the nation behind his Vietnam escalations, and the networks gave the president a slot at 9 p.m. Eastern time on Sunday, March 31.

After attending a church service with his daughter Luci and son-in-law Patrick Nugent that morning, Johnson paid an unexpected visit to the home of his vice president, Hubert Humphrey. The two men, accompanied by White House Chief of Staff James Jones, met privately in Humphrey's den. Johnson gave Humphrey two drafts of the speech he was scheduled to deliver that evening. "I could barely believe what I was reading," Humphrey wrote later. "One of them had Lyndon Johnson withdrawing from the 1968 election."[6]

The president told Humphrey he hadn't decided which version of the speech to use, even though the address was only several hours away. He asked his vice president to keep this possibility secret, but suggested that Humphrey start planning "your campaign for president."

In his address that evening, Johnson seemed unusually somber as he declared how much he wanted an honorable end to the Vietnam conflict. Near the end of the address, he made the surprise announcement that he would stop U.S. bombing in most of North Vietnam in order to move toward a negotiated settlement of the war. (He made good on this pledge, reducing most of the bombing and starting peace talks, but the war would drag on for several years and became a thorn in the side of Johnson's successor, Republican Richard Nixon.)

As he moved to the end of his allotted TV time, a weary-looking Johnson looked directly into the camera and said he wanted to devote his full time to the cause of peace, not politics. Then he dropped his bombshell. "I have concluded that I should not permit the presidency to become involved in the partisan divisions that are developing in this political year," Johnson said.

> With America's sons in the fields far away, with America's future under challenge right here at home, with our hopes and the world's hopes for peace in the balance every day, I do not believe that I should devote an hour or a day of my time to any personal partisan causes, or to any duties other than the awesome duties of this office—the presidency of our country. Accordingly, I shall not seek, and I will not accept, the nomination of my party for another term as your president.[7]

His decision threw the 1968 campaign into pandemonium—what Rep. Wright Patman, D-Tex., called a "Pearl Harbor in politics."[8]

Only a few White House aides, Johnson friends and family members knew that, for weeks, LBJ had been giving increased consideration to not seeking reelection. And in his private discussions with those close to him he discussed the pros and cons. "In these late evening talks, he gave several reasons for not running again," recalled Johnson chief of staff Jim Jones in an essay for the *Los Angeles Times* in 2008. For one thing, he wanted to spend more time with his grandchildren, which his aides believed was a sincere desire. LBJ also told aides that "his father and grandfather had both died at age 64, and he felt that he would not complete a second term as he would be 64 during the last year of that term," Jones recalled. LBJ had suffered a heart attack in 1955 and was always worried about a recurrence. It turned out that LBJ, 59, was prescient in this regard. He died at age 64 in retirement at his Texas ranch.[9]

"His fear was he was going to end up like Woodrow Wilson, incapacitated in the White House," said historian Kyle Longley, director of the LBJ Presidential Library in Austin, Texas. "I don't think he was afraid of death as much as he was incapacitation. He'd watched one of his grandmothers be incapacitated by a stroke, and he was afraid he was going to end up like that."[10]

Jones wrote,

> But I believe that the most important reason he decided not to run again was his passionate desire to conclude the Vietnam War honorably. His middle-of-the-night awakenings to get the casualties report; his ongoing concern about the safety of his son-in-law, Chuck Robb, who was a Marine officer in the thick of heavy combat; his personal sense of responsibility each time he met with troops soon to be heading to Vietnam; and his growing sense of the futility of achieving total victory—all of this had taken a toll on his vitality.
>
> In many of our discussions, he said that if he did not seek reelection, he would be free to explore all options to conclude the war. If he did run, however, politics would interfere.[11]

Historian Doris Kearns Goodwin, who knew Johnson well, wrote, "Abdication was thus the last remaining way to restore control, to turn rout into dignity, collapse into order."[12]

It reflected the very difficult political reality that LBJ faced in 1968. "Johnson knew by then it was an extreme situation—30,000 American troops had already died [in Vietnam]," says presidential historian and LBJ biographer Robert Dallek. "The war was seen as a stalemate . . . He was a smart enough politician to know it would've been a disaster and he would have been humiliated."[13] Likely rejection by his fellow Americans was something the proud LBJ couldn't abide. He didn't want to go down in history as a despised loser.

He admitted as much to key advisers. On Thursday, March 28, he told aide Harry McPherson, "I've asked Congress for too much for too long, and they're tired of me." He knew his political capital was badly depleted and he was facing possible defeat in 1968.[14]

Robert Caro, the noted LBJ biographer, adds another theme to explain Johnson's decision—fear of failure. "The one thing about Lyndon Johnson. He was afraid to fail," former Texas Gov. John Connally, a close LBJ friend, told Caro, who explains:

> Why was he afraid to fail? His brother Sam Houston Johnson said to me, "The one thing that was most important to Lyndon was not to be like daddy." His father had been a politician for a while, a successful politician, and had failed, lost the ranch and the family was plunged into not only bankruptcy, but into being the laughing stock of their town. Johnson, when he was Senate majority leader, had Bobby Baker as the man who counted [senators' likely] votes for him, and Baker says, "I learned never to let him fail on a [Senate] vote. Never." All the people who knew him best say that Lyndon was afraid to fail, to be like his father.[15]

Coming amid the setbacks in Vietnam, his defeat in 1968 would have been too much for Johnson to bear.

Vice President Hubert Humphrey entered the race with the support of the Democratic party establishment. Eugene McCarthy had the backing of many anti-war insurgents. Sen. Robert Kennedy, D-N.Y., brother of the assassinated President John F. Kennedy whom LBJ served as vice president, was running as another anti-war candidate with a very liberal domestic platform and strong charisma. But Sen. Kennedy was fatally shot by an assassin on the night he won the California Democratic primary, and many of his supporters sank into despair. Humphrey won the Democratic nomination at the party's divided convention in Chicago, where there was rioting in the streets, police violence against the demonstrators, and many arrests.

Another factor that had deepened LBJ's unpopularity was the racial tension that was spreading during 1968. On April 4, only a few days after he announced his withdrawal, the Rev. Martin Luther King, Jr. was shot as he stood on a balcony outside his room at the Lorraine Motel in Memphis. King, the most respected civil rights leader of the era and an apostle of non-violence, died that evening. A few hours later, riots including looting and arson broke out in Washington, less than a mile from the White House where LBJ watched the TV news coverage with alarm. During the next several days, riots erupted in more than 100 cities. Overall, 39 persons died, more than 2,600 were injured, 21,000 were arrested, and the property damage was estimated at $65 million.

These disorders ended whatever goodwill Johnson had gained from his withdrawal from the campaign and reduced whatever political strength he had, terminating any prospects for making progress legislatively.[16]

"The level of vitriol in the mail and the calls over all the race issues dwarfed anything we had on Vietnam," recalled LBJ domestic policy adviser Joseph Califano, Jr. later. "He was very conscious that he'd become an incredibly divisive figure because of his strong stand on the race issue"—a strong advocate of civil rights and racial equality.[17]

The rioting quickly broke his spirit, his advisers said.

That November, Republican Richard Nixon won the general election, and the Vietnam war dragged on for five more years.

"Richard Nixon's campaign and subsequent election opened a Pandora's Box of racially motivated resentment against economic justice, civil rights, and deep democracy that still reverberates to this day," writes historian Peniel Joseph. " . . . In resoundingly large ways that remain too often unappreciated, Johnson's decision not to run set the stage for a half century of debate, division, and discussion of the role of government in our constitutional democracy."[18]

Historian Clay Risen observed, "Johnson may be remembered as the Vietnam war president, but in his mind his greatest legacy was his efforts to improve the lives of African-Americans. And he had much to show for it: the 1964 Civil Rights Act, the Voting Rights Act, the War on Poverty, Head Start and more. But as the 1960s wore on he also saw himself in a race—against black militancy, against rising ghetto frustrations, against an increasingly conservative white electorate."[19] He later complained to Doris Kearns Goodwin: "Just a little thanks. Just a little appreciation. That's all. But look what I got instead . . . Looting. Burning. Shooting. It ruined everything."[20]

By this point, most Americans had little or no sympathy for him. But in retrospect, his withdrawal from the 1968 race was a blessing for the country. The United States was already being pulled apart, and Lyndon

Johnson spared the nation the intensified bitterness, anger and polarization that his candidacy would have wrought.

Precis

Lyndon B. Johnson's withdrawal from the 1968 presidential race showed the essence of his leadership—part high-minded idealism and part political calculation, always centered on LBJ the individual as a larger-than-life figure. He took bold action in withdrawing—adapting to changing circumstances such as the setbacks in Vietnam and his fading popularity at home. His withdrawal was a wise move because he could no longer unite the country, largely due to his false claims that the United States was on the verge of victory. He persevered in Vietnam, not wanting to be the first U.S. president to lose a war. But by then the conflict was a lost cause and he didn't recognize it. The fighting that Johnson hoped to end with an "honorable" peace agreement continued for five more years.

Notes

1. James R. Arnold, *Presidents Under Fire: Commanders in Chief in Victory and Defeat*, New York: Orion Books, 1994, p. 266.
2. Arnold, p. 270.
3. Betty Boyd Caroli, *Lady Bird and Lyndon: The Hidden Story of a Marriage That Made a President*, New York: Simon & Schuster, 2015, pp. 359–360.
4. Caroli, p. 360.
5. Lyndon B. Johnson oral history interview August 12, 1969, by William Jordan, LBJ Library.
6. Robert Mitchell, "A 'Pearl Harbor' in Politics': LBJ's Stunning Decision Not to Seek Reelection," *Washington Post*, Mar 31, 2018, washingtonpost.com/news/retropolis/wp/2018/03/31/a-pearl-harbor-in-politics.
7. Mitchell, ibid.
8. Mitchell, ibid.
9. Kenneth T. Walsh, "Peace Over Politics," *U.S. News & World Report*, March 30, 2018, usnews.com/news/the-report/articles/2018-03-30/lyndon-johnson-chose-peace-over-politics.
10. M.B. Roberts, "What Were the Real Reasons LBJ Decided Not to Run for Reelection in 1968?" *Parade*, Aug 30, 2018, parade.com/696849/m-b-roberts/what-were-the-real-reasons-lbj-decided-not-to-run-for-reelection–in-1968/.

11. Walsh, ibid.
12. Walsh, ibid.
13. Walsh, ibid.
14. Walsh, ibid.
15. Robert Caro, Interview Contained in Brian Lamb, Susan Swain and C-SPAN, *The Presidents: Noted Historians Rank America's Best—and Worst—Chief Executives*, New York: Public Affairs, 2019, p. 127.
16. When it ended: Clay Risen, "The Unmaking of the President," *Smithsonian Magazine*, April 2008, smithsonianmag.com/history/the-unmaking-of-the-president-31577203/.
17. Risen, ibid.
18. Peniel Joseph, "The stunning—and pivotal—decision by Lyndon Johnson," CNN, March 30, 2018, amp.cnn.com/2018/03/30/opinion/the-stunning-decision-by-president-lyndon-johnson-joseph/index.html.
19. Risen, ibid.
20. Risen, ibid.

Chapter Seven
Richard M. Nixon
The Watergate Scandal and National Disgrace

Richard Nixon waved to his White House staff for a final time as he left office and flew home to California on Aug. 8, 1974. Nixon made many mistakes in handling the Watergate scandal, which led to his resignation. (Richard Nixon Presidential Library and Museum)

The Watergate scandal was President Richard Nixon's most serious crisis. It brought out his worst qualities—among them, deceptiveness, arrogance and paranoia. It led to his leaving office in disgrace as impeachment proceedings gained momentum and seemed sure to succeed, partly because of his own flawed efforts at crisis management. He was the only president in U.S. history to resign.

ON JUNE 17, 1972, six men hired by Nixon's re-election campaign broke into Democratic National Committee headquarters at the Watergate office complex in Washington to gather intelligence on what the Democrats were planning as they prepared for the general election that November. A guard caught the intruders in the act.

This was the start of the scandal.

Only four presidents have faced formal impeachment charges— Andrew Johnson in 1868 because of the firing of a Cabinet member amid Washington's fiery post-Civil War divisions; Richard Nixon in 1973–74 because of the Watergate scandal and cover-up; Bill Clinton in 1998–99 for committing perjury in denying his affair with a White House intern, and Donald Trump in 2019–20 for abuse of power and obstruction of Congress. Johnson and Clinton were impeached by the House but acquitted by the Senate. Trump was impeached by the House and at the time this book went to press the Senate was considered likely to acquit him. Nixon was headed for impeachment but he resigned before it could happen.

"When *The Washington Post* reporters Bob Woodward and Carl Bernstein drew attention to the June break-in at the Democratic National Committee headquarters in 1972, they began an investigation into illegal activities waged by members of Nixon's reelection committee," says the Miller Center at the University of Virginia.

> The following February, the Senate launched a congressional investigation into the alleged misconduct of the burglars, and as the narrative unfolded over the next year, it became clear that the fears of criminal activities, wire-tapping, and abuses of power were validated—and even worse than many suspected.[1]

The Justice Department, pressed by Congress, named Archibald Cox as special prosecutor in May 1973, and under the law at that time he had enormous power and independence. "His assignment was monumental," wrote historian Barry Sussman.

He was given carte blanche to investigate as he saw fit in a public pledge by Elliot Richardson at the Attorney General's Senate confirmation hearings. Only the Attorney General could fire Cox, and then only for what Richardson said would be "extraordinary improprieties."[2]

Nixon was deceptive from the start. On May 22, 1973, he promised that, "Executive privilege will not be invoked as to any testimony concerning possible criminal conduct, in the matters presently under investigation, including the Watergate affair and the alleged cover-up." But this was not as all-encompassing a statement as it seemed. On May 25, Nixon told Attorney General Richardson during an Oval Office meeting that he had used the word "testimony" carefully and that he had meant it only to include oral testimony and not documents. This caused Richardson to worry about potential trouble in getting the president's cooperation with the investigation.[3]

Sussman wrote:

> It was a moment when the President was at his weakest—under pressure from every quarter in March and April, he had let go of H.R. Haldeman and John Ehrlichman [his top aides who were implicated in Watergate] only to be smashed by the Ellsberg revelations [which were disclosures by former government analyst Daniel Ellsberg about the U.S. government's history of lies about Vietnam], and the CIA testimony and the opening of Senate Watergate hearings in May. For a period of about a month, Nixon and his new chief of staff, Alexander Haig, under constant battering, submitted to requests for materials by both the Senate Watergate Committee and the Special Prosecutor.[4]

Cox was receiving incriminating information from cooperative witnesses including former Nixon aides John Dean, Herbert Kalmbach, Frederick C. LaRue and Jeb Magruder. And "Cox immediately extended the Watergate inquiry so broadly that the term 'Watergate' had little to do with much of his investigation; it was only a convenient label to attach to the many probes of the Executive branch under Nixon."[5]

> Cox was looking into the work of the White House plumbers [operatives trying to stop leaks of sensitive information from the White House], the early White House wiretaps, and illegal campaign contributions to Nixon, including those that allegedly had been a payoff

to Nixon by the dairy industry for the promise to raise milk price supports. He was investigating the role of the White House in the ITT merger plans, and dirty tricks aside from Watergate in the 1972 campaign. Much of his inquiry paralleled that of the Senate Watergate Committee, with one crucial difference: Cox worked through the criminal justice system and had the power, therefore, to follow his investigation through with criminal prosecutions. So while the Ervin Committee [in the Senate] gave public airing to the most sensational charges of corruption ever made about a presidential staff, Cox quietly began putting together material for indictments.[6]

During June, Haig called Richardson and expressed dissatisfaction with how far Cox was going. In July, it seemed that Cox might be looking into Nixon's purchase of his estate in San Clemente, California, and spending taxpayers' money to make improvements there. Haig warned Richardson that if Cox expanded his inquiry that far, he could be fired. From then on, Haig and other White House aides kept up the pressure on Richardson by complaining frequently about the extent of Cox's investigation and the possibility that national security programs could be improperly revealed. The White House stopped nearly all cooperation with the investigators.[7]

Cox had received no reply to his request for sensitive White House tape recordings and on July 20, he wrote asking for the tapes again. This time his request was officially denied. Charles Alan Wright, a University of Texas law professor advising Nixon about the Watergate inquiry, told Cox that the president would not give up the tapes to the special prosecutor or to the Senate committee investigating Watergate, which had separately requested tapes. Wright claimed executive privilege in order to maintain the confidentiality of presidential conversations and preserve "the effective functioning of the presidency."[8]

On July 23, Cox issued a subpoena to Nixon's lawyers. Nixon refused to allow the lawyers to comply, sending the issue of the tapes to the courts. On October 12, the U.S. Circuit Court of Appeals ruled that Nixon must turn over the tapes to lower court judge John J. Sirica, who was handling many Watergate-related issues.

The battle between Nixon and the congressional investigators also got more intense. Nixon and his aides altered transcripts of taped White House conversations to make him look innocent of orchestrating a cover-up and to exonerate him of various other allegations. White House officials then sent these altered transcripts to Congress. The discrepancies were quickly revealed, prompting outrage that Nixon was trying to distort reality in order to avoid impeachment.

"The televised Senate hearings in the summer of 1973," wrote a group of presidential scholars,

> brought the crimes of the Nixon White House—a break-in at the Watergate hotel, subsequent cover-up attempts and bribery, and a range of dirty tricks the president used to target his opponents and punish his enemies to gain person power—directly to the American people. The Watergate investigation, which played out in Congress, the courts, and the press over the next year, confirmed public suspicions of presidential abuses of power, and as a result, fundamentally altered the relationship of the presidency to the people, the press, and Congress.[9]

On October 19, 1973, Nixon found what he thought would be a clever way to save face and extricate himself from the increasingly damaging scandal. As noted, federal courts had ordered him to surrender the tapes of nine of his private conversations and Nixon had refused. But on October 19, he announced a "compromise" that would allow him to maintain the confidentiality he thought was necessary to conduct presidential business and at the same give special prosecutor Cox what he said he needed to continue his investigation.[10]

Nixon announced that he would submit summaries of relevant portions of tapes to Judge Sirica and allow Sen. John Stennis of Mississippi to listen to the tapes to authenticate what was provided to the judge. But Cox would have to agree not to use the judicial process to seek other tape recordings or additional records of Nixon's conversations in the future.[11]

His explanation fell flat. "Every shibboleth that has come to be equated with Nixonism was contained in this statement," historian Sussman argued.

> The President said he was seeking to assuage damages to the nation, making no mention of damages to himself. He invoked the threat of danger from foreign powers should an investigation of his own

honesty be pursued. He charged that those seeking to find the truth about Watergate, or those disturbed by the crimes that had become so apparent, were motivated by partisan interest and not by a desire to clean up corruption. Throughout, he attempted to give the appearance of being above the fray, and he concluded with a statement that he was cooperating with the Watergate inquiry when, in fact, he was defying a court order.[12]

The following day, Saturday, October 20, Cox refused Nixon's offer. Haig, Nixon's White House chief of staff, ordered Attorney General Richardson to fire Cox. Richardson replied that under the terms of Cox's appointment as special prosecutor, only the attorney general could fire him and he didn't wish to do so. Instead of obeying Nixon's order, Richardson resigned. Haig then ordered Deputy Attorney General William Ruckelshaus to fire Cox, and Ruckelshaus also refused and resigned. Solicitor General Robert Bork, the third-ranking official in the Justice Department, was named attorney general and he proceeded to fire Cox. Nixon then had his press secretary Ron Ziegler announce that the Office of Special Prosecutor had been abolished. FBI agents were sent to prevent Cox's staff members from taking files out of their offices, a move designed to protect Nixon from more damaging disclosures.

This overreach became known as the "Saturday Night Massacre." It resulted in a wave of anger against Nixon and within ten days more than a million letters and telegrams were sent to members of Congress, most of them demanding Nixon's impeachment. The president's actions and the public's reaction emboldened his critics and propelled the impeachment forward on Capitol Hill with legislators arguing that the president was clearly attempting to thwart the pursuit of justice.[13]

The episode was a disaster for the president. And it was a microcosm of Nixon's handling of the Watergate scandal, marked by arrogance, isolation, hubris, bad judgment and an unwillingness to believe that the president's enemies could thwart his enormous power and destroy his presidency.

The situation got worse for Nixon.

In November 1973, Nixon's lawyers claimed that two of the nine tapes being sought by investigators never existed. White House officials also said the tape of a conversation between Nixon and H.R. Haldeman three days after the original break-in arrests had an 18-and-a-half-minute gap in it. To the critics, this was more evidence of a White House cover-up.

Various impeachment resolutions were introduced in the Democrat-controlled House of Representatives that fall, but many legislators of both parties didn't want to deal with it at that time. They considered public reaction too unpredictable, partly because the impeachment process would be messy and divisive, and many legislators thought voters would tire of it or be appalled by it. A new special prosecutor, Leon Jaworski, was named by a court to succeed Cox.

For his part, Nixon and his allies argued that impeachment would be a partisan witch hunt, with Democrats attempting to nullify the 1972 presidential election in which Nixon won a second term with a historic majority.

In June 1974, as his credibility eroded, Nixon made a last-ditch effort to save himself. He flew to the Middle East and the Soviet Union to meet with other leaders and dramatize his mastery of foreign policy and national security issues. The subtext was the argument of the dwindling band of Nixon supporters that he was indispensable to the nation as commander in chief, and this was no time to remove him.

The argument failed, and the Watergate vise tightened.

ON JULY 14, 1974, the Supreme Court decided in an 8–0 vote that President Nixon was required to turn over the 64 tapes requested by Special Prosecutor Jaworski. In a 31-page opinion written by Chief Justice Warren Burger, the court decided:

> We conclude that the ground for asserting privilege as to subpoenaed materials sought for use in a criminal trial is based only on the generalized interest in confidentiality, it cannot prevail over the fundamental demands of due process of law in the fair administration of criminal justice. The generalized assertion of privilege must yield to the demonstrated, specific need for evidence in a pending criminal trial.[14]

Also on July 14, the House Judiciary Committee began to work out the language of an impeachment recommendation to Congress. The debate, which was very negative toward Nixon, was carried live on network television and had a wide audience. It served to deepen public distrust and animosity toward the president, and had the same effect on members of Congress. Whatever hope Nixon had of avoiding impeachment was rapidly fading.

On July 16, 1973, Haldeman's aide Alexander Butterfield had told a congressional hearing about the existence of a White House taping system, and on July 18, 1974, Jaworski formally requested the tapes of nine conversations—five of talks between Nixon and John Dean, the others between Nixon and Haldeman, Ehrlichman or Mitchell in the 13 days following the Watergate arrests of June 17, 1972. The Supreme Court ruled that Nixon must provide the tapes.

On July 19, 1974, the House Judiciary Committee led by Rep. Peter Rodino, D-N.J., acted dramatically. John Doar, the senior counsel to the Democrats, and Albert E. Jenner, Jr., the senior counsel to the Republicans, urged the full committee to endorse impeaching Nixon and sending the measure to the Senate on one or more charges. The lawyers listed obstruction of justice in the Watergate cover-up and related scandals; abuse of government agencies by the president; contempt of Congress and the courts by Nixon because he defied subpoenas; failure to observe his constitutional duty "to see that the laws be faithfully executed," and demeaning the presidency by underpaying his income taxes and using federal funds to improve his personal property.[15]

In all, there were 29 potential articles of impeachment, and they were presented in harsh terms. The first proposed article said:

> Beginning almost immediately after the burglary and continuing up to the present time, Richard M. Nixon, using the powers of his office, acting directly and personally and through his personal agents at the seat of Government and their immediate subordinates, has made it his policy to cover up and conceal responsibility for the burglary, the identity of other participants, and the existence and scope of related unlawful covert activities.
>
> The means of implementing this policy have included the subornation of perjury, the purchase of silence of those directly participating in the burglary, the obstruction of justice, the destruction of evidence, improper and unlawful interference with the conduct of lawful investigation by the Department of Justice, including the Federal Bureau of Investigation and the Office of the Special Prosecutor, improper and unlawful misuse of other agencies of the Executive branch, including the CIA, and the release of deliberately false and misleading statements from the White House and by the President.[16]

Doar concluded his report to the committee by declaring, "For all this, Richard M. Nixon is personally and directly responsible."[17]

Nixon's claims of executive privilege seemed less and less credible. Even some of his past supporters considered them simply a way to keep damaging information from Congress and the courts, rather than a genuine attempt to defend the Executive from assertions of power by the Legislative and Judicial Branches.

As historian Barry Sussman wrote,

> In the last week of July 1974, as the Judiciary Committee held its final deliberations in lengthy and spellbinding televised sessions it was apparent that [Nixon's survival] strategy had failed to move all but a few members of the committee. Nixon had given little in the way of assistance to the Judiciary Committee, generally defying their counsel's requests and subpoenas for evidence. Nevertheless, the committee, working largely from material gathered in earlier investigations by other bodies, presented an overwhelming case against him in the form of three articles of impeachment.[18]

The committee charged in three articles of impeachment that Nixon had, first of all, violated his constitutional oath to "faithfully execute the office of the President of the United States" and enforce the law. Second, he was charged specifically with obstructing justice, misusing executive power in various ways such as improperly using agencies of government such as Internal Revenue Service and the FBI for illegal activities. Third, he was charged with refusing to comply with Judiciary Committee subpoenas and thereby attempting to defy the constitutional power of the legislative branch.[19]

By July 30, the committee had approved all three articles of impeachment.

Nixon's worst setback in attempting to remain in office came with the release of new tapes showing his involvement in making the Central Intelligence Agency part of the Watergate cover-up. His critics called this revelation "the smoking gun" because the evidence was so damaging to the president's claims of innocence.[20]

The "smoking gun" disclosure referred to three of the 64 tapes that the Supreme Court ordered to be made public. There were tapes of meetings between Nixon and then-White House Chief of Staff H.R. Haldeman on June 23, 1972, and they showed conclusively that Nixon had taken part in the Watergate cover-up from the beginning. It turned out that six days after the first Watergate arrests, Nixon and Haldeman talked about ways to prevent the FBI from investigating what Haldeman called "productive areas."[21]

"Now, on the investigation," Haldeman said. "You know, the Democratic break-in thing. We're back . . . in the problem area because the FBI is not under control . . . They've been able to trace the money ... through the bank . . . and it goes in some directions we don't want it to go." Haldeman was referring to money paid illegally to the Watergate burglars, which the FBI was tracing back to Nixon's campaign.[22]

Haldeman suggested that the president order the CIA to contact FBI Director L. Patrick Gray "and just say, 'Stay the hell out of this. This is business here we don't want you to go any further on.'" Nixon replied, "All right. Fine." Nixon told Haldeman he should work on CIA Director Richard Helms and Deputy Director Vernon Walters to get their cooperation.

The president added:

> When you get these people [from the CIA] in, say: "Look, the problem is that this will open the whole Bay of Pigs thing." . . . Just say this is sort of a comedy of errors, bizarre, without getting into it . . . They should call the FBI in and say that we wish, for the country, "Don't go any further into this case, period."[23]

Actually, the Bay of Pigs reference was a lie. The Bay of Pigs was the site in Cuba where Cuban exiles attempted to invade the island and overthrow the rule of Fidel Castro, with U.S. assistance, under President John F. Kennedy. The operation failed miserably. As law professor Andrew Coan of the University of Arizona has written, "This was a complete fabrication. Nixon was not actually worried about national security or foreign relations. He was simply trying to protect his closest aides from criminal investigation and himself from untold political damage."[24]

This was obstruction of justice.

The tapes also showed that Nixon knew by June 23, 1972 that Nixon operative Gordon Liddy was involved in the break-in and bugging—and

Nixon failed to let the FBI know. The FBI later found out independently about Liddy's involvement.[25]

As Sussman wrote,

> For more than two years, the President had lied to the people about his role in the Watergate cover-up. As he relinquished the last three tapes, he admitted that he had kept them from the House Judiciary Committee with the awareness that they "presented potential problems ... that those passing judgment on the case did so with information that was incomplete and in some respects erroneous."[26]

Nixon's credibility was shattered among the Republicans in Congress whom he needed to ward off impeachment. Constitutional scholars Laurence Tribe and Joshua Matz write: "Even as the evidence against the president piled up, many Republican voters stood by him. Indeed, on the day he resigned from office, over 50 percent of registered Republicans approved of his performance."[27] But in Congress, the picture looked very different. At first, partisan loyalties had held firm. In February 1974, Representative William L. Hungate, D-Mo., bitingly remarked that "there are a few Republicans who wouldn't vote to impeach Nixon if he were caught in a bank vault at midnight."[28] By August, however, Nixon's support had collapsed. His threat to the nation was clear, and his compulsive lying had alienated allies.

A group of Republican Party elders finally concluded that Nixon had to go. On Wednesday, August 7, 1974, Sen. Barry Goldwater, Senate Minority Leader Hugh Scott, and House Minority Leader John Rhodes entered the Oval Office and met with the president. After some awkward pleasantries, Goldwater cut to the chase: "'[J]ust about all of the guys have spoken up and there aren't many who would support you if it comes to that.' One day later, Nixon announced his resignation."[29]

Goldwater privately expressed his frustration to White House Chief of Staff Alexander Haig, telling him that Nixon "has lied to me for the last time and lied to my colleagues for the last time." Goldwater's remark underscores the importance of a president being credible with key members of Congress. "History could not be clearer on this point," Tribe and Matz say. "Nixon resigned after repeatedly shooting himself in the foot."[30]

Nixon announced his resignation on August 8, and he left office on August 9. "By taking this action," he told the nation in a televised address from the Oval Office, "I hope that I will have hastened the start of the process of healing which is so desperately needed in America."[31]

THE MILLER CENTER summed up:

> Critics of the Vietnam War argued that the unfettered use of executive authority to wage war and deceive the American people on the progress of that war exposed pressing problems in expanding the institutional authority of the Executive Branch. And yet, the Watergate scandal, though perhaps a culmination of what historian Joan Hoff terms the "decline in political ethics and practices during the Cold War," did test the system of checks and balances designed by the Constitution to prevent abuses of power. In fact, the investigation began and continued because of actions taken by the press, Congress, the courts, and the Federal Bureau of Investigation—all government institutions which pushed back against the growing power of the presidency. As such, Watergate involved a battle between the president and each of these government institutions, leaving each of them fundamentally transformed in the wake of Richard Nixon's resignation.[32]

This resulted in a diminution of presidential power for years.

AS FOR NIXON, after leaving office he attempted with limited success to rehabilitate himself as an elder statesman and foreign-policy sage, both at home and abroad. He wrote well-received books and made carefully chosen appearances displaying his impressive knowledge of domestic and foreign policy. He even expressed the kind of contrition that might have made a difference in limiting the scandal if he had done it early enough during his presidency.

In a series of interviews with British broadcaster David Frost, released in May 1977, Nixon was at the same time defensive and contrite. Discussing his view of presidential power, he said, "When the president does it that means it is not illegal." Yet he admitted he had "let down" his friends and the American public and said, "I did abuse the power I had as president" even if his conduct wasn't illegal. He denied approving payments to silence the Watergate burglars but also conceded, "I said things that were not true." In a remarkable admission, he added: "I brought myself down. I gave them a sword, and they stuck it in. And they twisted it with relish. And, I guess, if I'd been in their position, I'd have done the same thing."[33]

Precis

Richard Nixon failed all the most important tests of crisis management in dealing with the Watergate scandal. He didn't take action to end the crisis by telling the truth after the initial break-in. He didn't adapt properly to changing circumstances even when his support in Congress began to crumble. Instead, he moved relentlessly to cover up and obstruct justice even when those tactics were backfiring. He put pragmatism—his political survival—ahead of principle. He persevered with his flawed public strategy of spreading falsehoods and stonewalling far too long. He undermined public confidence in the institution of the presidency and the federal government, and failed to save his job.

Notes

1. Miller Center, University of Virginia, millercenter.org/the-presidency/educational-resources/recasting-presidential-history/presidency-crisis. Accessed August 13, 2019.
2. Barry Sussman, "The Great Coverup," essay in Nathaniel May, ed., *Oval Office: Stories of Presidents in Crisis from Washington to Bush*, New York: Adrenaline, Thunder's Mouth Press, 2002, p. 154.
3. Sussman, p. 154.
4. Sussman, p. 155.
5. Sussman, p. 155.
6. Sussman, p. 155.
7. Sussman, p. 157.
8. Sussman, p. 157.
9. Miller Center, ibid.
10. Sussman, p. 152.
11. Sussman, p. 152.
12. Sussman, pp. 162–163.
13. Sussman, p. 153.
14. Sussman, p. 192.
15. Sussman, p. 186.
16. Sussman, pp. 186–187.
17. Sussman, p. 187.
18. Sussman, pp. 193–194.

19. Sussman, pp. 194–195.
20. Sussman, p. 196.
21. Sussman, pp. 196–197.
22. Andrew Coan, "Why William Barr Is Wrong on the Mueller Investigation," *Washington Post*, December 21, 2018, p. A21.
23. Coan, ibid.
24. Coan, ibid.
25. Sussman, p. 197.
26. Sussman, p. 197.
27. Jody C. Baumgartner and Naoko Kada, *Checking Executive Power: Presidential Impeachment in Comparative Perspective*, Westport, CT: Greenwood Publishing Group, 2003, p. 21.
28. Baumgartner and Kada, ibid.
29. Laurence Tribe and Joshua Matz, *To End A Presidency: The Power of Impeachment*, New York: Basic Books, 2018, p. 147.
30. Tribe and Matz, p. 148.
31. David Frost, *Frost/Nixon*, p. 254.
32. Miller Center, ibid.
33. David Frost, *Frost/Nixon: Behind the Scenes of the Nixon Interviews*, New York: Harper Perennial, 2007, pp. 254–256, 266–271.

Chapter Eight
Gerald R. Ford
The Pardon

Gerald Ford took the unusual step of testifying before a congressional subcommittee during October 1974 about why he pardoned Richard Nixon in the aftermath of the Watergate scandal and Nixon's resignation. Many legislators and voters remained suspicious of his motives, and the pardon was an important reason he lost his bid for a full term in the 1976 election. (Gerald R. Ford Library)

Gerald Ford's pardon of Richard Nixon probably cost him the presidency in the 1976 election. But Ford felt the pardon was the right thing to do, no matter the damage to his political future and his place in history. In retrospect, he was correct.

The seeds of the crisis were planted in February 1973 when former Maryland Gov. Spiro Agnew resigned as Nixon's vice president amid a tax evasion scandal. The critics believed that Nixon picked Ford, then a member of the House of Representatives from Michigan, as the new vice president because he believed Ford would eventually pardon him if the Watergate scandal worsened and Nixon had to resign because he was implicated in serious crimes. Many suspected a corrupt bargain, but Ford always denied such a quid pro quo.

As described in the previous chapter, the Watergate scandal focused on a botched 1972 break-in at the Washington headquarters of the Democratic National Committee, located at the Watergate office and residential complex. After the burglars were caught, President Nixon and his operatives attempted to cover up the crime and White House links to it by having officials commit perjury, pay hush money and destroy records.

Congress investigated the scandal for many months and in 1974 legislators began moving aggressively toward impeaching Nixon for obstruction of justice and other offenses. The quickened pace came after White House tape recordings and other evidence showed that Nixon knew in advance about, and perhaps authorized, the illegal break-in and wiretapping of the DNC offices. One of the most damning pieces of evidence was a tape recording on June 23, 1972, six days after the Watergate break-in, in which Nixon told his then chief of staff Bob Haldeman three times in a single day to have the CIA stop the FBI investigation of Watergate. This was obstruction of justice.[1]

Rather than face impeachment and possible removal from office, Nixon announced his resignation on August 8, 1974 and he left office the next day, August 9.

As constitutional law scholars Laurence Tribe and Joshua Matz have pointed out,

> By late 1973, impeachment was in the air and Nixon was on the defensive. But the cagey president had an ace in the hole: his vice president, Spiro Agnew. By almost every relevant measure, Agnew was painfully unqualified for our highest office. In private, Nixon and John Ehrlichman jokingly called him "the assassin's dilemma."

Nixon was sure that Congress wouldn't impeach if doing so meant elevating Agnew.[2]

Unfortunately for Nixon, Agnew was caught in his own corruption scandal and had to resign in October 1973. With Watergate hearings looming over him, Nixon deliberately sought a replacement unsuitable for the presidency. This led him to Representative Gerald Ford. As biographer Evan Thomas notes, "with the poor political judgment that increasingly afflicted him, Nixon believed that Ford provided him with a layer of protection against impeachment." At one point Nixon remarked that Ford was a "good insurance policy."[3]

Nixon had badly miscalculated. It turned out that Ford was far more popular and respected on Capitol Hill than Nixon thought. Most legislators apparently had little or no concern that then-Vice President Ford could rise to the occasion and they believed he would be a capable president if Nixon left office. But Nixon's departure left Ford in a deep quandary.

His concern for his predecessor was strong—this was clear from his comments when he was sworn in. "May our former president, who brought peace to millions, find it for himself," Ford said.[4]

As Ford adviser Donald Rumsfeld would write later:

> But it was that very question—how to bring peace to the long and bitter political battles of Watergate, which had been tearing the nation apart—that soon dominated the administration. While Ford made clear at his first Cabinet meeting that any talk of a pardon for Nixon should not be discussed publicly, the idea clearly was on his mind. Those of us close enough to observe it ourselves could see how tormented Ford was by the decision. And when he finally made it, it caught many of us by surprise and even led to angry outbursts from people inside the administration, at least one of which I found myself on the receiving end of.[5]

On the day Ford was sworn in as president, August 9, 1974, aides to Leon Jaworski, then the special prosecutor in the Watergate case, drafted a memo assessing whether to prosecute Nixon. Their memo said:

> In our view there is clear evidence that Richard M. Nixon participated in a conspiracy to obstruct justice by concealing the identity of those responsible for the Watergate break-in and other criminal

offenses... There is a presumption (which in the past we have operated upon) that Richard M. Nixon, like every citizen, is subject to the rule of law. Accordingly, one begins with the premise that if there is sufficient evidence, Mr. Nixon should be indicted and prosecuted. The question then becomes whether the presumption for proceeding is outweighed by the factors mandating against indictment and prosecution.[6]

Rumsfeld wrote:

The main arguments the aides cited in favor of Nixon's arrest, indictment and prosecution were: the "principle of equal justice," that the country would remain divided without a final disposition of charges, that the lack of action might encourage a future president to commit acts of lawlessness; and that a resignation alone might not be "sufficient retribution" for such criminal offenses. Among the factors cited that weighed against arrest, indictment and prosecution were: that the embarrassment and disgrace associated with resignation would be punishment enough; that prosecution would "aggravate" the nation's divisions and that pretrial publicity might make it hard, if not impossible, for Nixon to receive fair trial.[7]

Ford asked White House counsel Phil Buchen to get an estimate from Jaworski about much time a criminal prosecution would take. Jaworski replied that it would be at least nine months before Nixon could be brought to trial, and a trial would take many more months after that. Initial legal proceedings could reveal more negative information about the Nixon administration, further prolonging the prosecution.

Ford was also troubled by the questions asked by reporters at his first press conference as president on August 28. Ford had prepared to address a wide variety of topics, including negotiations with the Soviet Union on a nuclear arms agreement and the condition of the economy. Instead, the press conference was dominated by inquiries about Nixon and Watergate. Later, Ford asked an aide whether this was what he would have to face every time he met with members of the media.[8]

Ford believed he could not move beyond the scandal until Nixon's legal fate was resolved. Ford told his White House press secretary Ron

Nessen, "The country has so many other problems. I need to spend time working on other things."[9]

In addition, the new president was very sympathetic to Nixon, his longtime friend, who was in declining health. White House officials received periodic reports that the former president was despondent over his predicament. They were told that young people were throwing dog feces from the beach onto Nixon's beachfront estate in San Clemente, Calif. Pat Nixon, the former first lady, felt under siege and resorted to disguises such as wigs to avoid harassment when she went shopping.

The former president suffered a painful blood clot in his leg soon after leaving office. A doctor who examined Nixon advised reporters that the former president was "a ravaged man who has lost his will to fight" and described his condition as "critical." Ford came to believe that pardoning Nixon would be "the humanitarian—and the Christian—thing to do."[10]

Ford believed that Nixon had already paid an enormous price for his transgressions. He had given up the office he had always craved and that was the absolute center of his life. And Ford agreed with a 1915 Supreme Court case his aides had discovered, *Burdick v. United States*, which declared that a pardon had an "imputation of guilt," and that accepting a pardon was, in effect, "an admission of guilt." For a time, he kept a clipping of the Burdick ruling in his wallet.

The big announcement came on September 8, 1974. Ford said he was pardoning Nixon and it was fully within his powers as president, which was true. He gave his predecessor a full pardon for all offenses against the United States in order to allow the country to move beyond the scandal, and to render moot any questions about whether Nixon had paid enough of a price for his transgressions. This removed the possibility of Nixon being prosecuted for obstruction of justice and abuse of power for his role in the Watergate scandal.

In a ten-minute speech to the nation, Ford tried to explain what he had done and put the furor behind him. Speaking behind his big desk in the Oval Office, making use of the trappings of the presidency to invest his statement with as much gravitas as possible, Ford spoke calmly and seriously, "I have learned already in this office that the difficult decisions always come to this desk," he declared.

> To procrastinate, to agonize and to wait for a more favorable turn of events that may never come or more compelling external pressures

that may as well be wrong as right, is itself a decision of sorts and a weak and potentially dangerous course for a president to follow.[11]

He attempted to explain and justify his sympathy for Nixon and his family:

> Theirs is an American tragedy, in which we all have played a part. It could go on and on and on, or someone must write the end to it. I have concluded that only I can do that and, if I can, I must.

If Nixon were indicted and brought to trial, he argued, "the tranquility to which this nation has been restored by the events of recent weeks could be irreparably lost."[12]

It was the most controversial and unpopular presidential pardon in U.S. history. On the plus side for Ford, some Americans agreed with Ford that Nixon had suffered enough by leaving the presidency in disgrace. And many citizens appreciated Nixon's statement of contrition after Ford's announcement. Nixon released a statement that he had begun to think differently about the Watergate scandal since he left office, admitting that he was "wrong in not acting more decisively and more forthrightly in dealing with Watergate, particularly when it reached the stage of judicial proceedings and grew from a political scandal into a national tragedy."[13]

Nixon also said, "No words can describe the depths of my regret and pain."[14]

But Ford's pardon also outraged and angered millions, and thousands of letters and phone calls poured in condemning the action. White House Press Secretary J.F. terHorst resigned in protest.

Ford's arguments did little to mute the outrage and anger felt by many Americans who believed Nixon had wasted thousands of lives with his Vietnam war policies, and they couldn't forgive him for his lies and abuse of power in the Watergate scandal. As Rumsfeld observed, "Throughout the rest of Ford's presidency, fomented by Nixon critics in the media, where they were thick in number, suspicion about the circumstances surrounding the pardon lingered."[15] A *Time* magazine poll found that 71 percent of Americans believed Ford may not have told the whole truth about the circumstances of the pardon.

Ford testified before Congress to explain what he had done. But nothing worked to help him dig out from public opprobrium.

Ford never recovered politically. His job approval ratings declined and he lost the 1976 election to Democrat Jimmy Carter that fall.

OVER TIME, historians and many Americans have come to believe that Ford was correct in pardoning Nixon after all.

A high point for Ford came in 2001 when the John F. Kennedy Library awarded Ford the "Profile in Courage" award. At the award ceremony, Sen. Edward Kennedy, D-Mass., the slain president's brother, admitted he had condemned the pardon in 1974. "But time has a way of clarifying past events, and now we see that President Ford was right," Kennedy said at the ceremony. "His courage and dedication to our country made it possible for us to begin the process of healing and put the tragedy of Watergate behind us."[16]

Ford's pardon of Nixon showed that the new president could be a decisive, forward-looking leader willing to bear harsh criticism for the public good—a quality that is prized but rare in public life.

Precis

Gerald Ford took bold action to put the issue of Richard Nixon's resignation behind him and allow the country to heal. He adapted to changing circumstances by recognizing that the polarization over Nixon wasn't subsiding and he needed to issue a pardon to end the episode. He chose principle over pragmatism even though it involved a huge political risk, and Ford persevered despite being pilloried for it. Even though the pardon probably cost Ford the 1976 election, it did calm the nation because prosecuting Nixon for alleged Watergate crimes would have been such a divisive spectacle, just as Ford feared it would be. Ford's controversial pardon was a success, not for him but for the American people.

Notes

1. James Cannon, Gerald R. Ford, interview contained in Brian Lamb, Susan Swain and C-SPAN, *The Presidents: Noted Historians Rank America's Best—and Worst—Chief Executives*, New York, Public Affairs, 2019, p. 298.
2. Laurence Tribe and Joshua Matz, *To End A Presidency: The Power of Impeachment*, New York: Basic Books, 2018, p. 149.
3. Tribe and Matz, p. 149.

4. Gerald R. Ford's remarks upon being sworn in as the 38th president, August 9, 1974, p. 3, transcript provided by geraldrfordfoundation.org/40th/documents.
5. Donald Rumsfeld, "How the Nixon Pardon Tore the Ford Administration Apart," *Politico*, May 20, 2018, politico.com/magazine/story/2108/05/20/richard-nixon-pardon.
6. Rumsfeld, ibid.
7. Rumsfeld, ibid.
8. Rumsfeld, ibid.
9. Laura M. Holson, "Ford's Pardon of Nixon, Reviled Before Praised, Made Charity an Option," *New York Times*, Sept. 9, 2018, p. A14, nytimes.com/2018/09/08/us/politics/nixon-ford-pardon.
10. Rumsfeld, ibid.
11. Ford Pardons Nixon—September 8, 1974, YouTube video of Ford speech.
12. Holson, ibid.
13. "President Ford Pardons Former President Nixon," History.com, February 26, 2019, history.com/this-day-in-history/president-for-pardons-former-president-nixon.
14. Holson, ibid.
15. Rumsfeld, ibid.
16. Adam Clymer, "Ford Wins Kennedy Award for 'Courage' of Nixon Pardon," *New York Times*, May 22, 2001, p. A14.

CHAPTER NINE
JIMMY CARTER
THE IRANIAN HOSTAGE CRISIS

Jimmy Carter spent a year trying to win the release of U.S. hostages in Iran. Here he is shown attending a prayer service for the hostages at the Washington National Cathedral on Nov. 15, 1979. The hostage crisis was a key factor in his defeat for reelection in 1980. (AP Photo/ Ira Schwartz)

The Iranian hostage debacle of 1979–80 was Jimmy Carter's most damaging crisis, and in the minds of millions of Americans it was his biggest failure.[1]

It started with the deepening resentment among Iranians to the rule of Shah Mohammad Reza Pahlavi. He was widely despised in his own country because of his brutal use of the secret police (SAVAK), his attempts to reduce the influence of Islam, his secular orientation and his strong ties to the United States.

Islamic clerics led the opposition to Pahlavi, notably Grand Ayatollah Ruhollah Khomeini, whom the shah had exiled in 1964. The level of violence increased dramatically in 1978, and on September 8, the shah declared martial law and his army fired into a large crowd in Tehran, killing hundreds of protesters.

In January 1979, the tumult continued and the shah made the mistake of attempting to take a vacation abroad with his family. After he left Iran, Khomeini triumphantly returned to Tehran and helped to orchestrate the creation of a government parallel to the shah's. Iran was in chaos. The shah abdicated that same month amid increasing opposition at home, leaving enormous turmoil behind.

Carter and his aides misread the situation, seeing the turmoil as caused by pro-Soviet insurgents and failing to recognize that the revolt was at its core Muslim-inspired.[2]

At this time, Carter had many other problems to deal with, especially high inflation and gasoline shortages. The former shah's difficulties took a back seat to the economy but they proved to be a very serious dilemma for Carter, rivaling all the other problems he was facing. The shah had departed from Iran amid angry rioting against his brutal regime, traveling to Cairo, Egypt, then to the Bahamas, and finally settling in Cuernavaca, Mexico. But he desperately needed sophisticated medical care for what was diagnosed as malignant lymphoma and a blocked bile duct, and in October 1979 he requested admittance to the United States to get treatment.

Carter's advisers were divided on whether to grant admittance. "It would be a sign of weakness not to allow the shah to come to the States to live," said White House National Security Adviser Zbigniew Brzezinski at a key White House meeting. "If we turned our backs on the fallen shah, it would be a signal to the world that the United States is a fair-weather friend." Secretary of State Cyrus Vance disagreed, and the president at that moment sided with him. "It makes no sense to bring him here and destroy whatever slim chance we have of rebuilding a relationship with Iran," Carter said. "It boils down to a choice between the shah's preferences as to where he lives and the interests of our country."[3]

But as the shah's physical condition deteriorated, pressure grew on Carter to allow the former Iranian ruler to enter the United States to receive treatment in New York. Among his advocates were New York banker David Rockefeller and former Secretary of State Henry Kissinger. On October 19, 1979, Carter raised the subject at his weekly foreign affairs breakfast in the Cabinet Room. Vance, noting the shah's dire situation, changed his mind and urged Pahlavi's admittance as a humanitarian gesture. Carter remained skeptical. At this point, all his senior advisers wanted the shah to receive treatment in the United States.

Hamilton Jordan, newly appointed as White House chief of staff, added a domestic political consideration. "Mr. President, if the shah dies in Mexico, can you imagine the field day Kissinger will have with that?" Jordan said. "He'll say that first you caused the shah's downfall and now you've killed him."

Carter fumed, "To hell with Henry Kissinger. I am the president of this country."[4]

But Vance and Brzezinski, often at odds on other questions, pressed the matter, arguing that admitting the shah was the decent thing to do. The president changed his mind and decided to allow entry. But he added, with remarkable prescience, "What are you guys going to advise me to do if they overrun our embassy and take our people hostage?" No one replied and Carter made a final point: "On that day we will all sit here with long, drawn, white faces and realize we've been had."[5]

Some American diplomats and other leaders felt loyalty to Pahlavi because he had been a strong anticommunist and close U.S. ally for many years during the Cold War. His regime also spent lavishly on U.S.-made weapons. But the shah had angered millions of his own people, and some described his regime as a "reign of terror."[6]

When Carter allowed the shah to have medical treatment in New York in late October 1979, his decision triggered an outpouring of rage against the United States for helping the despised and exiled ruler, who had been considered by many Iranians as an American puppet. On Sunday, November 4, 300 college students managed to enter the grounds of the U.S. Embassy in Tehran, after a few of them climbed over a gate and opened the site to the mass of protesters. Iranian policemen who were supposed to be guarding the main gate did nothing to stop them. And U.S. Marines guarding the compound ran inside and locked the doors behind them, under the direction of civilian U.S. officials who didn't want to cause an international incident by firing on the crowd.[7]

The students quickly took control of the Embassy and seized 63 Americans. This began the episode known as the Iranian hostage crisis, which in some ways was Carter's undoing as president.

On November 6, Carter met with his full National Security Council—the advisers most responsible for keeping the nation safe and protecting America's security. Carter announced his goals in the mushrooming Iranian crisis: first, win the release of the hostages. Second, start planning ways to punish those responsible for the hostage seizure. Third, avoid any military operations on the ground in Iran, which Carter said would be too risky and very likely to fail. Secretary of State Vance explained various diplomatic initiatives that were under way, but Director of Central Intelligence Stansfield Turner argued that the chances of negotiating directly with the students who had invaded the Embassy were probably destined to lead nowhere, and the militants' leaders had warned that any U.S. attempt to rescue the hostages would result in their being killed. Defense Secretary Harold Brown admitted that any such rescue attempt would likely fail. Clearly, the situation was going from bad to worse, and the president had no good options.[8]

In order to remain focused on crisis management, Carter cancelled a planned trip to Canada on November 8. But this added to the impression of a president under siege. The sense of isolation was reinforced by Carter's decision to cancel all of his campaign activities in order to remain at the White House and focus on the crisis. This decision deepened the perception that the president was himself hostage to the hostage crisis, and unable to find a way out. He was calling attention to himself as a figure of futility, a ruinous image with his re-election on the line in November 1980, less than a year away.

Every action that Carter took seemed weak and too little, too late. On November 14, he announced economic sanctions against Iran, such as freezing Iranian accounts in U.S. banks and banning the purchases of Iranian oil. The Carter administration asked the International Court of Justice to endorse releasing the hostages and ordered a reduction in staff at Iran's Washington Embassy. During the Thanksgiving holiday, Carter asked Americans to pray for the hostages and ring church bells for them in solidarity. He promised not to light the National Christmas Tree until the hostages were released. It all seemed well-intentioned but hapless.

What Americans were paying attention to was the media coverage of the crisis, which had become a spectacle, especially on television. TV anchors such as CBS's Walter Cronkite began summarizing how many days the hostages had been in captivity, citing the number each evening during their nightly news broadcasts. ABC began a late-night broadcast anchored by Ted Koppel called *America Held Hostage*.

Some of Carter's advisers were urging him to act boldly to avoid seeming trapped and to alter the image that he was too passive and indecisive.

During a 48-hour period starting November 18, the Iranians released 13 of the hostages, all of them women or African Americans. But this good news was quickly overwhelmed by the ayatollah's announcement that if Carter did not extradite the shah, Iran would put the remaining hostages on trial.

Carter convened members of the NSC at the Camp David presidential retreat on November 23 to plan his response. The group reviewed the military's planning, which included air strikes on the Iranian oil industry and a naval blockade. But these were only contingency plans. There was serious disagreement on how to respond to Khomeini's threatened trials.

Secretary of State Vance, Defense Secretary Brown and Vice President Walter Mondale opposed any direct threat of retaliation for the threatened hostage trials. Brzezinski, Jordan and White House Press Secretary Jody Powell supported a tougher line. "Ham [Jordan] whispered to me that Carter simply would not be reelected president if he did not act firmly," Brzezinski wrote later.[9]

Carter took a half step—a direct threat but one delivered privately, through Swiss operatives. His message was: if the hostages were harmed, the United States would mine or blockade all Iranian harbors. This message was delivered and the Tehran rhetoric about trials became more muted, which Carter felt was a good sign.

Beyond this, Carter proceeded with his favored strategy of negotiation and imposing sanctions.

But at the seven-week mark of the crisis, few Americans seemed satisfied with Carter's incremental approach. Political scientist Betty Glad wrote later, "Carter had inflated the importance of the hostages to American foreign policy. Jimmy Carter helped create a feeling of emergency in the United States which suggested that the holding of hostages was a national security threat." And he "suggested that the whole nation had been hurt by this assault on its integrity."[10]

Denise Bostdorff, a scholar who has studied presidential rhetoric, said the public expected Carter to take pragmatic and realistic steps to free the hostages. His focus on airy theories and statements of ideal outcomes "reinforced his public image as a passive leader."[11]

Historian Bohn added: "Carter's suggestions that his critics were unpatriotic reinforced the president's message that America was in a dangerous conflict."[12]

It made matters worse for Carter when the Soviet Union invaded Afghanistan, a country adjacent to both Iran and the U.S.S.R., just after Christmas 1979, as the Iranian crisis simmered. The stakes suddenly got higher. Moscow was now playing a bigger role in the region, and any U.S. military action against Iran might precipitate a crisis with the Kremlin. At least this is what some of Carter's advisers feared. This left the president more committed than ever to a diplomatic effort, at least for the moment.

But the ayatollah rejected several diplomatic overtures designed to end the crisis, and Carter was becoming increasingly frustrated. So were both his allies and adversaries in Congress. When Vice President Mondale visited Capitol Hill in February to assess the level of support for the president's approach, he found many legislators grim, angry and demanding action. They weren't sure exactly what Carter should do, but they expected something decisive and bold. This pressure made Carter's job all the more difficult because so many of his diplomatic avenues were closing and he felt pushed into what he felt might be rash choices.

By mid-March 1980, as public and congressional frustration with the crisis intensified, Brzezinski began pushing aggressively for a hostage rescue mission and Carter began seriously considering it. On March 22, Carter held a day-long meeting at Camp David and listened as Air Force Gen. David C. Jones, chairman of the Joint Chiefs of Staff, gave a briefing on a draft plan for such a rescue.

Wearing casual clothing in front of a roaring fire, the group learned in detail of what was being proposed: eight Navy RH-53D Sea Stallion helicopters would be flown by Marine pilots from the aircraft carrier USS *Nimitz* in the Arabian Sea, travel nearly 600 miles at night to a secret landing strip inside Iran called Desert 1. Meanwhile, six Air Force C-130

Hercules propeller-driven transport planes would fly separately and meet the helicopters there. The C-130s would drop off fuel supplies and a rescue team from the Army's Delta Force and then the C-130s would leave Iran.[13]

The helicopters would refuel and fly to a hiding place in the local mountains until the following night. The rescue team would drive into Tehran during that second night using vehicles obtained locally by the CIA. The team would rescue the hostages and then board the helicopters that were to fly in and pick them up. They would proceed to an Iranian airfield captured by special forces and meet Air Force C-141 Starlifter jet transports there. The Delta Force team, the hostages and the helicopter crews would fly off in the C-141 aircraft, leaving behind the abandoned helicopters, presumably for the Iranians to find later.

It was a very intricate plan calling for an extraordinary degree of coordination and a large degree of luck. This made the mission a huge risk from the start.

Carter said he would think about it but gave no time frame for a decision.

On April 7, Carter convened an NSC meeting and said he would continue to ratchet up the sanctions against Iran. Among his immediate steps were breaking diplomatic relations with the Tehran government, banning all exports to Iran except for food and medicine, and expelling all Iranian embassy and consulting personnel.

On April 11, Carter convened another NSC meeting and announced at the beginning, "Gentlemen, I want you to know that I am seriously considering an attempt to rescue the hostages." General Jones and Secretary Brown then gave a detailed briefing on the military options, including the display of top-secret maps, indicating how far the planning had gone. At the end of the session, Carter said he would coordinate further with Secretary of State Vance, who was out of town, before making a final decision. But it was clear that he was poised to act when he ended the meeting by saying it was time to bring the hostages home.[14]

As the group left the Cabinet Room, White House Press Secretary Jody Powell said to Brown,

> Mr. Secretary, the president is going to go with this thing, I can sense it. If we can bring our people out of there, it will do more good for this country than anything that has happened in twenty years.[15]

Brown replied, "Yes, and if we fail, that will be the end of the Carter presidency . . . But we really don't have much choice, do we?"[16]

Carter consulted with Vance, who strongly opposed the rescue mission. The president gave Vance the opportunity to state his case in front of the other senior advisers and Carter. No one agreed with his view that diplomacy and sanctions should be given more time to work. Vance was to resign within a few days, since it was clear his standing was at a low point within the administration.

On Thursday, April 24, the hostage rescue mission began. At 4:45 p.m., Brown phoned Brzezinski and said, "I think we have an abort situation."[17] Actually, it was turning into a disaster. The rescue team reached Desert 1 but two of the eight helicopters were damaged and a third turned back to the *Nimitz*. Six helicopters were considered the minimum needed to do the job and only five were available. The commander at the scene recommended ending the mission.

Brzezinski interrupted Carter in the Oval Office and they talked privately in the president's study adjacent to the Oval. Carter called Brown at the Pentagon, received a quick briefing, and agreed to stop the mission. But it was too late, and Carter immediately realized his roll of the dice had failed. When he hung up, the president put his arms and head down on his desk, and neither he nor Brzezinski could muster any words for several moments.

The raid turned out to be even more of a calamity than what was reported to Carter initially. One of the helicopters at the Desert 1 site collided with a C-130 tanker as it was being prepared for refueling, and the resulting explosion and fire killed eight men. At 5:58 p.m., 73 minutes after the first report of a possible aborted mission, General Jones called Carter with word of the collision.

"Are there any dead?" Carter asked, his face draining of color. Told of the deaths, he said, "I understand" and hung up the phone as a handful of his senior advisers looked on, realizing that there were indeed casualties. Jordan ran into a restroom and vomited.[18]

Later, military expert Charles Kamps described the folly of the hostage rescue mission, code-named "Operation Eagle Claw." "[T]he things which did cause the mission to abort were probably merciful compared to the greater catastrophe which might have taken place if the scenario had progressed further than the Desert One rendezvous," Kamps wrote. ". . . In the realm of military planning there are plans that might work and plans that won't work. In the cold light of history it is evident that the plan for Eagle Claw was in the second category" and would have required several miracles to succeed.[19]

Carter quickly acknowledged the mission's failure publicly but there were no reprisals from Tehran. In fact, Khomeini allowed the release on July 11 of hostage Richard Queen, who was suffering from multiple sclerosis. But Iran's continued holding of the other hostages remained a huge embarrassment to Carter. The shah's death on July 27 also didn't alter the dynamic. Khomeini and his clerics used the seizure of the hostages to show strength and rally the support of militant Iranians against the "great Satan"—the United States.

As the November presidential election neared, the United States and the Iranian regime started to talk seriously about the release of the hostages, but the process was agonizingly slow because the distrust and animosities ran so deep. On September 22, Iraq invaded Iran as each country sought supremacy in the region. This further complicated the negotiations over the hostages, in part because the Iranian regime didn't want to show weakness during the war with Iraq, and some Iranian officials saw strong advantages in keeping the Americans as bargaining chips. On the other hand, before the hostage seizure Iran had ordered weapons and other military equipment from the United States which the regime desperately needed to defeat the Iraqis. As long as the hostages remained in custody, those weapons wouldn't be delivered.

Some Carter advisers have argued that representatives of Republican presidential candidate Ronald Reagan, who was running against Carter that autumn, made a deal with the Iranians to keep the hostages until after the election rather than give Carter a PR success by winning the release just before the balloting. None of this has been proven, however.[20]

On the Sunday night before the Tuesday election, Carter addressed the nation on television and said it was unlikely that a deal would be reached before the balloting. Carter said he wanted to be candid with the public. "But the fallout from the speech was not good, as the announcement confirmed perceptions that Carter was unable to resolve the crisis and was paralyzed in dealing with Iran," wrote historian Julian E. Zelizer. "Carter soon knew the speech had killed him. The failure to obtain the release of the hostages was highlighted by the media coverage of the anniversary of the start of the crisis, which happened to fall on Election Day."[21] Carter wrote later in his memoirs that the speech had released a "flood of related concerns among the people that we were impotent," not only in Iran but in dealing with the energy crisis, the troubled economy and the Soviet invasion of Afghanistan.[22]

Reagan won the election overwhelmingly with 489 electoral votes to Carter's 49. A big reason was the belief of many Americans that Jimmy Carter had botched the biggest crisis of his presidency.

There was an important postscript for Carter. The hostages were actually released on Reagan's inauguration day, January 20, 1981, minutes after Carter left office.

"With the exception of the wag-the-dog moment when he tried to rescue the hostages, President Carter patiently worked his way through the crisis," writes author Bohn.

> Nevertheless, the 444-day hostage ordeal allowed Jimmy Carter's critics to fashion a damaging caricature of a president in crisis. He was a weak-willed leader, they said, who was afraid to take bold action to free those people. When he had a little good news, he shamelessly used it to win a primary election over Ted Kennedy [the Massachusetts senator and brother of the slain President John F. Kennedy who unsuccessfully challenged Carter for the 1980 Democratic nomination]. When he had bad news, he wrapped himself in the American flag and from the Rose Garden called critics un-American. But when he finally did act, his penchant for involving himself in the military details doomed the rescue attempt to failure. The rest of the time, his critics argued, he just dithered and turned off the Christmas tree lights . . . Carter created high public expectations for decisive action by inflating the hostage situation into a veritable national emergency. His calls for prayer and church bells, coupled with his cancelation of campaign events, increased attention to what he did or didn't do. The insatiable TV coverage made the situation seem even more dire by bringing the suffering of the hostages and their families into American living rooms and dens.[23]

Bohn continued:

> On the other hand, multiple real-life forces—issues largely unseen or ignored by the critics—inhibited bold action and thus unfortunately contributed to the caricature. Among the factors that forced

cautious, incremental crisis management steps—muddling through—was Carter's dedication to keeping the hostages alive. Harbor mining and the destruction of oil refineries would bring hostages home in boxes. Moreover, air strikes could enflame the Muslim world with anti-American hatred, trigger an oil-supply emergency, strain relations with allies, and invite Soviet adventurism.[24]

Carter learned an important lesson, although it came too late to save his presidency. He told the *New York Times* in 1981 that the crisis taught him that "there are limits even on our nation's great strength. It's the same kind of impotence that a powerful person feels when his child is kidnapped."[25]

Most Americans considered the episode as a huge blemish on Carter's record. It showed that good intentions are no substitute for good judgment, and a president must sometimes refuse to be stampeded into hasty and reckless action no matter how intense the pressure.

Precis

Jimmy Carter failed a significant test of his leadership in the Iranian hostage crisis. He didn't take quick action once the crisis started, failing to immediately impose crippling sanctions on Tehran. He tried adapting to the changing circumstances—he acknowledged rising congressional and public pressure to act boldly—by launching a rescue mission. But it ended in disaster because it was so poorly planned. He made his top priority the safe release of the hostages and he persevered in working toward this objective but he seemed indecisive and passive. The hostages were released on the day Carter left office but by then the crisis had done lasting damage to Carter and the United States by making the president and the country look weak and vulnerable.

Notes

1. Michael K. Bohn, *Presidents in Crisis: Tough Decisions inside the White House from Truman to Obama*, New York: Arcade Publishing, 2016, pp. 132–151.
2. Julian E. Zelizer, *Jimmy Carter*, New York: Times Books, 2010, pp. 79–80.
3. Hamilton Jordan, *Crisis*, New York: G.P. Putnam's Sons, 1982, p. 29.
4. Jordan, p. 31.

5. Jordan, p. 32.
6. David Harris, *The Crisis*, Boston: Little, Brown, 2004, p. 28.
7. Bohn, pp. 135–136.
8. Bohn, p. 138.
9. Zbigniew Brzezinski, *Power and Principle*, New York: Farrar, Straus, Giroux, 1983, p. 483.
10. Betty Glad, "Personality, Political and Group Process Variables in Foreign Policy Decision-Making," *International Political Science Review*, Volume 10, Number 1, 1989, p. 42.
11. Denise Bostdorff, *The Presidency and the Rhetoric of Foreign Crisis*, Columbia: University of South Carolina Press, 1994, p. 161. Also see Bohn, p. 141.
12. Bohn, p. 141.
13. Bohn, pp. 144–146.
14. Bohn, p. 145.
15. Jody Powell, *The Other Side of the Story*, New York: William Morrow, 1994, p. 228.
16. Powell, ibid.
17. Bohn, p. 146.
18. Jordan, pp. 272–273. See also Bohn, pp. 146–147.
19. Gene Healy, "The Carter Legacy: What About the Failed Iran Hostage Mission?" *Newsweek*, September 13, 2015, newsweek.com/carter-legacy-what-about-failed-iran-hostage-mission.
20. Bohn, p. 148.
21. Zelizer, p. 123.
22. Jimmy Carter, *Keeping Faith: Memoirs of a President*, Fayetteville: University of Arkansas Press, 1995, p. 577.
23. Bohn, pp. 149–150.
24. Bohn, p. 150.
25. Terence Smith, "Putting the Hostages' Lives First," *New York Times*, May 17, 1981, p. 1.

Chapter Ten
Ronald Reagan
A Matter of Life and Death

Ronald Reagan was shot and almost died in an assassination attempt on March 30, 1981. His resolve, fortitude and grace under pressure impressed many Americans, and he received many get-well cards and messages, including this one from federal employees. He is shown admiring the huge get-well photograph during his hospital convalescence in a picture taken on April 8, 1981, about a week after the shooting. (Ronald Reagan Library)

There is nothing more important to any president, clearly, than a brush with death. Under such circumstances, a president's natural instincts in an emergency are on display, as are the individual's grace under pressure, character, bravery, strength, resilience and luck. All these factors go a long way toward illuminating a president's impulses and character.

Ronald Reagan was almost killed by a would-be assassin on March 30, 1981, only ten weeks after he took office. His reactions showed that he had mettle and that optimism was an essential part of his creed in both public and private. It also underscored the talent of his advisers, who generally handled the crisis with efficiency and good judgment.

The lessons he drew from the ordeal shaped his presidency and influenced the decisions he made for the remainder of his time in the White House, nearly eight years.

The nation's 40th president was shot by a deranged young man named John Hinckley, Jr. as Reagan walked to his limousine after giving a speech to a labor audience at the Washington Hilton Hotel, about 2:45 p.m. on a cold winter afternoon. This became a test of the highest urgency. Not only was Reagan's presidency at stake but his life was in the balance. It amounted to the ultimate crisis.

Reagan biographer Lou Cannon says the assassination attempt was one of the defining moments of the Reagan era. "He is sixty-nine days into his presidency," Cannon recalls,

> and all at once he's wounded. America sees this rather gallant man quipping, telling stories, using one-liners that would have seemed artificial in many circumstances, except this is a person who could have died from this wound. We found out later that the bullet just missed his aorta. Doctors have told me that many people never really recover fully from gunshot wounds, and here this man is well advanced in life. At this point he's just had his seventieth birthday, and he bounces back in a hurry. He became a mythic figure in America when he was quipping to the doctors, "I hope you're all Republicans" and those kinds of lines.[1]

HISTORY WAS AGAINST REAGAN. Four of his predecessors had been shot while in office—Abraham Lincoln, James Garfield, William McKinley and John F. Kennedy—and none survived. The fact was that, until Reagan, if a would-be assassin shot an incumbent president, he had always succeeded in killing the commander in chief.

An additional six of the 44 individuals who have been president were the targets of assassination attempts and survived close calls.

This means that one-tenth of the U.S. presidents, four of them, have been killed in office, and, more broadly, a total of ten or 22.7 percent of presidents have been either killed in or survived an assassination attempt.

The four who died:

- Lincoln was shot on April 14, 1865 as he watched "Our American Cousin," a stage production at Ford's Theater in Washington. He died the next day, April 15.
- Garfield was shot July 2, 1881 as he walked to a waiting train at the Baltimore and Potomac Railroad Station in Washington. He died on September 19, 1881.
- McKinley was shot on September 6, 1901 while shaking hands on a receiving line at the Pan-American Exhibition in Buffalo, New York. He died on September 14, 1901.
- Kennedy was shot on November 22, 1963 as he rode in an open convertible during a motorcade in Dallas, Texas. He died the same day.

Targeting the lives of America's presidents has been frequent, and luck plays a big role in the outcome.

President Gerald Ford survived two assassination attempts unscathed. On September 5, 1975, a woman pulled a pistol on Ford in a park in Sacramento, California, but was subdued before she fired the weapon. Seventeen days later, on September 22, another woman fired at Ford with a revolver outside the St. Francis Hotel in San Francisco. One shot missed and the other was deflected when a bystander grabbed the shooter's arm.

Harry Truman was the target of would-be killers in November 1950. Two Puerto Rican nationalists attempted an assassination to publicize their demands for Puerto Rico's independence from U.S. control. (The island was then and remains U.S. territory. It is not formally a state but governs itself). The two men tried to force their way into Blair House, a government building where Truman and his family were staying while the White House Residence was being renovated. They killed one guard and wounded two others; one of the attackers was killed and the other captured before they could enter the house and shoot Truman, who was taking an afternoon nap and wasn't hurt.[2]

In addition, Franklin D. Roosevelt was the target of an assassination attempt on February 15, 1933 when he was president-elect. An unemployed brick layer named Giuseppe Zangara fired a gun six times at FDR after the president-elect delivered a speech in a Miami park from the back seat of an open touring car. Five people were hit, but not Roosevelt. Chicago Mayor Anton Cermak, who was shot in the stomach, died of his wound.[3]

Another potentially lethal attack was directed at Theodore Roosevelt but he was not in office at the time. As a former president (he succeeded to the office as McKinley's vice president when McKinley died in 1901, and TR served for nearly seven years after that), he was attempting to restart his political career by running for the White House as a third-party candidate in 1912. He was hit in the chest as he arrived to deliver a speech in Milwaukee, Wisconsin, on October 14, but, miraculously, an eyeglass case and a thick speech text in the chest pocket of his jacket prevented the bullet from penetrating too deeply into his body and saved his life. He went on to talk for 90 minutes before seeking medical attention. Doctors thought surgery would be too risky so they left the bullet in his chest, and Roosevelt recovered.

Andrew Jackson was the first president to survive an assassination attempt. A deranged house painter tried to shoot Jackson on January 30, 1835 while Jackson was visiting the Capitol. Jackson went after the man with his cane, but the president was not hurt.[4]

Reagan's behavior was similar to FDR's. "All reports of Roosevelt's response to the shooting emphasized his composure and even his disdain at his brush with death," reports historian Robert Dallek. "He insisted that Cermak [the gravely wounded mayor] be transported in his car to the nearest hospital, where he waited until the mayor was out of the emergency room and he could speak with him." An aide said that privately he was "easy, confident, poised, to all appearance unmoved." And the public liked his grace under fire, increasing national confidence in him. "For his part," Dallek writes,

> Franklin viewed the assassination attempt as a blessing in disguise—a postelection rallying event carrying him into the presidency on a wave of sympathy and approval that he believed would greatly serve his initial presidential actions in the coming struggle with the Great Depression.[5]

REAGAN, like Roosevelt (Reagan's political hero as a young man), was very fortunate in several ways. One was the quick reaction of his chief bodyguard. If it were not for Jerry Parr, Reagan would surely have died.

In his autobiography, Reagan recalled that his speech at the Hilton Hotel to the Construction Trades Council "was not riotously received—I think most of the audience were Democrats—but at least they gave me polite applause." After the address, Reagan left the hotel through a side entrance and passed a line of news photographers and TV cameras. He had almost reached his limousine when he heard "what sounded like two or three firecrackers over to my left—just a small fluttering sound, *pop, pop, pop*." He turned to his Secret Service agents and asked, "What the hell's that?"[6]

At that moment, Jerry Parr, head of the president's Secret Service detail, grabbed the president by the waist and hurled him into the back of the limo, where he landed face down on an arm rest in the back seat. Parr jumped on top of Reagan to protect him, and the president immediately felt an excruciating pain in his upper back. "Jerry, get off," Reagan said. "I think you've broken one of my ribs." Parr shouted to the driver, "The White House," and then sat on the jump seat and the car sped off. Reagan tried to sit up on the edge of his seat and "was almost paralyzed by pain," he recalled. He coughed up "red, frothy blood" onto the palm of his hand, and he told Parr he thought the agent had not only broken a rib but caused the rib to puncture his lung. At this point, Parr saw the blood and told the driver to head for nearby George Washington University Hospital instead of the White House for emergency treatment. This quick thinking likely saved Reagan's life.[7]

A bullet, fired by Hinckley with a .22-caliber handgun, had bounced off the president's armor-plated limousine and pierced his chest under his left arm, which he had raised to wave to the crowd. The bullet lodged close to Reagan's heart, a very dangerous situation. Three men were wounded by three of the five other shots fired by Hinckley within 1.7 seconds at a distance of about 15 feet—Secret Service agent Timothy McCarthy, Washington police officer Thomas Delahanty, and White House Press Secretary James Brady, who suffered permanent brain damage.[8]

Weakening by the minute, the president still insisted on playing the role of the optimistic and dignified commander in chief. When his limo pulled up outside the emergency room, Reagan got out of the vehicle, hitched up his trousers, buttoned his suit jacket, and walked into the hospital, only to collapse when he shuffled into the lobby and was out of public view. Senior White House adviser Michael Deaver said the president showed "not even a would-be assassin was going to bring Ronald Reagan down."[9]

Deaver also told me in a 1994 interview that Reagan didn't want to show any weakness. "He believed it was part of the role of the President of the United States," Deaver said.[10]

By the time he reached the emergency room, he could barely breathe. "I was frightened and started to panic a little," Reagan recalled. "I just was not able to inhale enough air." He lost consciousness briefly and found himself lying face up on a gurney. His new blue pin-striped suit was being cut off his body. Doctors put a breathing tube in his throat, and he passed out again.[11]

Semi-conscious, he opened his eyes and saw his wife, Nancy, looking down at him. "Honey," he said, "I forgot to duck"—borrowing Jack Dempsey's famous quip to his wife after he was defeated by Gene Tunney for the heavyweight boxing title in 1926.[12] His sense of humor didn't fail him. Reagan's publicity-conscious aides passed these comments on to the news media, and the president's good cheer and fortitude during the crisis were widely reported, and served as an example for the country of how to behave in a personal life-or-death situation.

Seeing his beloved wife after he was shot gave him what he called "an enormous lift." Even though he was in deep distress, he was typically optimistic and his thoughts turned to the future. "I pray I'll never face a day when she isn't there," he wrote in his diary later, summarizing his thoughts at the moment of his greatest personal crisis, " . . . [Of] all the ways God had blessed me, giving her to me was the greatest—beyond anything I can ever hope to deserve."[13]

He saw signs of divine intervention. "Someone was looking out for us that day," he later wrote. He also observed,

> I thanked God for what he and they [members of his security detail, two of them having been shot that day] had done for me, and while I was waiting to be taken into the operating room, I remembered the trip I had made just the week before to Ford's Theater and the thoughts I'd had while looking up at the flag-draped box where Lincoln had died. Even with all the protection in the world, I'd thought, it was probably impossible to guarantee completely the safety of the president. Now I'd not only benefited from the selflessness of the

two men; God, for some reason, had seen fit to give me his blessing and allow me to live a while longer.[14]

Reagan noted that most of the doctors who helped save his life were attending a special meeting at the George Washington University Hospital that day and many of them would not ordinarily have been there when he was shot. It turned out that they were an elevator ride from the emergency room. Because of their proximity, a few minutes after Reagan arrived, the emergency room was filled with specialists in virtually every medical field, Reagan said. When one of the doctors said they were going to operate, Reagan quipped, "I hope you're a Republican." The physician looked at him and replied, "Today, Mr. President, we're all Republicans." He showed his sense of humor again when one of his nurses asked him how he felt. "All in all, I'd rather be in Philadelphia," he joked, referring to an old line from comedian W.C. Fields.[15]

What the physicians found was a 70-year-old man in extremis. Reagan was losing lots of blood and looked very weak and pale. After he collapsed in the hospital entryway, he was placed on a gurney and taken to the emergency room where the surgical team began desperate efforts to save his life.

The doctors worked deftly. They initially couldn't pinpoint the location of the bullet fragment, but an x-ray image showed it was lodged in lung tissue close to his heart. They removed it with considerable difficulty.[16]

As recounted by his savvy media team and widely reported, Reagan's grit and sense of humor were on display from the start, creating the indelible image of a man able to deal with the ultimate crisis, rising to the occasion with grit and determination.

"News of the attempted assassination dominated the airwaves that spring afternoon," writes political scientist Robert E. Gilbert.

> At first, it seemed to be 1963 all over again—shots fired at a president, pandemonium at the scene, the rush to the hospital, uncertain news reports of his condition. But this time there were important differences. The President was still alive and, although wounded, was cracking jokes to his wife and doctors. Reagan's gallant behavior helped assure the country that this time all would be well.[17]

Throughout his ordeal, the role of his staff and those around him was pivotal—as it tends to be in any situation where a president responds to a crisis.

While the doctors worked to save his life, providing him with anesthetic, removing the bullet and giving him transfusions, Reagan's advisers were considering what to do next.

White House Chief of Staff James Baker, presidential counselor Ed Meese and senior aide Michael Deaver rushed to the hospital. They and other Reagan advisers discussed invoking the 25th Amendment, which provides for the succession to the presidency when a president dies or cannot perform his duties. Section 3 allows the president to temporarily turn over his duties to the vice president. Section 4 allows the vice president and a majority of officers of the top executive-branch departments to inform Congress if a president is incapable of fulfilling his duties and authorizing Congress to decide if power should be transferred.[18]

Reagan went into surgery before he could transfer his powers under Section 3. Vice President George H.W. Bush was flying back to the capital from Texas and, unsure of Reagan's condition in the chaos of the moment, did not invoke Section 4.

Secretary of State Alexander Haig, a former general, took decisive action—too decisive, as it turned out. Haig interrupted White House spokesman Larry Speakes, who was updating the media about Reagan's status shortly after the president entered the hospital, and Haig announced, "As of now I am in control here." He wasn't.[19]

The Presidential Succession Act of 1947 provided that the first in line to take over presidential authority was the vice president, followed by the speaker of the House, the president pro tempore of the Senate, and only then, fourth in line of succession, the secretary of state. Other cabinet members disputed Haig, and White House officials quickly clarified the situation by announcing that Reagan remained in charge.

Dr. William Ruge, Reagan's White House physician, disagreed. "[T]here was a period of 10–15 hours when Ronald Reagan was unable to function as President and could not have responded to a crisis," Ruge said in the aftermath of the episode. "This was the period of time when the Amendment clearly should have been in effect." But Ruge said he was never asked specifically by Reagan's staff about invoking the 25th Amendment.[20]

Haig and Defense Secretary Caspar Weinberger suspected that the Soviet Union was somehow linked to the assassination attempt. They told aides the Soviets would have preferred that Vice President Bush, more moderate in his attitudes toward the U.S.S.R., step in as president. Weinberger ordered the U.S. military to go on "standby alert" because he thought Soviet submarines were closer than normal to the U.S. East Coast.[21]

Attempting to show that he was recovering quickly, Reagan signed a dairy bill the day after the assassination attempt. White House media managers released a series of photos designed to show Reagan on the mend. One depicted the president doing paperwork in his hospital bed. Another showed him meeting with aides. But some of these pictures were misleading. The White House staff photographer was carefully positioned on one side of Reagan so the pictures wouldn't show the tubes running into the other side of the president's body, to provide medication and anesthetic.

From the start of the crisis, his family members were also very much attuned to appearances. Michael Reagan, the president's oldest son, said the president's children didn't fly from California to Washington until nighttime "because if we were seen rushing to the airport, the press would have known that Dad was in serious condition." Nancy Reagan explained why she didn't spend the first night at the hospital by saying that if she had, "I'd be sending out a message to the world that Ronnie's condition was critical. It was, of course, but at that moment I didn't want people to know."[22]

Reagan returned to the White House from the hospital on April 11, less than two weeks after he was shot. This gave the White House media managers another opportunity to add to the larger-than-life image of Ronald Reagan and his supposedly miraculous recuperative powers. He walked unassisted from his car into the White House, and the photograph was sent around the world.

Reagan drew expansive conclusions from the attempted assassination. He later wrote in his diary: "Whatever happens now I owe my life to God and will try to serve him in any way I can."[23]

Less than a month after the shooting, Reagan spoke to a joint session of Congress to urge support for his economic program. It was his first major public appearance after the shooting and he looked remarkably well.

Reagan had proven himself as a man of strength and resilience, bravery and wit. "It showed his grace under pressure and his sense of humor," recalled Ken Duberstein, a Reagan adviser who became his White House chief of staff at the end of his second term, in 1988. "And the American people saw—here was a guy who made sense."[24] Reagan's personal courage and resolve, and his optimism that he would recover, impressed everyday Americans. As they saw their president's uplifting behavior, their support for him personally transferred to key parts of his agenda, such as his plan to cut taxes. He ended up getting this plan through Congress and even won over some opposition Democrats in the end.

REAGAN SAID later that he felt God had spared his life for two purposes—to destroy the Soviet empire of communism and be a catalyst to "lessen the risk of nuclear war."[25]

There were many manifestations of this, especially his desire to rid the world of nuclear weapons.

Historian Michael Beschloss writes:

> He worried that his defense buildup was overshadowing his wish to bargain with the Soviets. Especially after his brush with death, he wanted the Soviet leader, Leonid Brezhnev, to know how deeply he yearned for "a world without nuclear weapons."[26]

He sent a hand-written letter to Brezhnev to this effect. State Department hardliners tried to water it down but Reagan insisted on stronger language about promoting peace to convey his seriousness. He told an aide that after the assassination attempt he had decided, "I'm going to follow my own instincts."[27]

Reagan didn't get much conciliation from the Soviets initially. But during his second term, he formed a historical partnership with new Soviet leader Mikhail Gorbachev that paved the way for the dissolution of the Soviet empire, ended the Cold War and moved forward on arms control.

According to the scholars at the "We're History" web site:

> ... [T]he attempt on Reagan's life did alter his presidency. Hinckley shot Reagan just over two months into the president's first term. While he should still have been experiencing some post-inauguration

popularity, his public approval rating was low and Congress did not seem keen on his proposals to address the nation's economic malaise.

In the wake of the shooting, Congress, while not acquiescing to everything in Reagan's economic program, became more willing to try supply-side economics. Reagan's near-death experience also changed his outlook on the Cold War. While still openly hostile to communism, by his second term he began to pursue true nuclear arms reduction. In 1987, Reagan and Mikhail Gorbachev signed the Intermediate Nuclear Forces Treaty, which pledged to destroy a whole class of nuclear weapons, thus making it the first true arms reduction agreement. Finally, Reagan's ability to connect with the American people, so effectively demonstrated from his hospital bed, allowed him to weather more difficult public relations storms later in his presidency, especially the fallout from the Iran-Contra controversy.[28]

The assassination attempt had other wide-ranging consequences. The Secret Service greatly increased security protection for President Reagan. Heightened security also had followed other assassination attempts, such as those against Gerald Ford in 1975 and, of course, the murder of John F. Kennedy in 1963. In all these cases, the Secret Service placed restrictions on the president's activities. In Reagan's case, they insisted that he wear a bulletproof vest on more occasions than ever, surrounded him with more bodyguards and kept everyday Americans away from him, further isolating the nation's leader. The environment surrounding the president became more like an armed camp as the security bubble became more imposing. The Secret Service also exerted more control over his schedule to minimize risk by keeping him out of as many potentially dangerous situations as possible, such as wading into crowds or shaking hands with strangers.

First Lady Nancy Reagan was pleased with these arrangements but she remained deeply worried about her husband's safety. "Nothing can happen to my Ronnie," she wrote in her diary in the days after he was shot. "My life would be over." On the first evening while he recuperated in the hospital, she slept with one of his shirts and took comfort in the scent.[29]

She was so worried that she consulted with San Francisco astrologer Joan Quigley about ways to protect him. Based on Quigley's analysis of the position of the planets and the stars, Nancy insisted on adjusting the president's schedule to limit his travel to astrologically auspicious times and to avoid travel or public events during periods when Quigley thought the circumstances would be too dangerous. President Reagan went along to reassure his wife, who was so fearful for her beloved husband's life that she grasped at astrology as a way to keep him from harm.

The astrology connection was disclosed in a memoir by former White House Chief of Staff Donald Regan. He wanted to embarrass Mrs. Reagan after she lost confidence in the imperious official and pressured her husband to fire him, which the president did. "Virtually every major move and decision the Reagans made during my time as White House chief of staff," Regan wrote, "was cleared in advance with a woman in San Francisco who drew up horoscopes to make certain that the planets were in favorable alignment for the enterprise."[30]

It appears that Quigley's influence was not as all-encompassing as Regan suggested but focused instead on the timing of events, such as news conferences, speeches and trips outside Washington. This was a departure from the norm, to be sure, because usually astrologers have nothing to do with such decisions. But the episode showed how Reagan's near-death from the assassination attempt had many unforeseen and important effects on his presidency.

It also created sympathy for him from other political figures, including his partisan adversaries. House Speaker Tip O'Neill, a Democrat who had fought Reagan on many issues, showed up at the hospital when Reagan seemed well enough to receive political visitors. O'Neill was shocked to see how frail the president appeared. Teary-eyed, O'Neill knelt and kissed the president's face and the two rivals recited the Twenty-third Psalm, "The Lord is My Shepherd."[31]

A JURY found John Hinckley, Jr., the shooter, not guilty of his alleged crime by reason of insanity. He said he shot Reagan hoping to win the attention and affection of actress Jodie Foster after seeing her in the bleak and violent film *Taxi Driver*. Hinckley, 26, had written to Foster a few hours before he tried to kill Reagan and revealed his bizarre motivation. "I would abandon the idea of getting Reagan in a second if I could only win your heart and live out the rest of my life with you," Hinckley wrote.

> The reason I'm going ahead with this attempt now is because I cannot wait any longer to impress you. I've got to do something now

to make you understand in no uncertain terms that I am doing this all for your sake.[32]

After his insanity conviction, Hinckley was sent to a Washington-area mental hospital. After 35 years, he was released in 2016, at age 61, to the custody of his mother.

Reagan was magnanimous toward his would-be assassin. Discussing how he prayed for his White House Press Secretary James Brady and the other officials who had been shot by Hinckley, Reagan wrote:

> I didn't feel I could ask God's help to heal Jim, the others, and myself, and at the same time feel hatred for the man who had shot us, so I silently asked God to help him deal with whatever demons had led him to shoot us.[33]

Precis

Ronald Reagan handled the 1981 assassination attempt with strength and grace. The president and his inner circle were quick to reassure the country that the commander in chief would recover, and that he had admirable traits of resilience and fortitude that would enable him to weather the storm. He had surrounded himself with a talented staff to help him govern and these officials took effective action to keep the government running smoothly despite Reagan's near-death experience. He persevered in every way, and used the crisis to enhance his popularity and win support for his agenda. He also felt that God had saved his life for a purpose, which he believed was to serve as a peacemaker. Driven by this belief, during his second term Reagan began a partnership with Soviet leader Mikhail Gorbachev that helped to end the Cold War.

Notes

1. Lou Cannon, "Ronald Reagan," Interview Contained in Brian Lamb, Brian, Susan Swain and C-SPAN, *The Presidents: Noted Historians Rank America's Best—and Worst—Chief Executives*, New York: Public Affairs, 2019, pp. 118–119.
2. Robert Dallek, *Harry S. Truman*, New York: Times Books, 2008, p. 111.
3. "FDR Escapes Assassination in Miami," History.com, November 16, 2009, https://www.history.com/this-day-in-history/fdr-escapes-assassination-in-miami.

4. Dallek, *Harry S. Truman*, p. 111.
5. Robert Dallek, *Franklin D. Roosevelt: A Political Life*, New York: Viking, 2017, pp. 131–132.
6. Ronald Reagan, *An American Life*, New York: Simon & Schuster, 1990, p. 259.
7. Reagan, p. 260. Also see Robert E. Gilbert, *The Mortal Presidency: Illness and Anguish in the White House*, New York: Basic Books, 1992, pp. 185–190.
8. Sarah Katherine Mergel, "The Failed Assassination Attempt on Ronald Reagan," March 30, 2016, werehistory.org.
9. Mergel, ibid.
10. Kenneth T. Walsh, *Ronald Reagan: Biography*, New York: Park Lane Press, 1997, p. 98.
11. Reagan, p. 260.
12. Reagan, p. 260.
13. Reagan, p. 261.
14. Reagan, pp. 261–262.
15. Reagan, p. 261.
16. Gilbert, p. 188.
17. Gilbert, pp. 189–190.
18. Mergel, ibid.
19. Richard V. Allen, "When Reagan Was Shot, Who Was 'In Control' at the White House?" *Washington Post*, March 25, 2011, washingtonpost.com/opinions/when-reagan-was-shot-who-was-in-contol.
20. Gilbert, p. 190–191.
21. Michael Beschloss, *Presidential Courage: Brave Leaders and How They Changed America 1789–1989*, New York: Simon & Schuster, 2007, p. 284.
22. Gilbert, p. 190.
23. Reagan, p. 263.
24. Author's interview with Ken Duberstein, September 20, 2018.
25. Beschloss, p. 286.
26. Beschloss, p. 286.
27. Beschloss, pp. 286–287.
28. Mergel, ibid.
29. Beschloss, p. 284.
30. Jaime Fuller, "The Fix: Joan Quigley, and 5 Stories of Astrology in the White House," *Washington Post*, October 28, 2014, washingtonpost.com/news/the-fix/wp/2014/10/28/joan-quigley-and-5-stories-in-the-White-House.
31. Beschloss p. 284.
32. Gilbert, p. 185.
33. Reagan, p. 261.

Chapter Eleven
George H.W. Bush
The Persian Gulf War

George H.W. Bush's biggest presidential crisis was Iraq's invasion of Kuwait and the subsequent Persian Gulf War in early 1991, which he deftly led in order to force Iraq out of Kuwait. During the Thanksgiving holiday in 1990, as U.S. and allied military forces converged on the Gulf area, he visited troops in the field to maintain their high morale, one of his most important missions. (AP Photo/J. Scott Applewhite)

The biggest crisis of George H.W. Bush's presidency was the 1990 Iraqi invasion of Kuwait and the resulting 1991 Persian Gulf War. Bush immediately defined the invasion as an emergency that threatened the national interest and required bold action. He moved decisively to push Iraq out of Kuwait and end, at least temporarily, the threat of Iraqi ruler Saddam Hussein to the Middle East, the United States and its Western allies.

Bush organized a massive international coalition to force the Iraqis out of the small, oil-rich kingdom they had invaded. In the process, Bush showed personal traits that are indispensable in crisis management—prudence, an even-keeled temperament and an ability to use his vast governmental and foreign-policy experience to form one of the most impressive international coalitions ever organized. He also drew on his time as a young Navy lieutenant whose torpedo bomber was shot down by the Japanese in the South Pacific during World War II. He was very sensitive to the fact that as commander in chief, many soldiers might lose their lives or suffer serious injuries and that he would be ultimately responsible for what happened to them. This added to his caution and his desire to use overwhelming force to win the war quickly and at the same time limit casualties as much as possible. Bush's experience as a businessman also helped. His Zapata Oil Co. had constructed the first offshore oil well in Kuwait during the 1950s, giving him a familiarity with the region and its many religious, cultural and political traditions.[1]

Bush showed that a president could rally the country and the world behind his leadership. He won Congress's endorsement for the military operation and also got the United Nations Security Council to sign on after strenuous efforts to gain support.[2]

ON THURSDAY, AUGUST 1, 1990, Bush arrived in Aspen, Colorado, for a speech. In the hours before he arrived, Iraq invaded Kuwait, precipitating an international crisis.

Saddam Hussein claimed that revolutionaries had pleaded for his help to overthrow the emir of Kuwait. This was his pretext for invasion, and Hussein used it to justify sending 140,000 Iraqi troops and 18,000 tanks into Kuwait, easily defeating the kingdom's 16,000-man army. Within 12 hours, Iraq had taken the capital of Kuwait City and Saddam Hussein controlled 21 percent of the world's oil supply. Hussein announced that Kuwait was no longer a separate nation and had become the "Nineteenth Province, an eternal part of Iraq."[3]

Kuwait's neighbors, especially Saudi Arabia, were worried that they might be next. Many U.S. officials were concerned that Iraq was moving to take over access to and production of a critical amount of oil in the Middle East and to dominate as much of the region as possible.

This would give the Iraqis leverage to disrupt economies around the world, including the economy of the United States, subject other nations to blackmail, and give Iraq the pre-eminent position in the Middle East. With his 30 years of experience in government, including service as vice president under President Ronald Reagan and director of central intelligence, Bush didn't have to be told any of this. He grasped the situation from the start.

Keeping an appointment to speak on cold war diplomacy at the Aspen Institute in Colorado, Bush continued to make phone calls to world leaders in order to put more pressure on Iraq to withdraw. In Aspen, Bush also met with British Prime Minister Margaret Thatcher, who presented a united front with him at a joint press conference. "What happened is a total violation of international law," Thatcher told reporters.[4]

In the early hours of the crisis, the situation was murky, but Bush took the lead. He stepped off the government's G-20 executive-style aircraft at the Aspen airport (the big Air Force jet normally used for presidential travel was too big to land there), smiled, and walked briskly and purposefully from his plane, knowing that much of the nation and the world, including Hussein, would be watching the TV coverage to see how he was reacting.

Bush sped by motorcade to the mountain chalet of Henry Catto, U.S. ambassador to Great Britain. As his car moved along the icy roads, Bush used an amplified microphone in the car to say hello to bystanders. But he joked to aides that he noticed some of the spectators giving him the finger, not a good sign for a president who would need to rally the nation around him.[5]

At Catto's home, Bush asked White House National Security Adviser Brent Scowcroft, a mild-mannered and cerebral Air Force general who was traveling with the president to Aspen, about whether Bush's requested phone call to King Fahd bin Abdulaziz Al Saud of Saudi Arabia was being arranged as he had directed. "It's coming," Scowcroft told him.[6] Bush began pacing restlessly in a bedroom of Catto's chalet, practicing in his mind the lines he would use with the king, and picking up memorabilia and other objects from the table in the room and then replacing them.

That day, he also contacted President Hosni Mubarak of Egypt, King Hussein of Jordan, Jaber Al-Ahmad al-Sabah, the emir of Kuwait, and others. Bush told aides how well they had gotten along when he gathered with Middle Eastern leaders during a recent meeting at the palace in Riyadh and on a sultan's yacht on the Bay of Oman. Bush told how he applied suntan lotion to King Hussein's forehead before boating in the Gulf of Acaba. In the United States, he had treated Mubarak to a hotdog at a Baltimore Orioles baseball game. Bush's point was that he knew these men well, and now he expected his warm relationships with them to help him organize an alliance against Iraq. In the process, he would offer them U.S. military support to protect their countries from Saddam Hussein.[7]

After talking by phone to King Fahd, Bush was told that British Prime Minister Margaret Thatcher was at that moment arriving in town for her previously scheduled speech at the Aspen institute. He rushed to the driveway as she emerged from her limousine and they greeted each other warmly.

Thatcher, it turned out, was eager to confront Saddam. "No small country will ever be safe if we allow him to succeed," she told Bush as they met in the living room of the Catto chalet. "And Hussein will never stop with Kuwait. We must act together—all of us." Bush agreed and added that one country should not be allowed to invade another without provocation.[8]

Thatcher, nicknamed "The Iron Lady" in Great Britain, caused a controversy when the U.S. media reported that she had told Bush not to "go wobbly" about confronting Saddam Hussein. The media made it sound as if she was trying to toughen up a reluctant president, but White House Press Secretary Marlin Fitzwater said her words were designed to summarize their mutual determination, not bolster Bush's resolve. "*We must not go wobbly, George,*" Thatcher had said. Bush liked the phrase so much that he used it himself in public a number of times.[9]

Bush and some of his key advisers immediately understood the stakes. They feared that a permanent Iraqi takeover of oil-rich Saudi Arabia would be next—a possibility raised by U.S. intelligence. Occupation of Saudi Arabia would give Iraq control of 40 percent of the world's known oil reserves.

Bush moved decisively. Only a few hours after learning of the invasion he signed an executive order freezing $100 billion in Iraqi property and assets in the United States and in other countries. He also moved the USS *Independence* Carrier Battle Group, which included two aircraft carriers and a guided missile destroyer, from the Indian Ocean to the Persian Gulf.[10]

He quickly turned to personal diplomacy, drawing on his years as a diplomat when he served as U.S. ambassador to the United Nations, U.S. envoy to China, and eight years as vice president when he conducted many diplomatic missions for President Ronald Reagan. On August 3, he spoke to every leader of the Western Alliance by phone as he constructed a coalition against Iraq. He quickly persuaded France, Japan, the United Kingdom, West Germany and seven other nations to join the United States in freezing Iraqi assets.[11]

Parlaying his close relationships with world leaders into action at the United Nations, Bush persuaded the UN Security Council, within hours of the Iraq invasion of Kuwait, to pass UN Resolution 660, which condemned Iraq's invasion, called for its immediate withdrawal and promised sanctions if Hussein did not pull out. This resolution passed unanimously, with Yemen abstaining. On August 6, the UN passed Resolution 661 calling for a complete prohibition of trade with Iraq and authorizing nonmilitary steps to enforce the sanctions. Even the Soviet Union went along, based in part on Bush's positive relationship with reform-minded Soviet leader Mikhail Gorbachev, who was angling for more U.S. aid to help his economically challenged country even though the Soviet Union had been an ally of Iraq.[12] With Gorbachev's support, Bush had a much freer hand to punish Iraq and, eventually, to go to war with Baghdad and not worry about causing a confrontation with Moscow.

On August 3, two days after the Iraqi takeover of Kuwait, Bush convened the National Security Council in the White House Cabinet Room. Bush wanted his senior advisers to dissect the issues involved in the invasion and discuss what the United States should do about it.

Scowcroft, a four-star Air Force general, set a tough tone, declaring, "We must not allow this to succeed." Bush announced that the invasion "is absolutely unacceptable." William Webster, the director of central intelligence, reported that Iraqi forces were within eight miles of Saudi Arabia. Colin Powell, a four-star Army general who was chairman of the Joint

Chiefs of Staff, said, "We need some U.S. forces in Saudi Arabia as a signal that an invasion of Saudi Arabia means a conflict with the United States."[13]

Richard Darman, director of the Office of Management and Budget, asked, "Are we prepared to fight to back that up?" Bush responded, "I haven't heard the military options that would allow such a decision." He didn't want to lean too far in one direction about using the military because this might inhibit the discussion by suggesting his mind was made up. The president wanted "independent views," Fitzwater observed later in his diary.[14]

But it turned out that Bush had already made his decision. Fitzwater asked Bush later for the precise moment when the president concluded that the United States needed to liberate Kuwait. Bush said he arrived at that conclusion on the first day of the crisis, August 1, when Iraq invaded Kuwait.[15]

On Sunday, August 4, at Camp David, the official presidential retreat in Maryland's Catoctin Mountains, the NSC met again in the Laurel Lodge conference room to discuss specific military options. Bush wanted to intervene with Saudi support but the Fahd regime had not signed on as yet, not even in the phone call that Bush had with the king from Aspen the previous Friday. Bush decided not to exert any public pressure but instead to wait a few more days "for the Arab world to absorb their situation," he told aides.[16]

Norman Schwarzkopf, Jr., a four-star Army general and the commander of U.S. troops in the Middle East, told the NSC about his plan for a ground attack from Saudi Arabian soil into Kuwait. It would involve 100,000 U.S. troops, a call-up of the Reserves, 500 tanks and countless air strikes, all with the goal of pushing Iraq out of Kuwait. Schwarzkopf suggested it would take 7 to 12 months to do the job.

On Wednesday, August 8, Bush told the nation he was ordering the deployment of the 82nd Airborne Division and two squadrons of F-15 fighter jets to Saudi Arabia. This was designed to scare off Saddam Hussein from invading Saudi Arabia and reassure the royal family that he was serious about protecting the kingdom. Bush explained that "a line has been drawn in the sand" and said Americans sought "the immediate, unconditional, and complete withdrawal of all Iraqi forces from Kuwait."[17]

Through it all, Bush took the long view, something that is very difficult to do in a crisis when immediate concerns tend to crowd out thoughts of the future.

One of his most important goals was to end what he privately called the "Vietnam syndrome"—a reluctance by U.S. officials to use military force abroad and risk getting the United States bogged down in another morass like the Vietnam war. And so, as war became more likely, he made every effort to ensure that the United States and its allies would win a quick and overwhelming victory.

Bush often told his aides not to worry too much about the daily news coverage, which raised doubts about his war strategy, such as whether sanctions would force Iraq to withdraw from Kuwait, whether the American military was ready for an invasion, and whether Bush was taking Iraq's military too lightly. On January 2, 1991, Bush called White House Press Secretary Fitzwater into the Oval Office at 8:49 a.m. to discuss their communications strategy. He urged Fitzwater not to get obsessed with winning every news cycle. "I don't care what the press says," Bush said. "I only care what Saddam thinks. I have an audience of one. And he must not see any flexibility, any waver of our commitment."[18]

PRIVATELY, BUSH DID HAVE CONCERNS. On December 31, 1990, New Year's Eve, Bush wrote an emotional letter to his five adult children—addressing it to "Dear George, Jeb, Neil, Marvin and Doro"—reflecting a father's desire to reassure his kids about the correctness of what he was about to do. The note also revealed the commander in chief's worries about the safety of the soldiers he would send into battle.[19]

> When I came into this job I vowed that I would never ring [sic] my hands and talk about "the loneliest job in the world" or ring [sic] my hands about the "pressures or the trials."

Having said that I have been concerned about what lies ahead. There is no "loneliness" though, because I am backed by a first rate team of knowledgeable and committed people. No president had been more blessed in this regard.[20]

Bush added:

> We have waited to give sanctions a chance, we have moved a tremendous force so as to reduce the risk to every American solider if force has to be used, but the question of loss of life still lingers and plagues the heart.

My mind goes back to history: How many lives might have been saved if appeasement had given way to force earlier on in the late '30s or earliest '40s? How many Jews might have been spared the gas chambers, or how many Polish patriots might be alive today?

. . . I look at today's crisis as "good" vs. "evil"—yes, it is that clear . . . Principle must be adhered to—Saddam cannot profit in any way at all from his aggression . . . and sometimes in your life you have to act as you think best—you can't compromise, you can't give in.

So, dear kids, better batten down the hatches.[21]

Bush overcame his concerns and began the invasion less than three weeks later. As historian John Robert Greene points out:

> Bush was completely sincere in his hatred of Saddam; it was easy for him to equate the Iraqi dictator's actions to those of the 1940s' dictators whom he had risked his life to defeat. But there was an equally important national security reason for Bush's actions, one that [Secretary of State] James Baker highlights in his memoirs. "We *had* responded to a clear violation of international law . . . and we *were* dealing with a megalomaniacal personality. But it was also true that we had vital interests at stake . . . We had to make sure we could maintain a secure supply of energy."[22]

DESPITE LARGE demonstrations at home against the possibility of war at the end of 1990 and early 1991, Bush reaffirmed the final UN deadline of January 15, 1991 for Iraq to withdraw from Kuwait. Economic sanctions weren't working, and war seemed inevitable. After prolonged debate, both houses of Congress voted in a bipartisan way on January 12, 1991 to support the president if he decided to go to war. The House voted 250 to 183 that day against an antiwar resolution, and the Senate also defeated the anti-war measure, 52 to 47. This was a big political victory for George H.W. Bush.[23]

"We didn't plan war, we didn't seek war but if conflict is thrust upon us, we are ready and we are determined," Bush said. Yet the crisis was taking its toll on him. His aides and friends said he looked older, weary, worried.[24]

At 3 a.m. in Iraq on January 17, 1991 (7 p.m. in Washington on January 16, a day after the deadline, Bush went to war in what the Pentagon called "Operation Desert Storm." Bush set precisely the right idealistic note when he announced that, "The liberation of Kuwait has begun."[25]

The American campaign began with a furious air attack on Iraqi troops and positions—5,000 bombing sorties in the first two days in both Kuwait and Iraq.[26] All this was brilliantly illustrated on the world's TV sets night after night, day after day, in a profusion of satellite and other aerial videos of the high-tech war, lighting up the skies of Baghdad and elsewhere with lethal pyrotechnics.

An ABC News poll found that 83 percent of Americans in mid-January approved of Bush's job performance and the war. This would increase to 89 percent approval in March. The air war lasted 42 days and was very effective in destroying the Iraqi communications networks, oil refineries, air defenses, weapons plants and other military facilities. The initial phase of the war revealed that the Iraqis might have had a strong conventional military but they were no match for a true superpower. The United States used modern technology such as Stealth bombers, cruise missiles and laser-guided "smart" bombs which Iraqi forces couldn't cope with.

Meanwhile, the United States and its allies were assembling a huge ground force to drive Iraq from Kuwait to supplement the air war if Hussein refused to move out after the bombardment. A month later, Bush was poised to send in that force.

On Tuesday, February 19, 1991, Bush summoned Fitzwater into the Oval Office and privately told him:

> I want you to know that we're going in Saturday night [February 23] at 8 p.m. Just so you don't get crossways on this. Please don't say anything to anybody. If you have questions, ask me. Not everyone knows, even some you might think know.[27]

On February 22, 1991, Bush and American allies gave Iraq 24 hours to begin withdrawing from Kuwait or a ground attack would soon begin. Hussein, believing that Bush and his allies were bluffing and underestimating the coalition's military strength, refused to withdraw.

Bush also decided on a last-minute ruse to ease Saddam Hussein's mind and make him think a ground attack was not imminent. The president went to Camp David on February 23 for what was billed as a period of rest, allowing TV coverage of his departure. But he came back after several hours to preside over the attack from the White House and address the nation.

On February 24, the ground war began, focusing on defeating Iraqi forces in Kuwait and southern Iraq. Bush had led the way in amassing an allied force of 750,000 in the Gulf area, including 540,000 U.S. personnel and military contingents from Great Britain, France, Germany, the Soviet Union and several Middle Eastern countries. Iraq had a force of 300,000 occupying Kuwait and many hundreds of thousands of troops in Iraq.

Bush gave the military brass what it wanted in the run-up to the war and let them pursue the fight as they saw fit. It was a brilliant exercise in delegation of authority and America's military leaders, a very talented group, justified the commander in chief's trust in them.

One key to maintaining Arab support for the coalition was keeping Israel, detested by millions of Arabs, out of the war. "[F]rom the point of view of Washington, Israel could not be a part of the coalition," wrote historian Greene. "If it entered the war, neighboring Arab states would be forced to decide whether to declare war on the hated Israel, a quandary that Saddam hoped would present itself."[28] The Israeli government of Prime Minister Yitzhak Shamir did not enter the war, and Bush constantly reassured the Israelis that the United States would protect them from Iraqi missiles and other attacks—and this is what happened.

The ground invasion went extraordinarily well; the U.S. military performed brilliantly and totally outclassed the Iraqis. On February 24, the first day of the ground war, things were going so well for the United States and its allied forces that there was only one confirmed U.S casualty, as of 5 p.m., and the Iraqis were in retreat from Kuwait.[29] The most important part of the battle plan was to avoid a head-on collision with Iraq's entrenched forces and instead take a "left hook" or wide swing around the western flank of Iraqi forces. This surprised the Iraqis, gained ground extremely fast with minimal U.S. and allied casualties and cut off Iraqi escape routes and supply lines to and from Baghdad, the Iraqi capital.

On February 25, Hussein began to hedge his bets very seriously, floating different ideas designed to cause Bush to call off the devastating attacks. One was to promise an Iraqi withdrawal from Kuwait. But the Americans thought this wasn't serious and came with very unpalatable stipulations. Among them were refusal to restore the Kuwaiti government or pay reparations, and leaving behind their front-line artillery, which would allow Hussein to keep a strong war-making capability.

Bush wanted a decisive military victory for the United States and its allies, which he thought would be an excellent tonic for the country.

Bush already could see that the victory would be a triumph. As a veteran of World War II in the Pacific he wanted a big, splashy ceremony in which Saddam Hussein would surrender to U.S. military leaders, as the Japanese had formally surrendered aboard the U.S. warship *Missouri* to end World War II.

On February 28, Bush and his coalition partners halted the ground assault and declared a ceasefire after Iraqi troops retreated en masse from Kuwait. It was six weeks after the start of the air bombardment and 100 hours after the start of the ground war. On March 6, Bush told Congress and the American people, "Aggression is defeated. The war is over." An estimated 22,000 Iraqi soldiers had been killed along with many civilians. 148 Americans died in combat and the rest of Bush's coalition lost 92 soldiers in action; 458 Americans were wounded.[30]

But the war had taken a toll on the 67-year-old commander in chief. He was aging visibly, losing weight, his complexion sallow and dark circles under his eyes. He was so focused on the war that he was making careless mistakes in other parts of his life. At 8 p.m. on February 25, Bush lit a fire in the Oval Office fireplace without opening the flue, and the room filled with smoke. Fitzwater called a staff engineer to rush over from his home and stop the smoke by switching on a chimney fan inside the flue. (Until the engineer arrived no one could locate the switch to turn on the fan.) Finally, the smoke cleared in time for Bush to have a national-security meeting in the Oval at 10 p.m.[31]

INITALLY, Bush was lionized. "I can't think of another president who could have pulled this off," commentator Fred Barnes, a longtime Bush critic, wrote in the *New Republic*.[32]

Bush was particularly proud of having exorcized what he called "the Vietnam syndrome"—an unwillingness of Americans to fight another major foreign war after the stalemate and eventual U.S. defeat in Vietnam.

"After Vietnam, when many wondered if the American people had lost their will, they did so without fully appreciating the role of the commander in chief," wrote historian James R. Arnold.

> Slowly, the lessons of history showed that Lyndon Johnson had deliberately refrained from mobilizing the American will to fight the

[Vietnam] war. Still, it remained uncertain whether the American character had undergone a profound transformation. It was an issue at the core of the Gulf War.

The Gulf War answered the question about American will. The outpouring of support for the men and women sent to Saudi Arabia, the hundreds of thousands of packages addressed to "Any Serviceman," revealed that the public had indeed changed since Vietnam, but perhaps in a way no one had anticipated. In this conflict they demonstrated an ability to separate debate about the wisdom of entering a war from concern over the welfare of those who had to fight the battles.[33]

Bush should also be credited for what he prevented from happening, as historian Bohn has pointed out. The war prevented Saddam Hussein from controlling 20 percent of the world's oil reserves and kept Iraq from emerging as the dominant Arab state in the region.[34]

But the post-war planning didn't go so smoothly. On March 1, Bush's war cabinet met to discuss the new political realities in the region, and there were immediate disagreements. The goal of Bush and most of his advisers was a "big new permanent presence" of combat forces in the Persian Gulf, said a participant. But Vice President Dick Cheney said key ally Saudi Arabia and other Gulf nations wanted only some U.S. presence to bring stability and security. The disagreements ran deep, and the president dropped the grand idea of a permanent pro-American coalition stabilizing the region.[35]

Saddam Hussein wasn't forced from power, and his military brutally ended uprisings of Kurds in the north of Iraq and Shiites in the south. Bush had encouraged these rebellions but didn't help the rebels once they started fighting. He decided to let the Iraqis sort things out for themselves. The insurgencies ended badly, with Saddam still in control.

THE PRO-WAR EUPHORIA and Bush's popularity didn't last long. One factor was that Saddam Hussein was still a thorn in the side of the United States and his regional neighbors, even though his power had been greatly depleted. Another problem for Bush was the collapse of his grand hope for a "new world order"—a concept that he had discussed at length with National Security Adviser Brent Scowcroft while fishing near his seaside estate in Kennebunkport, Maine in August 1990, just after the crisis began. Bush saw the likelihood that the United States would take the lead in setting policies around the globe for a new international coalition that would include not only traditional U.S. allies such as the

United Kingdom and France, but also Arab states that helped in the Gulf War. But these hopes dissipated as age-old enmities in the Middle East, including Arab hated of Israel, rose to the surface, and domestic support for a long-term, high-cost military entanglement in the region eroded.

Finally, Americans quickly shifted to domestic concerns, especially the troubled economy. Most didn't believe Bush, even though he was an effective military leader, was able to deal with such issues successfully. This was another lesson of the Bush presidency. Crisis management during a war can be brilliant but domestic concerns generally supersede foreign ones.

Bush went on to suffer a rapid erosion in his approval ratings and would lose his Republican bid for re-election to Democratic nominee Bill Clinton in 1992. After having seen his approval ratings soar from 43 percent in September 1990 to nearly 90 percent in March 1991, Bush received only 37.5 percent of the popular vote 20 months later in the November 1992 election.[36] It was a colossal fall from grace and power illustrating that a president must constantly prove himself or he will draw voters' disaffection and scorn.

YET BUSH's CAMPAIGN to force Iraq from Kuwait was a prime example of how war can be waged effectively in the modern era and how a commander in chief should behave at a time of crisis. He didn't force Iraqi leader Saddam Hussein from power—for which he was later criticized—but he understood that to do so would have required a larger U.S. commitment than the country was willing to bear. And it would have placed the United States in the untenable position of creating a new Iraqi government in a fractious, violent country and defending that government. As president a decade later, Bush's son George W. Bush learned these lessons to his chagrin when he did force Hussein from power.

On a personal level, Bush proved he had the leadership skills to forge a coalition against Iraq. He had confidence in his own judgment but he carefully delegated responsibility where appropriate and declined to micro-manage the conduct of the war as President Lyndon Johnson had done with negative consequences in Vietnam. Bush proved himself a good judge of personnel and he left operational decisions to the military commanders, many of whom he knew and trusted. And Bush demonstrated the ability to understand that he was risking people's lives and needed to do everything possible to minimize casualties and still achieve victory.[37]

"Bush was very much a man for whom World War II had been a defining experience of his youth," journalist and military historian Rick Atkinson told PBS in a 1996 interview.

> ... He was a man for whom shades of gray and nuances were annoying. He was fundamentally a man who viewed life in black and white terms. That's why it was much more comfortable for Bush to talk about this as a moral crusade.[38]

Added historian James R. Arnold:

> [Lyndon] Johnson's Vietnam legacy had a large bearing on how President George Bush conducted the war against Iraq. Bush drew certain strategic lessons from the Vietnam War regarding the perceived wisdom of leaving military matters in the hands of the generals; the importance of fighting with great force, unfettered by political constraints; the desirability of applying unrelenting force without pauses for discussion and negotiation; and the importance of managing the press to try to control public response to the war. He established the broad strategic outline and apparently made several crucial decisions—when to start the war, when to end it—on his own.[39]

Above all, Bush believed in the use of overwhelming force to score a decisive victory and then bring the troops home. In an interview published in *U.S. News & World Report* on December 31, 1990, just prior to the onset of hostilities, I asked Bush how he saw the coming struggle. He replied succinctly and in his distinctive ungrammatical way: "In, out, do it, do it right, get gone. That's the message." He was very cognizant of the problems that arose from the limited war in Vietnam in the 1960s and 1970s. "Never fight a war with a hand tied behind our back," he told me. "Never send a kid into battle unless you're going to give him total support. Don't send him in underequipped. Don't send a mission in undermanned. Don't send them in where you tell commanding officers what they can't do."[40]

Precis

George Bush performed well under crisis conditions. He took bold action when appropriate. He adapted to changing circumstances, notably by not occupying Iraq after it became clear that Saddam Hussein's forces had been thoroughly defeated. This spared the United States years of fighting with no good outcome. He persevered. He insured victory by insisting on using overwhelming force. And he set forth a clear goal, pushing Iraq out of Kuwait, and achieved this objective in brilliant fashion. Bush showed in the Persian Gulf War that the U.S military was capable of starting and succeeding in a big, complicated intervention half a world away. In this sense, the Gulf War ended the "Vietnam syndrome," a belief held by many U.S. citizens and leaders that the United States couldn't successfully wield military power around the globe and that, as with Vietnam, the results of such an operation would be disastrous. Bush proved the doubters wrong.[41]

Notes

1. John Robert Greene, "The Presidency of George Bush," in Nathaniel May, ed., *Oval Office: Stories of Residents in Crisis from Washington to Bush*, New York, NY: Thunder's Mouth Press, 2002, p. 236.
2. Kenneth Walsh, "The Lessons of the First Gulf War Still Linger 25 Years on," *U.S. News & World Report*, January 17, 2016, usnews.com/news/articles/2016-01-17/the-lessons-of-the-first-gulf-war-still-linger-25-years-on.
3. Greene, p. 236.
4. Greene, p. 237.
5. Marlin Fitzwater, *Tales from Holland Creek*, self-published, 2018, p. 203.
6. Fitzwater, p. 203.
7. Fitzwater, p. 204.
8. Fitzwater, p. 204.
9. Fitzwater, p. 205.
10. Greene, pp. 236–237.
11. Greene, p. 237.
12. Greene, pp. 237–238.
13. Fitzwater, p. 204.
14. Fitzwater, p. 205.
15. Fitzwater, p 205.
16. Fitzwater, p. 205.
17. Greene, p. 241.
18. Fitzwater, pp. 238–238.
19. Walsh, "The Lessons of the First Gulf War Still Linger 25 Years On."

20. Walsh, ibid.
21. Walsh, ibid.
22. Greene, p. 248.
23. Greene, p. 253.
24. Author's contemporaneous interviews as a White House correspondent during the crisis.
25. Andrew Rosenthal, "War in the Gulf: The Overview," *New York Times*, Jan. 17, 1991, p. A1.
26. Fitzwater, p. 242.
27. Fitzwater, p. 251.
28. Greene, pp. 242–243.
29. Fitzwater, p. 252.
30. Greene, pp. 255–256.
31. Fitzwater, pp. 254–255.
32. Greene, pp. 263–264.
33. James R. Arnold, *Presidents Under Fire: Commanders in Chief in Victory and Defeat*, New York: Orion Books, 1994, p. 286.
34. Michael K. Bohn, *Presidents in Crisis: Tough Decisions inside the White House from Truman to Obama*, New York: Arcade Publishing, 2016, p. 198.
35. Fitzwater, pp. 258–259.
36. Greene, p. 264.
37. I made these points in a *U.S. News & Report* article on the 25th anniversary of the Persian Gulf War in January 2016. See usnews.com/news/articles/2016-01-17/the-lessons-of-the-first-gulf-war-stil-linger-25-years-on.
38. Rick Atkinson, oral history of the Gulf War, Frontline on PBS, Jan. 9, 1996, pbs.org/wgbh/pages/frontline/gulf/oral/atkinson/1/html.
39. Arnold, p. xi.
40. Kenneth T. Walsh, "Very Clearly, Good Vs. Evil," *U.S. News & World Report*, May 16, 2008, usnews.com/news/national/articles/2008/05/16/very-clearly-good-vs.-evil.
41. Walsh, "The Lessons of the First Gulf War Still Linger 25 Years On."

Chapter Twelve
Bill Clinton
Impeachment and Scandal

Bill Clinton was impeached by the House of Representatives on December 19, 1998 because of his improper relationship with former White House intern Monica Lewinsky, which he initially denied. Clinton persuaded the country to separate his personal failings from his public leadership, and he avoided removal from office by the Senate, which acquitted him on February 12, 1999. (White House Photographic Office, Clinton Presidential Library (Digital Library))

Bill Clinton's sex-and-lies scandal almost cost him his presidency over his willingness to lie about an affair with former White House intern Monica Lewinsky.

It was a profound crisis for Clinton, showing his character flaws in mortifying detail. His private behavior and falsehoods led to his impeachment by the House of Representatives in late 1998, but he managed to win acquittal by the Senate in early 1999. As a case study in crisis management, his handling of the ordeal revealed serious ethical shortcomings, but also underscored Clinton's amazing political talents and his survival instinct—illustrating the larger pattern of Clinton's public life and presidency.

His problem was that he had the affair with Lewinsky in the first place and proceeded to lie about it under oath. His opponents were looking for a sword with which to strike him down and with the Lewinsky scandal he proceeded to give them a lethal weapon. Everything that happened later stemmed from his own fundamental errors.

IT ALL STARTED with a land deal that had nothing to do with Clinton's libido. Independent Counsel Kenneth Starr was appointed by a special panel of three federal judges to investigate a failed real-estate deal in which Bill and his wife Hillary Clinton had invested, years prior to his election to the presidency. Starr found evidence of other types of wrongdoing involving Clinton, which the law allowed him to pursue. Chief among them, he discovered that President Clinton had an affair with Lewinsky. And Starr determined that the president lied about it under oath in a separate sexual harassment case brought against Clinton by former associate Paula Jones, focusing on misconduct prior to his presidency.

It is now clear that Clinton made a fundamental mistake when he failed to agree to a quick out-of-court settlement in the Jones case. It would have spared him the temptation to lie in the first place.

The details that emerged about Lewinsky were salacious. In November 1995, Lewinsky, then a 22-year-old intern working in the West Wing, recalled flirting openly with the 49-year-old president. At a birthday party for a staff member, she realized her underwear was showing above her pants and decided to "up the game." She later recalled:

> I knew [the president] was walking out of a room, and instead of putting my trousers up, like I would have done in any other instance, I didn't. It was unnoticeable to everybody else in the room, but he noticed.[1]

On another occasion, Clinton asked her some questions and she was delighted that he showed an interest in her. She blurted out, "You know, I have a crush on you." He laughed and asked if she wanted to go "to the back office," and she did. The office was dark and Clinton asked to kiss her, and she said yes. Later that evening, Clinton found her alone in the West Wing and asked if she wanted to meet him again in the "back study," and she did. Their relationship "became more intimate from there," she recalled in a media essay years later. Federal investigators led by Starr issued a report that said Lewinsky gave Clinton oral sex and they performed other intimate acts during a period of a year and a half.[2]

"The nine 'sexual encounters' Monica Lewinsky would catalog with an Excel spreadsheet were so hurried, furtive, and one-sided, that Clinton would claim they abstained from 'sexual relations,'" wrote historian Gil Troy. "Anguished, struggling, Clinton would confess to Dick Morris [his pollster] that he tried to 'shut my body down . . . sexually'" but "sometimes I slipped up and with this girl I just slipped up."[3]

Clinton's key advisers and friends couldn't believe this was happening. It was so sordid and salacious, selfish and stupid. "I never believed that Bill Clinton would actually risk his presidency—a job he had studied, dreamed about, and prepared for since he was a kid—for something so frivolous, so reckless, so small," wrote Dee Dee Myers, Clinton's first-term press secretary.[4]

Clinton at first denied it all. "I did not have sexual relations with that woman, Miss Lewinsky,"[5] he declared angrily in a memorable Oval Office comment to reporters. Lewinsky later wrote, "With that, the demonization of Monica Lewinsky began. As it so often does, power throws a protective cape around the shoulders of the man, and he dictates the spin by denigrating the less powerful woman."[6] Clinton defenders called her a stalker and an infatuated, deluded young woman who was not to be believed.

Since then, the cultural atmosphere has changed. There is more public acceptance of women who accuse men of unwanted or improper sexual attention, sexual harassment and using a position of power to take advantage of women. It's called the "MeToo" movement. In March 2018, Lewinsky referred to this new environment when she wrote in *Vanity Fair* that she considered the affair "a gross abuse of power," adding: "He was my boss. He was the most powerful man on the planet."[7]

Bill Clinton agreed to be questioned before a grand jury by Special Council Starr and his team of prosecutors on August 17, 1998. Specifically, Clinton was facing allegations that he had lied under oath and obstructed justice in fighting the sexual harassment lawsuit filed by Paula Jones, a former Arkansas state employee. She claimed that Clinton, while he was Arkansas governor, lured her to his hotel room, dropped his pants and tried to pressure her to perform oral sex. It was Clinton's denial under oath that he had sex with Lewinsky—a side issue in this lawsuit—that led to the perjury charges against him in the impeachment crisis.

During questioning by Starr's team, Clinton tried to hide the improper sexual relationship with Lewinsky after he became president.

The Starr interrogation of Clinton took place in the Map Room of the White House, where President Franklin Roosevelt had kept track of military engagements during World War II. It was a tension-filled encounter, with Clinton's lawyers facing a squad of prosecutors, including Starr. The interrogation, which lasted four hours, was seen live on closed-circuit television by a grand jury in a local courthouse. But it wouldn't be released to the public for another month.[8]

That evening, Clinton addressed the nation, supposedly to apologize for his transgressions. But his four-minute mea culpa was grudging, and aides said later that he was too angry for his own good.

"As you know," Clinton said as he looked somberly into the camera,

> in a deposition in January I was asked questions about my relationship with Monica Lewinsky. While my answers were legally accurate, I did not volunteer information. I know that my public comments and my silence about this matter gave a false impression. I misled people, including even my wife.[9]

If he had stopped there, with this mea culpa, it might have satisfied many key critics. But Clinton went on to attack Starr for conducting an improper and unfair inquisition into his private behavior. The president said he had "misled" the public because of his embarrassment about what he had done and to keep his wife and daughter from knowing about his illicit behavior. He added:

> The independent counsel moved on [from its initial, limited investigation] to my staff and friends. Then into my private life. And the

investigation itself is under investigation. This has gone on too long, cost too much, and hurt too many innocent people . . . Even presidents have private lives. It is time to stop the pursuit of personal destruction and the prying into private lives and get on with our national life.[10]

Clinton's later assessment, contained in his autobiography, was accurate. "Everyone knew I had to admit that I had made an awful mistake and had tried to hide it," he wrote. "The question was whether I should also take a shot at Starr's investigation and say it was time to end it. The virtually unanimous opinion was that I should not." But anger contorted Clinton's judgment, and he attacked Starr anyway.[11]

It didn't work. "His intuition for the right words and right tone rarely failed him as critically as it did on this evening, when his judgment was warped by a toxic combination of fatigue and anger," wrote journalist John F. Harris. " . . . His words dripped, not with remorse, but with fury at Starr and his investigation."[12]

There was an enormous negative reaction to the speech. Even fellow Democrats said Clinton was not sufficiently contrite. The critics said he was still casting blame elsewhere rather than accepting the fact that his own conduct had created the crisis. It was, they said, his own sins that had dragged the country through the mud and jeopardized his presidency.

White House Press Secretary Joe Lockhart admitted:

> It was a bad day, a day when we took a step back politically. We were disappointed in getting the truth. Many of us were disappointed that the political strategy that we should have taken wasn't implemented. But . . . we doubled down on our resolve: "Well, we've just got to fight our way out of this."[13]

The crisis would get worse. His testimony was videotaped and sent to the House of Representatives, which released it the following month. This provided riveting if salacious TV, as if the White House had become a sleazy reality show. The president was forced to admit far more details of his affair than he expected or was comfortable with.

Clinton summed it up later. "I asked to make a brief statement," he wrote in a memoir.

> I admitted that "on certain occasions in 1996 and once in 1997" I engaged in wrongful conduct that included inappropriate intimate

contact with Monica Lewinsky; that the conduct, while morally wrong, did not constitute "sexual relations" as I understood the definition of the term that Judge [Susan Webber] Wright accepted at the request of the [Paula] Jones lawyers; that I took full responsibility for my actions; and that I would answer to the best of my ability all of the O.I.C.'s [Office of Independent Counsel's] questions relating to the legality of my actions, but would not say more about the specifics of what had happened.[14]

Explaining why he had gotten so furious, Clinton added:

Starr and his interrogators did their best to turn the videotape into a pornographic home movie, asking me questions designed to humiliate me and to so disgust the Congress and the American people that they would demand my resignation, after which he might be able to indict me.[15]

He also was rattled because Starr disclosed to Clinton advisers before the testimony the existence of a blue dress worn by Lewinsky during one of her intimate sessions with Clinton. It was stained with the president's semen, which was confirmed by a positive DNA test. This was a hugely embarrassing moment for the president.

Clinton apologized a few more times in the next few weeks. On these occasions, he didn't make excuses. At an East Room prayer breakfast in late August 1998, he told a group of ministers,

As you might imagine, I have been on quite a journey these last few weeks to get to the end of this, to the rock-bottom truth of where I am and where we all are. . . . I don't think there is any fancy way to say that I have sinned.[16]

He added: "But God can change us and make us strong at the broken places."[17]

Still, he was in deep trouble with Starr and with many members of Congress, and he knew it.

Journalist Joe Klein wrote:

And so began the most lurid month in the history of the American presidency, a month punctuated by the release of the Starr Report [on Clinton's misbehavior and lies] and the televising of Clinton's grand jury testimony in mid-September, a deranged time when even the most level-headed members of the political and journalistic communities seemed to come unhinged.[18]

On Monday, September 21, Clinton's testimony to the grand jury was finally released. Millions of Americans watched the spectacle of their president answering questions about his most intimate experiences with Lewinsky. He was smart and poised but he lost credibility with several comments in which he tried to wriggle away from telling the truth or admitting he had lied. He said oral sex wasn't sex. He explained that he had misled prosecutors about the affair by saying he wasn't having sex with Lewinsky in the present tense, making it appear that he had never done it at all, even though he had indeed performed the alleged acts in the past. This was his infamous line to the grand jury: "Well, it depends on what your definition of 'is' is."[19] His linguistic trickery brought a torrent of ridicule down on him.

Clinton had his defenders even when things looked the worst for him. "If character failures rose to the level of constitutional principle, Clinton would be a goner," wrote journalist William Greider in *Rolling Stone* several weeks before Clinton was impeached by the House.

> But they don't (the founders understood our human frailties and designed a government to offset them). The impeachment saga will thunder on, perhaps for months, as blood sport for partisans. But I do not believe that the Starr report convinces us that this president's wrongs against the republic approach Richard Nixon's or justify the equivalent of regicide.[20]

THE NEXT PART OF THE CRISIS was the most perilous for the Clinton presidency—the impeachment debate in Congress.

Clinton's strategy was to have his aides lobby one legislator after another, arguing that his misbehavior was a private matter and wasn't relevant to his ability to perform his duties as president. In public, Clinton channeled questions about the Lewinsky scandal and the Starr investigation to his outside lawyer, David Kendall, and to volunteer defenders such as Washington attorney Lanny Davis, a former White House aide who left to practice law outside government. Davis in particular became a very frequent guest on cable-TV talk shows, sometimes appearing four times a day. These shows gave enormous coverage to the scandal.

The president avoided talking about his affair and his lies, and returned again and again to the theme that he was working hard every day to improve the lives of the American people. It was a smart political strategy.

Mark Penn, one of Clinton's pollsters, said:

> We basically went back on campaign footing. That meant finding issues, finding communications, running the message, just like a campaign—but not about impeachment. The polling principle was: Keep the president's approval above 50 percent at all costs, because above 50 percent, people are reticent to kick the president. Below 50, it's to people's political advantage to kick a political figure . . . We always had this distinction between public behavior and private life. In his public life he was an exceptional president. In his private life—[21]

Clinton continued to adopt policies and take official actions that were popular. On August 20, he authorized the launch of cruise missiles at suspected al Qaeda terrorist targets in Afghanistan and Sudan in retaliation for the bombing of the U.S. embassies in Kenya and Tanzania. Critics said these cruise attacks were designed to divert attention from the Lewinsky scandal. They were compared to the plot of a newly released fictional movie, *Wag the Dog*, about military action taken by a president to divert attention from a sex scandal. Clinton also ordered military action against potential weapon sites in Iraq in December.

Clinton's Republican opponents said these actions were minimal and didn't have much effect on terrorists or the Iraqi government. But they did serve Clinton's political purposes by showing he was not paralyzed or gravely weakened by the sex scandal and was capable of decisive action.

"The question you really have in a crisis is: Can the business keep operating while you resolve the crisis, or not?" Penn said.

> If it can't keep operating, then you have to dissolve it regardless of whether you're innocent or guilty. If you can keep it operating, if you can make decisions and prove to people that you can supply the product or function, then even if you're guilty on some of it, it's okay. And that really became what the strategy was. The strategy was that he would do the job of president. He would talk about the other stuff as little as possible.[22]

The broader lesson was that after he owned up to the sex-and-lies scandal, Clinton found a way to save himself by compartmentalizing. He managed to persuade the country to separate his personal life, in which millions considered him a rogue, and his public leadership policies, where millions liked what he was doing. Most Americans thought that, with the economy doing well and the country at peace, he was going a good job. Despite his character problems, by the end of his presidency, about 60 percent of Americans told pollsters they approved of his job performance.[23]

Clinton also benefited from the country's financial well-being. "With the U.S. economy booming, voters were reluctant to turn an incumbent president out of office," says political scientist Brandon Rottinghaus. "Party unity was another factor in the survival of Clinton. [President Richard] Nixon gradually lost the support of his Republican allies [during the Watergate scandal] while Clinton maintained relatively strong support from his Democratic allies in Congress."[24]

Based on the Starr report, the House of Representatives impeached Clinton on two counts on December 19, 1998. The House voted 228 to 206 to impeach Clinton for perjury to a grand jury, and 221 to 212 to impeach him for obstruction of justice. On February 12, 1999, after a five-week trial, the Senate voted 55 to 45 to acquit him of perjury and 50–50 on obstruction of justice. The prosecution needed a two-thirds majority of 67 votes to convict on each charge, and it fell far short.

On April 12, 1999, U.S. District Court Judge Susan Webber Wright found President Clinton guilty of civil contempt of court for giving "false, misleading, and evasive answers that were designed to obstruct the judicial process," a reference to his "intimate contact" with Lewinsky, and for his "willful failure" to tell the truth. Wright's decision forced Clinton to reimburse Paula Jones' lawyers $89,484 for their work on the case and caused the Arkansas Supreme Court to disbar him.[25]

Clinton remained in office until the end of his second term in January 2001, succeeded by Republican George W. Bush. Many political scientists and journalists say that people by this time were sick and tired of the Clinton reality show and wanted to try something different. Bush, during his campaign, had promised not to demean the office of president, a reference to Clinton's scandal, and this proved to be an appealing slogan. Al Gore, Clinton's vice president and the Democratic nominee, ran a relatively weak campaign and couldn't escape the Clinton tarnish even though he had nothing to do with the Lewinsky scandal.

There were more humiliations to come. On January 19, 2001, Clinton's last day in office, he agreed to publicly acknowledge his misconduct, accept a five-year suspension of his Arkansas law license, and pay a $25,000 fine. He also would be disbarred from the U.S. Supreme Court.[26]

THE REVELATIONS and admissions in the Clinton-Lewinsky scandal were unique—the stuff of sensational TV soap operas and salacious reality shows. Much of the country already was troubled by the culture's hedonism and self-absorption, and Clinton's personal life and his endless lies and excuses, his cynicism and narcissism, seemed to illustrate a troubling erosion of values in American society.

Clinton's lack of shame and his self-indulgence deepened the country's cynicism about the presidency. His separation of his private behavior and his flawed character from his policies, in a strange twist, paved the way for Donald Trump's election to the White House in 2016. Trump was an extremely flawed individual in moral terms, but millions of voters overlooked this because they liked his policy proposals—precisely what had happened with Bill Clinton. The irony was that all this helped Trump defeat Clinton's wife, Hillary, who was the Democratic presidential nominee in 2016 and who could never escape from the large shadow of scandal associated with her husband.

Precis

Bill Clinton effectively managed the political side of his worst crisis by taking action when he had to, adapting to changing circumstances and persevering. But he abandoned principle through his lies and deceptions and by conducting himself improperly in the first place. He saved his presidency but failed to save his reputation, and he undermined faith in government and the institution of the presidency.

Notes

1. Allyson Chiu, "'Bill Clinton Should Want to Apologize': Monica Lewinsky Opens up about Scandal in New Documentary," *Washington Post*, Nov 14, 2018, washingtonpost.com/nation/2018/11/14/bill-Clinton-should-want-to-apologize-monica-lewinsky-opens-up-about-scandal.

2. Chiu, ibid.
3. Gil Troy, *The Age of Clinton: America in the 1990s*, New York: Thomas Dunne Books, 2015, pp. 217–218.
4. Joe Klein, "The Natural," excerpt in Nathaniel May, ed., *Oval Office: Stories of Presidents in Crisis from Washington to Bush*, New York: Thunder's Mouth Press, 2002, p. 271.
5. Bill Clinton video from Jan. 26, 1998, washingtonpost.com/video/politics/bill-clinton-i-did-not-have-sexual-relations-with-that-woman, accessed Jan 25, 2018.
6. Chiu, ibid.
7. Chiu, ibid.
8. Peter Baker, "When the President Testified: People in the Room Recall Clinton's 1998 Interrogation," *New York Times*, May 29, 2018, nytimes.com/2018/05/29/us/politics/clinton-testimony-grand-jury.html.
9. David A. Graham and Cullen Murphy, "The Clinton Impeachment, as Told by the People Who Lived It," theatlantic.com/magazine/archive/2018/12/clinton-impeachment/573940/.
10. Klein, p. 236.
11. Graham and Murphy, ibid.
12. John F. Harris, *The Survivor: Bill Clinton in the White House*, New York: Random House, 2005, p. 342.
13. Baker, ibid.
14. Baker, ibid.
15. Baker, ibid.
16. Harris, pp. 348–349.
17. Harris, pp 348–349.
18. Klein, p. 273.
19. Baker, ibid. Also see Klein, p. 274.
20. William Greider, "Clinton and Character," *Rolling Stone*, October 29, 1998, rollingstone.com/politics/politics-news/Clinton-and-character-240816/.
21. Graham and Murphy, ibid.
22. Graham and Murphy, ibid.
23. Klein, p. 275.
24. Lesley Kennedy, "Why Clinton Survived Impeachment While Nixon Resigned After Watergate," History.com, Oct. 1, 2018, history.com/news/clinton-impeachment-lewinsky-scandal-nixon-resigned-watergate.
25. Troy, p. 249.
26. Troy, p. 249.

Chapter Thirteen
George W. Bush
9/11 and the Global War on Terror

While he was on live television attending an education event on September 11, 2001, George W. Bush was informed that a second hijacked commercial airliner had hit the second World Trade Center tower in New York. He seemed shaken at this moment, but handled the immediate crisis well. However, he went on to make some unpopular, highly criticized decisions on long-range Middle Eastern policy. (Paul J. Richards/AFP/Getty images)

George W. Bush was ill-prepared for a foreign-policy crisis when he became president in January 2001. He had been governor of Texas for eight years, and aside from some dealing with neighboring Mexico he didn't have any experience on global issues.

When terrorists hijacked four commercial airliners on September 11, 2001, he was forced to deal with a crisis of enormous consequence. Two of the planes crashed into the World Trade Center in New York City and one hit the Pentagon in Washington. The fourth hijacked airliner went down in the Pennsylvania countryside after the passengers attempted to seize control of the jet from the terrorists. Three thousand people were killed and 6,000 injured in the four coordinated attacks. Americans suddenly felt unsafe and under siege.

Bush's response was a sterling example of effective crisis management. He demonstrated that even a neophyte president with little or no national or international experience in governing can perform admirably under harrowing conditions if the president surrounds himself with top-notch advisers, if he or she listens to smart advice, and if the president has good instincts.

Bush over-reacted after his appropriate initial response. His subsequent decisions, especially the war he waged against Iraq and the U.S. occupation of that country, are widely considered major blunders that got the United States bogged down in hostile, faraway places. But Bush did well in the initial crisis.

ON 9/11, Bush was in Sarasota, Florida, scheduled to address students at the Emma E. Booker Elementary School about his initiative to strengthen the country's education system. American Airlines Flight 11 struck the north tower of the World Trade Center at 8:46 a.m., as Bush's motorcade approached the school. After he arrived, at 8:55 a.m., a White House aide and Navy captain who was in communication with military officials in Washington ran to the presidential limousine and approached President Bush and White House Chief of Staff Andy Card as they walked to the school's entrance. "Mr. President, an aircraft has hit one of the World Trade Center towers in New York," the aide said. "Fire and smoke are coming from a point about four-fifths of the way up. We have no further information at this time." Bush replied, "Thank you, captain. Keep me informed."[1]

Bush proceeded inside, took a phone call confirming the aide's account of the World Trade Center crash, and entered a classroom where he sat with 16 second-graders. Card received word of the second attack on the twin towers and walked up to Bush, who was being filmed by news organizations, and whispered into his right ear, "A second plane hit the second tower. America is under attack." Bush seemed numb, frozen in place, befuddled—not a reassuring image for a president amid a crisis. He joined in a prearranged reading with the schoolchildren from a book called *The Pet Goat*, "A . . . girl . . . got . . . a . . . pet . . . goat." Press Secretary Ari Fleischer, standing with reporters and photographers in the back of the room, beckoned to the president and held up a legal pad on which Fleischer had written in big block letters, "DON'T SAY ANYTHING YET." Bush nodded slightly in agreement.[2]

Bush continued with the group reading and after a few minutes excused himself and walked briskly to a holding room at the school. He asked to speak immediately to Vice President Dick Cheney, who was at the White House.

From the start, Cheney was Bush's go-to adviser. During the 2000 campaign, Bush had said, "Mark my words. There will be a crisis in my administration and Dick Cheney is exactly the man you want at your side in a crisis."[3] For his part, Cheney welcomed this role.

But in the immediate aftermath of the World Trade Center attacks, neither Cheney nor Bush knew exactly what was going on. Bush, realizing that the world was waiting for his reaction, decided to read a vague statement drafted by Communications Director Dan Bartlett and Fleischer. At 9:30 a.m., less than an hour after the first hijacked airliner hit, Bush stood at a podium set up for him in the elementary-school library, began fidgeting and said on live television, "Ladies and gentlemen this is a . . . difficult moment for America." He spoke for less than two minutes and announced, "Terrorism against our nation will not stand."[4] This phrase, that terrorism "will not stand," was similar to the one his father had used in 1990 regarding Iraq's invasion of Kuwait as a prelude to the Persian Gulf War.

There were rumors that more terrorist attacks were ongoing or imminent, that the White House would be hit, or the State Department, or the presidential retreat at Camp David, or Air Force One, the president's 747 jet. Under these conditions, Cheney advised Bush not to return immediately to Washington. Bush agreed.

Air Force One took off from Florida at 9:54 a.m., leveled off at 45,000 feet, far higher than the altitude of commercial flights so any hijacked airliners would have a difficult time targeting it, and headed north. Bush, in consultation with his advisers, decided he would fly to Barksdale Air Force Base near Shreveport, Louisiana, a base for B-52 bombers and an extremely secure location. In addition, Bush wanted to address the nation on live television and at the time Air Force One didn't have an adequate live broadcast-transmission capability. Barksdale at least had the equipment to videotape his remarks, which could then be sent immediately to the TV networks. Air Force One banked to the left and headed west toward the Louisiana base.

At about this time, Cheney asked Bush to authorize the military to engage and possibly shoot down other hijacked airliners, and Bush gave the go-ahead. He later said he realized the gravity of his order, but felt it would be better to shoot down a commercial airliner that had been seized rather than allow it to hit other targets as the other hijacked planes had hit the World Trade Center and the Pentagon.

The president and his top aides got another scare when Cheney called on a secure line at 10:32 a.m. and reported that someone had phoned the White House and said "Angel," the code name for Air Force One, would be "next." Cheney reasoned that if the caller knew the code name, this might be a serious threat. What he didn't realize was that the caller didn't actually use the word "Angel" but instead referred to "Air Force One," indicating no special knowledge of the plane. "Angel" was used by the military official who passed along the threat to Cheney on a secure line. The threatening call, U.S. officials later concluded, was a prank. But this incident showed how chaotic the situation was and how much danger everyone around the president thought they were in. The commander in chief and his staff were engulfed by what soldiers call "the fog of war," a common occurrence during combat operations.[5]

Television commentators began questioning where the president was. The impression was sinking in that he was hiding. Bush and White House officials feared this might raise concerns around the country that the situation was even more dire than it was, or that Bush was uncertain what to do or scared about appearing publicly.

The Secret Service was refusing to allow anyone to disclose Bush's location and what he was doing, ordering secrecy to keep him safe. The small group of reporters and photographers who were allowed to remain on Air Force One were expressly forbidden by White House officials from reporting their location or using cellphones.

The blanket of secrecy was lifted, however, as Air Force One landed at Barksdale at 11:45 a.m., and a local TV station went ahead and broadcast the arrival. At this point, Bush had approved the grounding of all other air traffic, so sighting Air Force One was a dramatic moment indicating that the president was probably secure.

Military drivers took Bush and his aides in a Dodge Caravan to the base headquarters, and the president phoned Cheney to coordinate information and discuss what to do next. Bush walked to a conference room where he read comments drafted by press secretary Fleischer. Standing in front of two American flags and portraits of famous Air Force personnel, Bush spoke for two minutes, hoping to reassure the country that things were under control and he was firmly in charge. Attempting to project resolve and strength, he declared, "Make no mistake, the United States will hunt down and punish those responsible for these cowardly acts."[6] But with little information available as to exactly what had happened and who was responsible, he seemed uncomfortable and uncertain.

Bush was getting impatient, eager to return to the White House. "I want to go back home ASAP," he told Card. "I don't want whoever did this holding me outside of Washington." But the chief of staff and others persuaded him to stay away from Washington until they were sure he would be safe en route and when he arrived. Bush reluctantly agreed. Air Force One took off at 1:37 p.m. and headed to Offutt Air Force Base near Omaha, Nebraska, where he could take refuge in an underground bunker used by the Strategic Command.[7]

At 3:30 p.m., Bush convened a meeting at Offutt of his National Security Council from the bunker, with members of his team joining him by video teleconferencing. Among those participating were Cheney, National Security Adviser Condoleezza Rice, Defense Secretary Donald Rumsfeld, Director of Central Intelligence George Tenet, and FBI Director Robert Mueller. Sitting next to the president were Card and Admiral Richard Mies, the head of Strategic Command.

It was a dream team, at least at the start of the crisis. It showed that Bush realized from the start his dearth of international experience and named seasoned veterans as senior advisers to make up for it. At the top of the list was Vice President Dick Cheney, who had served his father George H.W. Bush as defense secretary and had been White House chief of staff under President Gerald Ford, and before that a U.S. representative from Wyoming. Bush named Donald Rumsfeld, former defense secretary under Ford, to resume his leadership of the Pentagon. And George W. Bush brought in Army Gen. Colin Powell as secretary of state. Powell had been Ronald Reagan's White House national security adviser and served as George H.W. Bush's chairman of the Joint Chiefs of Staff during the Persian Gulf War and during the collapse of the Soviet Union.

Tenet reported that intelligence sources had intercepted conversations among associates of al-Qaeda terrorist leader Osama bin Laden boasting about the day's attacks. Tenet said he was almost certain that al-Qaeda was responsible for the hijackings.

"Get your ears up," Bush told Tenet. "The primary mission of this administration is to find them and catch them." Bush also announced that he was returning to Washington, adding: "We will find these people. They will pay. And I don't want you to have any doubt about it."[8]

As he grasped the situation and understood what he was dealing with, Bush's confidence and swagger were returning. On the way back to Washington, he dropped by the press cabin on Air Force One to talk with the small media contingent to send another stern warning. "We're gonna get those bastards," he said. "No thug is gonna bring our country down."[9]

After his plane landed at Andrews Air Force Base outside Washington at 6:42 p.m., Bush boarded a helicopter for the flight back to the White House. As the chopper approached the capital, the pilot flew over the nearby Pentagon and Bush saw the still-smoldering building that had been hit by the hijacked airliner, and he grew angrier. He told an aide that they were looking at the reality of war in the twenty-first century. Bush arrived at the White House at 6:54 p.m. and immediately reviewed a draft of his planned speech to the nation scheduled for 8:30 p.m. He interrupted his preparations to talk with First Lady Laura Bush, who was in the underground White House command center and bomb shelter called the President's Emergency Operations Center (PEOC) and they talked briefly with Vice President Cheney and his wife, Lynne.

He practiced his speech, then walked to the Oval Office, sat at his desk and began. "Good evening," he said somberly. "Today, our fellow citizens, our way of life, our very freedom came under attack in a series of deliberate and deadly terrorist acts." In his seven-minute address, he aimed to reassure Americans that they would triumph over the evil represented by the horrendous acts of 9/11, praised the rescuers in New York and Washington and pledged that the government would bring those responsible to justice. He added: "We will make no distinction between the terrorists who committed these acts and those who harbor them."[10]

In the 12 hours since the attacks of that morning, Bush had steadied himself. He drew confidence from the unrattled, smart counsel of his advisers and realized that what the nation and much of the world wanted from him was a show of strength, resolve and defiance to the terrorists he would later call the "evil doers." He wasn't sure what the details of the U.S. response should be, but he knew it was vital for him to show he was in command. On that first evening, he told his senior advisers:

> I want you all to understand that we are at war and we will stay at war until this is done. Nothing else matters. Everything is available for the pursuit of this war. Any barrier in your way, they're gone.[11]

At one point, Rumsfeld warned that international law generally supported the use of force to prevent possible follow-up attacks but not for reprisal. "No!" Bush replied angrily. "I don't care what the international lawyers say, we are going to kick some ass."[12]

From then on, he met often with what he called his "war cabinet," which included Card, Cheney, Powell, Rice, Rumsfeld, Tenet and Gen. Hugh Shelton, chairman of the Joint Chiefs of Staff, and occasionally other senior officials such as Attorney General John Ashcroft and Mueller. These individuals would frequently disagree among themselves but Cheney emerged as Bush's chief wartime consiglieri. Bush trusted him fully and respected his vast experience.

Some critics still weren't sure Bush was up to the job during those first few days. After all, he had no real foreign-policy experience and had benefited from his father's connections all his life. It wasn't clear if he had the right stuff to be a wartime president or to handle this major crisis.

But he went a long way toward easing the doubts on September 14, when he visited Ground Zero, where the World Trade towers had stood. As the ruins of the building smoldered around him, he began addressing the first responders while standing on a burned-out fire truck. As he started to speak, the first responders shouted that they couldn't hear him, so he grabbed a bullhorn and, as volunteer fire fighter Bob Beckwith stood next to him, he declared dramatically, "I can hear you! The rest of the world hears you! And the people—and the people who knocked these buildings down will hear all of us soon." The crowd reacted with loud prolonged chants of "USA! USA!"[13]

This is exactly what the country wanted to hear at that moment—a spontaneous expression of strength and resolve and a promise to take action to punish the evil doers. Bush passed a big test. He showed that he could be an effective, even inspirational crisis manager during a time of trial and national emergency.

BUT BUSH, over the long term, over-reached and made some wrong-headed judgments, such as launching the invasion of Iraq to find "weapons of mass destruction" that, it turned out, weren't there.

Within hours of the 9/11 attacks, members of Bush's "war cabinet" were privately pressuring him to move extremely aggressively against real and suspected terrorists and their patrons. On September 12, the drumbeat for war got more intense at Bush's two meetings with his war cabinet. Rumsfeld asked the group, "Do we focus on bin Laden and al-Qaeda or terrorism more broadly?" Powell replied, "The goal is terrorism in its broadest sense, focusing first on the organization that acted yesterday." Cheney added: "To the extent we define our task broadly, including those who support terrorism, then we get at states. And it's easier to find them than it is to find bin Laden."[14]

Bush, who prided himself on his decisiveness and operating from his "gut," welcomed the aggressive attitude. "I want to get moving," Bush told his advisers on September 12. He was delighted that day when the United Nations Security Council endorsed action to fight terrorism without any elaboration. Two days later, on September 14, the U.S. Congress authorized the president to use military force against those who committed or aided the attacks on 9/11. The House endorsed the use of force 420 to 1, and the Senate, 98 to 0. NATO leaders reaffirmed the alliance's Article 5, which said an attack against one member is an attack against all members.[15]

During a later war cabinet meeting at Camp David on September 15, in a conference room at Laurel Lodge, Tenet distributed a packet of documents entitled "Going to War." He proceeded to describe using CIA covert action and military special-operations forces to help local militias overthrow the Taliban, a group of terrorists who were training in Afghanistan, considered a terrorist haven.

General Shelton offered three military options in Afghanistan in addition to Tenet's plans: a limited cruise missile strike; a cruise missile attack combined with attacks by bombers and other aircraft, and, as the third option, all of the above in addition to the use of more special operations units and some Army and Marine fighters.

On September 17, Bush revealed his decision at another war cabinet meeting. "It starts today," he announced. He ordered everyone to go ahead with Shelton's third, most aggressive option in Afghanistan and said, "We're going to rain holy hell on them." Bush added, ominously, "I believe Iraq was involved [in the 9/11 attacks], but I'm not going to strike them now." He asked Rumsfeld to make plans for future military intervention in Iraq.[16]

All this put Bush on a path to an ever wider military commitment, just what his father had sensibly avoided in 1991. He grew increasingly eager to hit at Iraq, in part because he believed that his father should have toppled the country's dictator Saddam Hussein during the Gulf War. Hussein had continued to make trouble for the United States ever since. There was little or no evidence that Hussein was behind the 9/11 attacks, but Bush had a hunch that Hussein was somehow to blame, administration officials said.

In any case, Bush considered Hussein and Iraq to be an international menace. He escalated his rhetoric at his State of the Union address on January 29, 2002 when he referred to Iraq, Iran and North Korea along with their "terrorist allies" as "an axis of evil, arming to threaten the peace of the world. By seeking weapons of mass destruction, these regimes pose a grave and growing danger."[17]

Throughout the first half of 2002, Bush targeted Iraq with verbal attacks, constructing a public case for war. He tried, with little evidence, to link Iraq with the 9/11 hijackings and, using his bully pulpit, managed to persuade many Americans of his argument. By early 2003, a Knight Ridder poll found that 44 percent of Americans believed most or some of the 9/11 hijackers were Iraqis.[18] They weren't. Actually, most of them had connections to Saudi Arabia, a U.S. ally.

The news media discredited these connections between Iraq and the 9/11 terrorists, and Bush began to use another argument to build support for war with Iraq. Senior administration officials, including Cheney and Powell, claimed Iraq had weapons of mass destruction, biological and chemical, and was on the verge of acquiring nuclear weapons. As mentioned, no such WMD were found during or after the invasion, but Bush was at this time hell-bent on invasion, hoping to rid the world of someone he genuinely considered a menace.

On March 19, 2003, U.S. forces and American allies invaded and occupied Iraq on Bush's orders. The war went well initially for the United States but gradually it became a costly morass.

Even though terrorist leader Osama bin Laden was killed during a daring U.S. raid ordered by President Barack Obama in May 2011, the terrorist threat remains today, although it has been diminished. Hussein was captured and executed, and President Barack Obama removed U.S. combat forces from Iraq in 2011. But Iraq remains unstable, and American forces remain in Afghanistan as they continue attempting to root out terrorists. The United States is entangled in the region, costing thousands of American lives and draining billions of American dollars. Most Americans say these conflicts haven't been worth the cost and the effort, according to the polls.

Historian Michael K. Bohn concludes that Bush's long-range decisions amounted to

> an unevenly resourced attempt at nation building . . . and the resultant quagmire still plagues America. Bush's larger action, the Global War on Terror, as he called it, had grander goals and resources and it prevented further major attacks on the United States. However, some of the president's harshest critics consider his decision to include the invasion of Iraq in that strategy to be the biggest foreign policy blunder in modern American history.[19]

George W. Bush proved to be a better crisis manager in the moment than a creative thinker or geopolitical strategist over the long term.

Precis

George W. Bush excelled at taking action, and he did well as commander in chief in the days and weeks following the 9/11 terrorist attacks. During this period, he was the strong, tough, perseverant leader that the country wanted and he inspired confidence that he would keep the country safe. Over the long term, he had trouble adapting to changing circumstances. He adhered to his original principle that democracy would flourish in Iraq and elsewhere, which turned out to be wrong. Most important, while he succeeded in his short-range goal of defeating Iraq and removing Saddam Hussein, he left behind a costly mess for his successors to deal with in Iraq and Afghanistan.

Notes

1. Michael K. Bohn, *Presidents in Crisis: Tough Decisions inside the White House from Truman to Obama*, New York: Arcade Publishing, 2016, pp. 213–214.
2. Bill Sammon, *Fighting Back*, Washington: Regnery, 2002, p. 86. This section on the events of 9/11 is also based on my reporting at the time as White House correspondent for *U.S. News & World Report*.
3. Sammon, p. 2.
4. Bohn, p. 215.
5. This section is based on my reporting at the time as the White House correspondent for *U.S. News & World Report*.
6. George W. Bush, "Statement by the President in His Address to the Nation," Sept 11, 2001, https://georgewbush-whitehouse.archives.gov/news/releases/2001/09/20010911-16.html.
7. Sammon, *Fighting Back*, p. 119.
8. Dan Balz and Bob Woodward, "America's Chaotic Road to War: Bush's Global Strategy Began to Take Shape in First Frantic Hours After Attack," *Washington Post*, Jan 27, 2002, p. A1.
9. Sammon, p. 126.
10. Bush, ibid.
11. Richard Clarke, *Against All Enemies*, New York: Free Press, 2004, p. 24. This passage is also based on my own reporting at the time as White House correspondent for U.S. News & World Report.
12. Bohn, p. 224.
13. I accompanied Bush to the site and observed this incident as White House correspondent for *U.S. News & World Report*.
14. Bohn, pp. 225–226.
15. Dan Balz and Bob Woodward, "We Will Rally the World," *Washington Post*, January 28, 2002, p. A1.
16. Bob Woodward, *Bush at War*, New York: Simon & Schuster, 2002, pp. 97-99.
17. "President Bush Addressing the Nation" Text of Address to Joint Session of Congress, September 20, 2001, washingtonpost.com/wp-srv/nation/specials/attacked/transcript.
18. Bohn, p. 231.
19. Bohn, p. 232.

Chapter Fourteen
Barack Obama
Ending the "Great Recession"

Barack Obama was dealt a bad hand when he took office in January 2009 as the economy went into meltdown because of a financial crisis he inherited. He handled this complicated and dangerous situation well and ended up celebrating the recovery of the initially endangered U.S. auto industry, which he helped to rescue with a federal bailout. (AP Photo/Paul Sancya)

As with Franklin D. Roosevelt in 1933, Barack Obama inherited a deep economic crisis and a troubled nation when he took over the presidency on January 20, 2009. And as with FDR, Obama realized that what the nation wanted and needed was immediate action. That's what he delivered in a careful, deliberate manner, all the while projecting optimism that he would find a way out of the emergency.

The conditions that Obama faced were horrendous. The economy was losing hundreds of thousands of jobs per month. In mid-September 2008, three months before he took office, Lehman Brothers, a major trader of and investor in mortgage-backed securities, went bankrupt, with liabilities of about $600 billion. Several other important financial institutions were teetering on the brink of collapse, such as the AIG insurance company, the massive Citigroup bank, and investment banks such as Goldman Sachs, Morgan Stanley and Merrill Lynch.[1] Mortgage behemoths Freddie Mac and Fannie Mae were placed in government conservatorship.

"The pain of the recession was not theoretical, not a matter of numbers in ledgers," wrote journalist Michael D'Antonio.

> Layoffs, foreclosures, ruined retirement accounts, and shuttered businesses were making it more difficult for millions of people to provide themselves with food and shelter. (Two signs of economic pain could be seen in the rising use of antidepressants and declining rates of pregnancy.) The Great Recession was draining the resources available for business to grow and for the government to perform its basic functions, including antiterrorism efforts and environmental protection . . . Rising unemployment. Markets in free fall. Credit frozen. The economy shrinking. It was too easy to imagine that the recession could become a depression with the kind of suffering not seen since the 1930s.[2]

Ever the methodical planner, Obama began the process of deciding what to do during his campaign—a year before he would take office. He quickly concluded, rightly, that the financial and mortgage lending industries had largely brought all this on themselves through a series of complicated and risky decisions that overextended the financial system. It would take an equally complicated and politically risky series of policies to fix the problem.

Starting in January 2008, as then-Senator Obama was preparing to run in the Democratic presidential primaries, he held a half-hour conference call every couple of weeks with senior economic advisers to discuss the dire condition of the economy. Participants included former Fed Chairman Paul Volcker, investors Warren Buffett and Mark Gallogly and, most important, Larry Summers, who had been Bill Clinton's Treasury secretary. (Obama would name Summers as director of the National Economic Council after he became president in January 2009.)[3]

During these calls, Summers would frame the issues in an authoritative and compelling way. His communication skills and mastery of the material caused Obama to give Summers enormous respect, as so many others had done before him, including Clinton and his Vice President Al Gore.[4]

The candidate was a quick study. "Obama specialized in restating what he had been told, crisply and sonorously," recalled Reed Hundt, an economic adviser who participated in some of the calls.

> He kept his own views in reserve . . . Distance came naturally to Obama. He was an outsider by birth and upbringing. He chose his persona quite consciously. He became who he thought he should be. Like Gore he learned to keep his vulnerable self backstage. Like George W. Bush and unlike Bill Clinton, he expected to be treated with respect. More than any politician I have known, he kept his cool. He was cocky but many liked that touch of edginess. Obama showed that he had a destiny.[5]

Obama learned that the ongoing Great Recession—marked by a huge decline in economic growth—could be traced to the approval of thousands of subprime mortgage loans as lenders, seeking to meet the demand for houses, loaned money on far less restrictive terms than in the past. As housing prices surged in North America and Western Europe, more financial institutions acquired thousands of these risky mortgages, often in the form of mortgage-backed securities, in hopes of making quick profits in the booming housing industry. There was a vast surge of debt.

Subprime mortgage lenders began to collapse and declare bankruptcy. The problem snowballed and the market for these subprime mortgages dried up. There was no way to sell them to recoup the initial investments, leading to more bankruptcies, loss of jobs, and a steep decline in the stock market.[6]

President George W. Bush, a Republican who would leave office in January 2009, had initiated a rescue of the banking system. His effort included the Troubled Asset Relief Program (TARP), approved by Congress in 2008, that committed the federal government to spend $700 billion to bail out the bankers.[7]

But the economy was getting worse. Obama decided he had to do more. He appeared to agree, at least initially, with his incoming White House chief of staff Rahm Emanuel who famously told a corporate leaders' forum, "You never want a serious crisis to go to waste. And what I mean by that is an opportunity to do things that you think you could not do before."[8]

The choices were unpalatable. Many liberals in his own Democratic party wanted Obama to punish the financial industry, clamp down on banks and lenders with new regulations, throw greedy fat-cat offenders in jail, and have the government support refinancing of large numbers of unsustainable mortgages so everyday people wouldn't lose their homes. On the other hand, many conservatives were suspicious or outright opposed to massive government intervention, trusting market forces to stabilize the situation. And Obama from the start was concerned about what he could actually get Congress to approve, especially if it appeared that he was creating make-work jobs that wouldn't last and if he seemed to be setting up a colossal giveaway program.

Through it all, Obama showed a talent for selecting talented advisers and delegating important work to them, and he displayed good judgment in assessing their counsel.

Obama surrounded himself with many former economic and political advisers to President Clinton, including former Treasury Secretary Summers, former Undersecretary of the Treasury Timothy F. Geithner, former White House Budget Director Jack Lew, former senior Clinton White House adviser Rahm Emanuel, and former White House Chief of Staff and Commerce Secretary Bill Daley. All of them returned to government as advisers to Obama in various senior capacities and were instrumental in developing his economic plan in late 2008 and early 2009. Obama also reappointed Ben Bernanke, who had been President Bush's nominee, as chairman of the Federal Reserve, to provide continuity.

"His advisers had convinced him to impart confidence by his words, decisions, and personnel choices," Hundt wrote in a detailed analysis of Obama's handling of the financial meltdown. "Critically, he must not seek reform of the financial sector at that time. Banking executives had enough to worry about already."[9]

They didn't always agree on the details, but what Obama did was to assemble a team that essentially represented the establishment wing of the Democratic party. The result was an agenda that sought to restore the pre-meltdown status quo in the financial industry. Obama sought above all to save the nation's major financial institutions. And, to the disappointment of liberals, he did so without making fundamental reforms in economic policy and the structure of America's economic institutions to help the middle class and the poor.

At the same time, Republicans condemned Obama's emerging fiscal stimulus, arguing that it would create gargantuan deficits and increase inflation. GOP legislators also opposed the re-regulation of the financial industry and ridiculed the proposed bailout of the auto industry.

AS THE OBAMA economic plan was taking shape, his political campaign enjoyed great success. On November 4, Obama won the presidential election with 53 percent of the popular vote over Republican nominee John McCain, who had 46 percent. And Obama won a huge majority in the Electoral College. The Democrats also ended up with big majorities in the House and Senate, meaning that Obama would have a friendly Congress to consider his ideas.

The unemployment rate was 6.5 percent on Election Day and the economy was shedding jobs at an alarming rate. Obama's advisers convinced him that one of his top tasks, again, was to reassure business leaders that he would work fast to end the calamity, and they should be confident about the future.[10]

Obama held a news conference in Chicago, his hometown, on November 7 and announced that a "fiscal stimulus plan that will jump-start economic growth is long overdue." He promised to help business recover from "the spreading impact of the financial crisis" and set a "central goal of stabilizing financial markets," including efforts to help families avoid foreclosures on their houses. He assigned top priority to ending bank runs and restoring the profitability of the big banks.[11]

In December, Obama was still developing his stimulus plan. One of his biggest challenges was determining how much the government should spend. On December 2, the president-elect told the National Governors Conference in Philadelphia he wanted a recovery plan that created or saved 2.5 million jobs. He didn't make clear if this target was for one year or longer. If it was one year, his advisers estimated that the stimulus would need to reach $250 billion. But on December 5, Obama said he wanted a stimulus initiative that would cover two years, which some of his advisers said would cost $500 billion.[12]

Then, on December 5, the U.S. Bureau of Labor Statistics reported that 533,000 jobs had been lost in November, up from 240,000 in October. In later revisions, the BLS said the real job loss in October was nearly 500,000 and in November it exceeded 800,000.[13]

The crisis was worsening, again.

At a key meeting on December 16, 2008, about a month after he won the presidency and three weeks before his inauguration, Obama was still in learning mode, but he was impressing his advisers. Christina Romer, an economics professor who would become chairwoman of the Council of Economic Advisers under Obama and attended this meeting, told an interviewer,

> The president-elect was brilliant. I called my husband afterward and said, "You cannot believe this man." We were all exhausted and he was still going strong. It was lots of substance, but he didn't really tip his hand. He listened. He asked questions. He obviously heard and understood everything.[14]

In a crucial decision, Obama accepted the advice of his political advisers not to allow the stimulus package to come close to $1 trillion. The thinking was that $1 trillion—an arbitrary number seemingly plucked from the air—would sound like too much money, and attaching this price tag to a legislative package in Congress would doom such a measure.[15]

The centerpiece of Obama's program came under the campaign slogan of "hope and change." It was a $787 billion economic stimulus package known as the American Recovery and Reinvestment Act of 2009, designed to create thousands of jobs. He pushed hard for it and, working with a Democratic majority in Congress, he won passage in the House on January 28—eight days after he took office—by a 244–188 margin, and in the Senate on February 10 by 61–37. After a conference committee ironed out differences between the two bills, Obama signed the $767 billion measure into law on February 17. It consisted of 45 percent spending, 37 percent tax cuts, and 18 percent state aid.[16]

At the same time, Obama authorized Treasury Secretary Timothy F. Geithner to stabilize the financial system with billions of dollars and the powers authorized by bailout legislation that Bush had obtained. Federal

Reserve Chairman Bernanke infused the banking system with funds to prop up weak financial institutions.[17]

Unemployment would rise again and remain at between 9 and 10 percent until late in Obama's first term, when it began to decline. But the collapse of the banking industry was stopped—a huge achievement.

In their 2019 book reviewing the crisis, three of the architects of the federal response, Ben. S. Bernanke, Timothy F. Geithner and Henry M. Paulson, Jr., said Americans today may not understand how desperate conditions were in 2008 and 2009. "The United States government—two successive presidents, Congress, the Federal Reserve, the Treasury Department, and thousands of public servants at a variety of agencies—had to confront the worst financial crisis in generations," Bernanke, Geithner and Paulson wrote.

> . . . We helped shape the American and international response to a conflagration that choked off global credit, ravaged global finance, and plunged the American economy into the most damaging recession since the breadlines and shantytowns of the 1930s . . . [W]e fought the fire with an extraordinary barrage of emergency interventions, escalating from conventional and then unconventional loans to government rescues of major firms and government backstops for vital credit markets.[18]

They added:

> When the fire kept raging, we persuaded Congress to give us even more powerful tools to fight it, including the authority to inject hundreds of billions of dollars of capital directly into private financial institutions . . . We eventually helped stabilize the financial system before frozen credit channels and collapsing asset values could drag the broader economy into a second depression. Even so, the economy suffered a major downturn, and unprecedented monetary and fiscal stimulus would be needed to help jumpstart the recovery . . . Americans who aren't bankers or investors still rely on a functioning credit system to buy cars and homes, borrow for college, and grow their businesses. Financial crises that damage the credit system can create brutal recessions that hurt ordinary families as well as financial elites. Today, much of the American public remembers the

government's interventions as a bailout for Wall Street, but our goal was always to protect Main Street from the fallout of a financial collapse. The only way to contain the economic damage of a financial fire is to put it out, even though it's almost impossible to do that without helping some of the people who caused it.[19]

The impulses of Obama and Roosevelt in dealing with their separate economic calamities were similar. Each favored bold action and tried to rally the country behind their ideas, even if the ideas were largely untested. But in some ways, Obama's challenge was more daunting than Roosevelt's. In FDR's more innocent and trusting time, the president was able to more easily rally the country behind him and generate enough public trust to push through many legislative and executive programs. But Obama didn't have these options. The nation and Congress were so divided and cynical—and opposition Republicans in Congress were so determined that he would fail—that it was impossible to generate the kind of unity and trust that propelled FDR and sustained his agenda.

In his first inaugural address, delivered in 1933, FDR accurately saw most of the country as ready for bold leadership and willing to follow a president who moved decisively. Roosevelt said Americans recognized "our interdependence" and were willing to "move as a trained and loyal army." He said the voters "want direct, vigorous action" and "have made me the present instrument of their wishes." He expressed the willingness to use his unilateral executive power if Congress wouldn't go along with his programs.

In contrast, Obama knew that the country's polarization required a more limited approach. As a result, his vision was considerably more restrained, pragmatic and cautious than Roosevelt's. "The question we ask today," Obama declared in his first inaugural address 76 years after Roosevelt's,

> is not whether our government is too big or too small, but whether it works—whether it helps families find jobs at a decent wage, care they can afford, a retirement that is dignified. Where the answer is yes, we intend to move forward. Where the answer is no, programs will end.[20]

"Our economy is badly weakened, a consequence of greed and irresponsibility on the part of some but also our collective failure to make hard choices and prepare the nation for a new age," Obama said in his inaugural address (on January 20, 2009). "Homes have been lost; jobs shed; businesses shattered." Underscoring the problems of providing affordable health care, improving education and climate change, he added:

> These are the indicators of crisis, subject to data and statistics. Less measurable but no less profound is a sapping of confidence across our land—a nagging fear that America's decline is inevitable, and that the next generation must lower its sights.

Today I say to you that the challenges we face are real. They are serious and they are many. They will not be met easily or in a short span of time. But know this, America—they will be met.[21]

Obama has defended this limited vision ever since. He told an interviewer in 2018:

> The dynamic you had at that juncture [in 2009] is that the actions that are necessary to save the financial system are by any definition bad politics . . . The crisis awakens people to that sense that the game is rigged, "This economy is not working for me." And in that kind of environment if you've got irresponsible politicians who want to take advantage of that and start scapegoating people who don't look like you and start trafficking in conspiracy theories, yeah, there is going to be more of an audience for that and it tests our democracy in ways that are troubling.[22]

Obama went on to say one big problem in 2009 was that greedy, irresponsible banks and mortgage lenders had advised millions of everyday Americans that they could buy houses they really couldn't afford. "It was a bum deal for people," Obama argued, " . . . and suddenly folks are getting wiped out." But the answers on what to do and how to rally congressional and public support were elusive, and Obama's GOP opponents were only too happy to attempt to obstruct him, then blame him for inaction.

Analyzing Obama's first few months in office, journalist Martin Wolf noted that the economy was "in free fall" and Wolf cited a later report from Obama's Council of Economic Advisers:

> It is easy to forget how close the US economy came to an outright depression during the crisis. Indeed, by a number of macroeconomic

measures . . . the first year of the Great Recession . . . saw larger declines than at the outset of the Great Depression in 1929–30.[23]

While Obama was the first African American president and was widely expected to move aggressively to help blacks improve their economic standing, he wisely chose not to portray his agenda in racial terms. He didn't want to be seen by whites as playing favorites. At a news conference marking his 100th day in office, Obama said he wasn't assisting only black people. "Keep in mind that every step we're taking is designed to help all people," he said. He added that blacks and Latinos would benefit from his programs because they were the "most vulnerable" in bad times, but that whites would benefit too.[24]

Historians have noted that Americans gained confidence in FDR's leadership because they liked and trusted him even if they weren't sure if his prescriptions would work. Obama, among the most likeable of presidents, seemed to gain in approval for the same reason—his personal appeal. Like Roosevelt, he radiated good cheer and empathy.

OBAMA'S INITIAL REVIEWS were positive and they have mostly stayed that way. The exceptions to what amounted to his middle-of-the-road, Establishment-favored course were Republican partisans who opposed Obama's aggressive and strong use of federal power, and liberal reformers who wanted far more government intervention.

"He had to use a lot of time and energy avoiding political disaster," says political scientist Bill Galston, a former White House domestic adviser to President Bill Clinton. "During his first three months, I'd give him an A-plus."[25]

By the end of his first 100 days in office, 65 percent of Americans approved of the job Obama was doing and only 29 percent disapproved, a very healthy rating compared with other presidents at a similar time in their administrations. (John F. Kennedy had 74 percent approval in April 1961, the highest among modern presidents for the same period, and President Donald Trump had 41 percent approval in April 2017, the lowest of the modern era, according to the Gallup research organization.)

ONE OF OBAMA'S KEY DECISIONS was to bail out the auto industry, which illustrated his crisis management skills in microcosm. This bailout was vital because so many Americans were dependent either directly or indirectly on the auto industry and "the entire supply chain feeding into it," says Galston.[26] The car companies, their suppliers and related businesses accounted for more than 3 million jobs.[27]

Obama moved boldly to rescue General Motors and Chrysler, two massive employers in Michigan and elsewhere that were tottering on the brink of collapse. Obama favored loan guarantees to the parent companies and their subsidiaries and suppliers. The wisdom of all this was seriously debated at the time and Obama was widely second-guessed for meddling in the economy and risking billions of taxpayer dollars. "The president . . . made some very tough decisions that at the time were politically very unpopular," said Steven Rattner, a senior economic adviser to Obama during the bailout.[28]

Journalist Michael D'Antonio wrote:

> The carmakers were in deep trouble caused in part by their own blunders and in part by the Great Recession, which had made consumers so frightened that sales of cars and light trucks had dropped 20 percent in a year. Chrysler and General Motors would soon be unable to pay their workers.[29]

One long-range problem was that the U.S. carmakers weren't making vehicles that Americans were eager to buy, as consumers increasingly preferred foreign competitors, whose vehicles were better made and had superior fuel economy. Yet millions of middle-class Americans and many communities depended on the U.S. automakers for their livelihood.

Obama, typically, was hands-on. He studied economic data and reports about the auto industry's financial condition. He held meetings with key advisers and ordered them to describe everything that could go wrong with an auto industry rescue.

David Axelrod, Obama's chief political strategist in the White House, told the president-elect that Americans didn't agree that government should bail out auto companies, according to the polls. "I was in the room when he made the decisions about the auto bailout," Axelrod recalls. "I had all the polling data. I told him that even people in Michigan, even in Michigan (home of the auto industry), were opposed."

Obama replied:

> If we can get the automobile companies to use our leverage [public funds to take them through bankruptcy, and allowing them to write

off debts and some obligations to unions] to get them to rationalize their businesses [such as by paying labor less] and to create cars for the 21st Century, they can become a source of renewal for the manufacturing sector, so I think it's worth the risk."[30]

The bailout worked. GM and Chrysler avoided bankruptcy. U.S. automakers had sold 16.5 million cars in 2014, the highest annual sales since before the economic collapse. GM and Chrysler and related companies had paid back most of the government bailout money.

In January 2015, Obama traveled to Michigan for a victory lap. Obama told applauding auto workers at a Ford assembly plant in Wayne, Michigan that the industry rescue had helped to save the U.S. economy. "Now this is the heartbeat of American manufacturing—right here," the president said. Recalling his decision to bail out the auto industry, he said, "It was not popular. Even in Michigan, it wasn't popular. But that bet has paid off for America, because the American auto industry is back."[31]

The auto industry achieved record sales in 2015, and as of 2016, Obama's final year in office, 640,000 auto industry jobs had been created.[32]

OBAMA HAD OTHER ACCOMPLISHMENTS during his first few months, such as signing into law the Lilly Ledbetter Fair Pay Act making it easier to file lawsuits for equal pay, and signing a law expanding health insurance coverage for children. But he focused most of his time and energy on the economy. This was a crucial and correct setting of priorities.

Obama decided to delay his push for comprehensive health care reform until the stimulus package passed, a gamble that he would be able to somehow amass enough influence to get both approved. And he did so. Congress eventually passed his landmark $940 billion health-insurance bill, known as the Affordable Care Act or Obamacare, over intense Republican objections, in March 2010. This provided health insurance for an estimated 20 million adults and 3 million children, and the growth of health-care costs slowed.[33]

Overall, Obama handled the economic crisis well.

"There may be significant areas of the country that aren't feeling it, but overall, the U.S. is far and away the closest of the developed economies to being 'normal' again," said Lucy O'Carroll, a chief economist at Aberdeen Asset Management at the end of his administration.

His was a presidency defined more by dealing with the hand that he was dealt, rather than tackling head-on much of what he aimed to in his stump speeches. On the whole, he finessed it in a methodical and measured say, which served his country well.[34]

Obama eventually decided to ask for second stimulus package, and Congress gave it to him in December 2010, the month after Republicans won control of Congress because of a heavy turnout of anti-Obama voters.

Obama then adapted to the changed political circumstances and compromised with GOP legislators. He agreed to extend George W. Bush's tax cuts on upper-income people and to reduce estate taxes in return for extended unemployment benefits, cutting payroll and other taxes, and enacting various tax credits. The budget cost was about $900 billion over two years—$100 billion more than the stimulus passed in February 2009.[35]

Obama went on to win re-election in 2012. He was in this way rewarded for his strong, stable and resilient leadership during the financial crisis.

"All in all, you have to give Obama pretty high grades for coming into the presidency in the middle of a white-hot financial crisis, with no executive experience, and putting the country back on the road to recovery," said Democratic pollster Geoff Garin, a veteran adviser to Democratic congressional and presidential candidates.[36]

His policies, while justified, also had serious downsides in that they exacerbated social tensions. Axelrod, who was President Barack Obama's chief political strategist, recognized the rising public anger and cynicism in 2009, when Obama had just taken office:

> There is a sense on the part of a lot of Americans that they work hard every day, they meet their responsibilities, they pay their bills, they take care of their families. Above them they see people who acted recklessly or worse and they are not accountable. They get bailed out, they continue to make fortunes. The same group of people feel like below them there are people who get handouts, who aren't meeting their responsibilities. That's the most primal force in American politics today.[37]

This was precisely the political dynamic that gave rise to Donald Trump's election in 2016.

It's no coincidence that white men became a principal constituency for Trump. He rode to the White House on a wave of grievance from middle-aged white men and others, partly because these voters felt left out of the federal response to the economic meltdown.

Obama didn't do everything right. No president does. But he led the country through a dangerous economic storm and proved his mettle as a crisis manager.

Precis

Barack Obama took bold action. He adapted to changing circumstances. He balanced the principle of helping every economic interest with emphasizing what worked, which was bailing out the big financial institutions even though this was unpopular. Obama showed impressive political skills in persuading the Democratic majorities in Congress to approve the American Recovery and Reinvestment Act of 2009, which contained his controversial economic stimulus package. He helped to shore up the financial sector through re-regulation, and rescued the auto industry. Obama's adaptability, sound judgment, and preference for quiet deliberation—his signature leadership traits—carried him and the country through what became a global economic meltdown and big declines in world markets. He persevered. And he achieved success.

Notes

1. Simon Johnson, "The Crisis Last Time," *The American Prospect*, March 29, 2019, prospect.org/article/crisis-last-time.
2. Michael D'Antonio, *A Consequential President: The Legacy of Barack Obama*, New York: Thomas Dunne Books, 2016, pp. 27, 37–38.
3. Reed Hundt, *A Crisis Wasted: Barack Obama's Defining Decisions*, New York: Rosetta Books, 2019, p. 52.
4. Hundt, p. 53.
5. Hundt, pp. 53–54.
6. For more detailed explanations of the causes of the Great Recession, see "Great Recession," History.com, August 21, 2018, history.com/topics/21st-century/recession, and "Crash Course," *The Economist*, September 7, 2013, economist.com/schools-brief/2013/09/07/crash-course.
7. D'Antonio, p. 37.
8. Rahm Emanuel interview with the *Wall Street Journal*, November 19, 2008, youtube.com/watch?v=_mzcbXi1Tkk.
9. Hundt, pp. 53–54.

10. Hundt, p. 87.
11. Hundt, p. 87–88.
12. Hundt, pp. 125–126.
13. Hundt, pp. 126–127.
14. Hundt, p. 166.
15. Hundt, p. 171.
16. Hundt, p. 182.
17. Josh Zumbrun, "Financial Crisis, Regulatory Agenda Shaped Obama's Economic Legacy," *Wall Street Journal*, January 18, 2017, wsj.com/amp/articles/financial-crisis-regulatory-agenda-shaped–obamas-economic-legacy/2017/01/17.
18. Ben S. Bernanke, Timothy F. Geithner and Henry M. Paulson, Jr., *Firefighting: The Financial Crisis and Its Lessons*, London: Profile Books, 2019, pp. 1–2. Bernanke was chairman of the Federal Reserve. Geithner was secretary of the Treasury under President Barack Obama. Paulson was secretary of the Treasury under President George W. Bush.
19. Bernanke, Geithner and Paulson, ibid.
20. C-SPAN: President Barack Obama 2009 Inauguration, January 20, 2009, video.
21. See note 20.
22. "Panic: The Untold Story of the 2008 Financial Crisis," *Vice News* on HBO, December 7, 2018.
23. Martin Wolf, "How Barack Obama Rescued the US economy," *Financial Times*, January 10, 2017, ft.com/content/b5b764cc-d657-11e6-944b-e7eb37a6aa8e.
24. Sam Tanenhaus, "100 Days in the Footsteps of F.D.R. and L.B.J.," *New York Times*, May 2, 2009, https://www.nytimes.com/2009/05/03/weekinreview/03tanenhaus.html.
25. Author's interview with Bill Galston, May 7, 2019.
26. Author's interview with Bill Galston, May 7, 2019.
27. D'Antonio, p. 60.
28. David Kiley, "As Obama Takes Victory Lap Over Auto Industry Rescue, Here Are the Lessons of the Bailout," *Forbes*, January 20, 2016, forbes.com/sites/davidkiley5/2016/01/20/obama-takes-victory-lap-over-auto-industry-rescue/#3119f0a13e83.
29. D'Antonio, p. 59.
30. Hundt, pp. 307–308.
31. D'Antonio, p. 80.
32. Kiley, ibid.
33. Martin Wolf, "How Barack Obama Rescued the US economy," *Financial Times*, January 10, 2017, ft.com/content/b5b764cc-d657-11e6-944b-e7eb37a6aa83.
34. Wolf, ibid.
35. Hundt, p. 248.
36. Author's interview with Geoff Garin, May 22, 2019.
37. Hundt, p. 309.

Chapter Fifteen
Donald Trump
A New Era of Perpetual Crisis

Donald Trump's presidency has been one crisis after another, some of them self-inflicted. A billionaire real-estate developer and reality-TV star, he entered office in January 2017 without any government experience, and it showed. (Saul Loeb/AFP/Getty Images)

In 2016, Donald Trump was elected the 45th president of the United States in a major upset. He had never run for public office before and created a cult of personality based on his reputation as a billionaire real-estate developer who knew how to make deals and a political outsider who would break up the Washington establishment. Trump, a quasi-conservative Republican and former TV reality-show host, tapped into the enormous sense of grievance felt by white middle- and working-class voters, especially men, who believed the country's leaders no longer listened to them or respected them. This propelled Trump to victory over Democrat Hillary Clinton, the former first lady and secretary of state.

As president, Trump immediately became the disrupter in chief, following up on his campaign promises to defy the power brokers and take on various elites. They included Democratic Party leaders, fellow Republicans who disagreed with him, the mainstream news media, Hollywood celebrities who mocked him, entrenched bureaucrats whom he labelled part of an anti-populist "deep state," and foreign leaders who didn't bend to his will. With his distinctive blond mane, his endless one-liners, his stream of insults, and his brazen disregard for civility and tradition, he held the media's attention and became an inescapable presence in the nation's consciousness—a consummate showman.

His core supporters were willing to overlook his many faults, such as his history of adultery, his years of making degrading remarks about women and treating them crudely, his demeaning of people and institutions that stood in his way, and his falsehoods. Trump managed to keep his political base happy with his constant attacks on the status quo and by adopting policies they loved, such as opposition to abortion, curbing immigration, cutting taxes and regulations, and naming conservatives to the Supreme Court and lower courts. He also benefited from the relatively strong economy and gains on Wall Street, which he said were due to his leadership.

He was unique in that, unlike his predecessors, Trump sought to create crises in order to dramatize his concerns or confuse his opponents, and then end each crisis on his own terms. All this was designed to make him look like a bold leader who did things his own way.

Trump's presidency became a series of political emergencies, both real and concocted. None of them was on the scale of the profound crises that other presidents had faced, such as the Civil War, the Depression and the Great Recession. Trump was lucky to avoid this kind of calamity during his first three years, which is the span of time covered by this book.

But he was always spoiling for a fight, escalating battles and using angry, off-the-cuff remarks that offended and alienated allies and adversaries. He was prone to making rash decisions that turned existing policies upside down with little apparent thought about the consequences. He lived for the moment in just about everything, adopting an "America First" foreign policy that infuriated U.S. allies and promoting domestic tax policies that helped mostly the rich and corporations and vastly increased annual deficits and the national debt.

"He's an agitator, and as a result he thrives in crisis," said Rutgers political scientist Ross Baker.[1] No one could predict how long his good fortune would last in avoiding a catastrophe, but his high-wire act clearly disturbed many Americans.

Trump said he was intent on keeping his campaign promise to "drain the swamp" in Washington of liberals, Establishment elites, lazy and meddlesome bureaucrats and anti-Trump legislators—a very popular concept among his core supporters. They represented about 40 percent of the electorate, according to opinion polls during his first three years. "With his constituency, there was a sense there was nothing worth saving, nothing to be valued in government," Baker said. "This chaos theory of government, that's crisis-driven, was seen as a positive development by Trump supporters."[2] It remained an open question how many of his core voters would stay with him during the election year when he would be, in effect, asking to be rehired and when he would have a clear Democratic alternative to contend with.

Through it all, Trump displayed a disdain for the way constitutional government is supposed to operate, with a system of checks and balances so no individual or institution gets too much power. This was the intention of the founders. He believed he could rush into big policy shifts because he was smarter than everyone else and could trust his instincts instead of looking into the issues in detail or listening to the wise counsel of others. His way of dealing with crises brought out the worst in him— such as narcissism, hubris and always looking for easy answers to complex problems. And it deepened the impression that Trump was most interested in winning every battle at all costs while humiliating his adversaries, to deter them from challenging him again.

This was not a recipe for compromise and getting things done in Washington or building relationships to help him govern over the long term.

Trump also was doing something unprecedented in the presidency— openly undermining the credibility of the news media, including the *New*

York Times, Washington Post, CNN and NBC, for running critical stories about him and his policies. Other presidents such as Richard Nixon had attacked individual news organizations, but Trump was attempting to cast doubt on the mainstream media as an institution so his followers would believe only him, not the Fourth Estate.

Trump admitted as much in an interview with CBS journalist Lesley Stahl after his victory in the 2016 election. Stahl told Trump his repeated attacks on the press were getting "tired" and "boring," and Trump replied, "You know why I do it? I do it to discredit you all and demean you all so that when you write negative stories about me no one will believe you."[3]

MOST IMPORTANT in terms of crisis management, Trump generated a constitutional crisis centering on alleged abuse of power. Many Democrats, who took control of the House of Representatives in the 2018 mid-term election, favored starting immediate impeachment proceedings against him in 2019. But they initally backed off, fearing that impeachment would divert attention away from what they considered their winning issues for the 2020 campaign, such as improving health care, expanding educational opportunities, and helping the middle class economically.

These issues, they argued, had given them the House majority in the mid-terms, and they wanted to use them again when Trump was on the ballot. House Speaker Nancy Pelosi, D-Calif., initially pointed out that the Republican-controlled Senate would refuse to remove Trump from office if the House impeached him, and the impeachment process could make the Democrats look petty and overly partisan.

Others argued that the Democrats had a constitutional duty to pursue impeachment. Historian Julian Zelizer, calling the situation "a crisis for democracy," pointed out in late May 2019 that Trump and his Cabinet:

> have put on a first-class demonstration in how to subvert the congressional right to oversight. The administration has offered justifications for ignoring subpoenas and preventing testimony that wouldn't pass muster in an episode of "The Simpsons." When Republicans controlled the House, their response to this kind of abuse was to ignore it and attack the investigators. [Then-]Speaker Paul Ryan's apparent calculation was that it was more important to protect the interests of the party by keeping Trump in place and insulating him from oversight than it was to hold him accountable . . . Now the Democrats are the ones with power in the House and they watch as the president's behavior only gets worse.[4]

Zelizer added:

> If the Democrats voted for articles of impeachment, that in itself would be a huge blow to the historical legacy of this President and permanent part of the record with both parties being forced to say where they stand on his use of power. Even if Senate Republicans decided to keep the President in power, that vote would be an extremely important statement for the country. It would be a public statement about what is right and what is wrong.[5]

At first, majority Democrats in the House opted for caution and didn't move to impeach Trump, only to investigate him and see what turned up. Still, the investigations kept the shadow of corruption hanging over his presidency. No one could be sure what the Democratic probes would find.

DONALD TRUMP was above all a showman and a dramatist, and this is the way he governed. He had been the star of a popular national television show, *The Apprentice*, followed by *Celebrity Apprentice*, in which he assessed the talents of people who wanted to work for him and delighted in firing them in front of millions of viewers. He understood the media's and the public's fascination with celebrity and the culture's attraction to conflict. As president, he gave America both.

Following this pattern, his White House became another reality series, created by and starring Trump and featuring drama, suspense, sudden firings and resignations, disagreements and clashes, bizarre plot twists, and no clear idea about where the show was headed. He loved to be the disrupter in chief and keep everyone guessing about what he would do next. Much of his governing strategy was based on dealing with crises that he manufactured himself. One of them was declaring a national emergency at the U.S. southern border with Mexico, which was surely a regional crisis but not a national one. Yet Trump set forth one policy after another for reducing the flow of migrants, including a threat, never implemented, to totally close the U.S.–Mexico border. This gambit was also part of his 2020 re-election strategy as Trump regularly lambasted immigrants in order to stir up his hard-core conservative supporters.[6]

He used Twitter, the social media platform, to go over the heads of the mainstream media. It was his favorite form of presidential communication. He could dominate the news and the national discourse with a stream of comments and policy pronouncements, insults and accusations, sent directly to millions of Americans who followed him on Twitter. In this way, he avoided the filter of what he called the "fake" news media, which he said was biased against him and was the "enemy of the people."[7]

"I would say that what sets Donald Trump apart from virtually all of his predecessors—first of all, I don't think you can exaggerate the reality TV element," says historian Richard Norton Smith,

> To Trump, this is all a performance, and every episode is a news cycle. It isn't that he has long-term vision that he wants to implement. He wants to win the day. Beyond that, and inseparable from that, is the fact that unlike virtually every president, this is someone who defines himself by his enemies and who seems curiously deflated if he doesn't have a foil to play off. None of us is a prophet, but it's hard to believe that it's a formula for successful governance.[8]

Historian Doug Brinkley says:

> We've never had a president that's a business person like Donald Trump. CEOs have a board to report to, and President Trump never had a board in his life. He was his own boss, kind of like a family kingpin. He got used to just barking orders, and people would jump. And, obviously, being president, that's tough because we have a Justice Department, FBI, a State Department; there's protocol. If he's had a deficit as president, it's constantly trying not to abide by the rules. We often call it an "unprecedented" presidency, but it's really just that he's somebody who has never in his life had to take orders, or follow protocol, from anybody else.[9]

In keeping with his campaign slogan—"Make America Great Again"—Trump described himself as a nationalist and a champion of putting "America first." He withdrew the United States from international trade agreements and removed the United States from a global pact designed to limit climate change. He said these arrangements allowed other countries to take advantage of the U.S.A. He pulled out of a deal negotiated by his predecessor Barack Obama's administration to limit the Iranian nuclear program. Trump said the agreement was too weak. He cozied up to the dictatorial regimes in North Korea, Russia and China. He presided over disruptions and occasional chaos in government by hiring and then ousting important aides and by shifting policy suddenly and dramatically.

He criticized his own cabinet choices, such as his first attorney general, Jeff Sessions. Trump eventually fired Sessions for being too independent and for what Trump considered bad judgment. Trump replaced him with William Barr, a former attorney general under President George H.W. Bush who seemed more likely than Sessions to protect the president from legal troubles—just what Trump wanted.

All these traits were evident in two of the most revealing crises of Trump's presidency—his handling of a government shutdown in 2018-2019, and his dealing with an embarrassing federal investigation into alleged collusion between Trump's 2016 campaign and the Russian government.

In both cases, Trump emerged as a bombastic attention-seeker who often slipped into demagoguery and delighted in undermining institutions and individuals who stood in his way. He made a habit of blaming others for his own shortcomings and failures, and relished the crisis of the moment because it put him in the spotlight.

ONE OF TRUMP'S MOST CONTROVERSIAL acts came when he triggered a 35-day partial shutdown of the federal government in 2018–2019—the longest such shutdown in history. This episode served as a paradigm of the Trump presidency, illustrating his weaknesses as a leader, his erratic approach to problem solving and his lack of empathy.

Trump initially indicated that he would accept a year-end spending bill to fund the government, even though it didn't meet all his specifications. The Republican-controlled Senate went ahead and approved the measure. Then Trump overplayed his hand and said he would refuse to sign such legislation unless it contained $5.7 billion for a wall between the United States and Mexico. This project had been one of his key campaign promises during the 2016 campaign. Actually, he had pledged that he would somehow force Mexico to pay for the wall, but its government refused, so Trump turned to Congress to get funding, knowing that the Democrat-led House would rebuff him. A congressional deadlock on the funding bill ensued.

Running out of money, the government began to shut down on December 22, 2018, just before the year-end holidays. Federal workers were furloughed in growing numbers; public services declined, and there were increasing concerns about safety, including questions about whether the shutdown was making air travel inconvenient and unsafe. When officials at LaGuardia Airport in New York said they were grounding planes because of staff shortages, it seemed that the air travel system might be starting to collapse. All this intensified the pressure on President Trump to give in.

A *Washington Post*/ABC News poll released on January 13, as the shutdown entered its fourth week, found that 53 percent of Americans said Trump and the Republicans in Congress were mostly responsible for the shutdown. Only 29 percent blamed Democrats in Congress, and 13 percent blamed all sides equally.[10]

"The public response had clear effects in Congress," journalist Perry Bacon reported.

> Congressional Republicans had been unified behind the president in the early stages of the shutdown, but cracks started to emerge as it dragged on. In public, this was demonstrated . . . by six Senate Republicans voting for legislation put forward by Senate Democrats that would fund the government without money for the wall. And, in private, disagreement with the president's strategy extended beyond those six. A meeting between Senate Republicans and Vice President Mike Pence . . . reportedly turned into a venting session, with some senators scolding Pence for the White House's strategy. Among the critics was Majority Leader Mitch McConnell, who has the power to bring forward legislation, whether Trump likes it or not.[11]

Unlike his past negotiations as a businessman, he had much less ability to intimidate and bulldoze his opponents. Many of them, including House Speaker Nancy Pelosi, D-Calif., and Senate Minority leader Chuck Schumer, D-N.Y., had solid constituencies of their own and they were very resistant and in some cases immune to Trump's bullying and blandishments. They also pointed out his inconsistencies and his frequent falsehoods—something he wasn't accustomed to.

"Donald Trump was elected president partly by assuring the American people that 'I alone can fix it,'" wrote Philip Rucker and Josh Dawsey in the *Washington Post* during January 2019 when the shutdown was a month old.

> But precisely two years into his presidency, the government is not simply broken—it is in crisis, and Trump is grappling with the reality

that he cannot fix it alone. Trump's management of the partial government shutdown—his first foray in divided government—has exposed as never before his shortcomings as a dealmaker.

The shutdown also . . . accentuated several fundamental traits of Trump's presidency: his shortage of empathy, in this case for furloughed workers; his difficulty accepting responsibility, this time for a crisis he had said he would be proud to instigate; his tendency for revenge when it comes to one-upping political foes; and his seeming misunderstanding of Democrats' motivations.[12]

Argued Republican strategist Mike Murphy, who regularly criticized Trump:

What really drove him [during the 2016 campaign] was "Art of the Deal" [a Trump book about his business career], that he could get stuff done in D.C. and deal with the knuckleheads. People saw him as some sort of business wizard. That's all disintegrating. It's like McDonald's not being able to make a hamburger.[13]

Author James B. Stewart observed in the *New York Times*:

With the government shut down over Mr. Trump's demand for funding a border wall, the loss of a Republican majority in the House of Representatives and scant legislative achievements beyond the 2017 tax cut, his presidency is emerging as a case study in how not to govern.[14]

Stewart added that Trump's most loyal supporters gave him "credit for being himself" and for taking on the liberal elites in Washington but this was outweighed by his many faults as a manager such as his inconsistencies, his unpredictability, and his insistence on antagonizing so many others.[15]

After the Democrat-controlled House and the Republican-controlled Senate agreed on compromise legislation to reopen the government in mid-February, Trump at first sent mixed messages about whether he would sign or veto the bill. He reluctantly signed it. It was clear that all along he had no endgame strategy for ending the shutdown, no bottom line. He knew how to provoke the fight, the easy part, but not how to end it.

Trump was the clear loser in the battle over the wall and the shutdown, and this contradicted the image he relished of always being the winner in everything he did.

THE CONFRONTATION in Washington didn't stop when the shutdown concluded.

Trump, stung by his legislative defeat, kept calling attention to what he called the national-security crisis at the U.S.–Mexican border. He said tens of thousands of illegal immigrants, many of them criminals, rapists and drug dealers, were flooding across the border and endangering national security. This appeared to be a huge exaggeration. Yes, migrants from Central America were trying to enter the United States. The overwhelming majority of them were not criminals. They simply wanted a better life for themselves and their families, and many were seeking asylum from oppression and violence back home.

But the exaggeration suited Trump's political purposes to exploit fears. He used the crisis argument to officially declare a national emergency on February 15, 2019. This declaration, he said, gave him unilateral authority to shift billions of dollars from different government accounts to the project of building a wall, even though Congress hadn't approved the funds. This was of questionable legality, since the Constitution gives Congress the power of the purse. A protracted court battle followed that hadn't been resolved as this book went to press.

But Trump repeatedly used the issue to appeal to his hardline base. "We're going to confront the national security crisis on our southern border, and we're going to do it one way or the other," he announced at the White House. "It's an invasion. We have an invasion of drugs and criminals coming into our country."[16]

Opposition Democrats condemned him. "This is plainly a power grab by a disappointed president, who has gone outside the bounds of the laws to try to get what he failed to achieve in the constitutional legislative process," House Speaker Pelosi and Senator Schumer argued in a joint statement.[17]

In the short term, Trump's ornery, disruptive stance during the shutdown showdown damaged his reputation. His weaknesses as a negotiator—his vacillation mixed with petulance and vituperation, his Manichaeism, and his utter lack of collegiality—had been exposed. And this emboldened his political adversaries and media critics to challenge him more than ever. This became clear when Congress, in February 2019, amid the shutdown debate, approved legislation preserving large tracts of public land from development, in defiance of the president's wishes.

In the longer term, the immigration issue continued to be a source of deep frustration for President Trump. He was being whipsawed by various courts of law as his anti-immigration policies were challenged. On January 15, 2019, a U.S. District Court judge in New York blocked Trump's attempt to add a citizenship question to the 2020 Census, widely seen as part of Trump's plan to make it harder for undocumented workers to get federal aid and vote. In June, the Supreme Court agreed with the judge in another defeat for Trump. Federal courts also stopped Trump's attempt to end a deferred-action program designed to protect young undocumented immigrants and stymied his attempt to bar some Central Americans from seeking asylum in the United States.

Trump's immigration policies were "creating more havoc," said Marielena Hincapié, executive director of the National Immigration Law Center. "Rather than solve problems, Trump is manufacturing 'crises.'"[18]

THE TRUMP ROLLER-COASTER RIDE led to considerable instability in his administration, a serious drawback that hindered efficiency. One-third of his top White House appointees left their jobs during his first year in office, far higher than normal. For his top 12 appointees, the departure rate was 50 percent. During his second year, the total turnover rate reached 83 percent, according to the Brookings Institution.

In late-2019, Trump was governing with his third White House chief of staff, his fourth national security adviser, second secretary of state, second attorney general, second defense secretary, third White House press secretary, and sixth communications director. And there was turnover in many other positions in Trump's administration.

He announced the resignation of Defense Secretary James Mattis amid evidence of a deep rift between the president and his military chief over many aspects of policy. These included the value of America's international alliances, which Mattis believed Trump was undermining. Trump also announced that he was ordering the immediate withdrawal of U.S. troops from Syria. This was widely criticized as a dangerous move toward instability in the region that would enhance the influence of Iran, Russia and terrorist groups, which would fill the void left by the U.S. pullout. Within a few weeks of his announcement, however, senior U.S. officials said Trump really didn't mean an immediate withdrawal of these troops and would be more cautious than he had indicated originally. It was another bewildering flip-flop.

The pressures intensified as 2019 progressed. One big reason was that the opposition Democrats now held the majority in the House based on their victories across the country in the midterm elections of November 2018. Many of the wins in individual House districts were considered rejections of Trump. As he knew, the ascendant House Democrats would be empowered by their majority status to investigate the president, his administration, his businesses, his family and his campaign. The House Democrats were also moving ever closer to impeaching Trump for alleged high crimes and misdemeanors. The president and his aides were clearly upset and thrown off balance.

AS HIS PROBLEMS INTENSIFIED, Trump seemed to grow more irate and more willing to violate the norms of Washington. A particular irritant, which sometimes seemed to be an obsession, was the investigation of Special Counsel Robert Mueller, appointed by the Justice Department to look into possible illegalities in the 2016 election. The suspicion was that Trump and his campaign operatives had cooperated with the Russians to ensure the defeat of Democratic nominee Hillary Clinton and that, as president, Trump obstructed justice to prevent Mueller's investigators from finding the truth.

President Trump didn't react well to the Mueller probe from the beginning. He was meeting with advisers in the Oval Office in May 2017 to discuss a replacement for James Comey, the FBI director whom Trump had just fired, when Attorney General Jeff Sessions left the room to take a phone call. When he returned, he told Trump that Robert Mueller had just been appointed as special counsel to assume control of the investigation into possible Russian interference and alleged obstruction by the president to thwart any probe. Trump immediately saw it as a big setback and a grave crisis. "Oh, my God," he declared as he slumped in his chair. "This is terrible. This is the end of my presidency. I'm fucked."[19]

He added: "Everyone tells me if you get one of these independent counsels, it ruins your presidency. It takes years and years, and I won't be able to do anything. This is the worst thing that ever happened to me."

Trump turned to his attorney general and said, "How could you let this happen, Jeff?" Sessions didn't reply.[20]

Mueller, a former FBI director, was actually appointed by Deputy Attorney General Rod Rosenstein who took over that authority after

Sessions recused himself from overseeing the investigation because of a potential conflict of interest—he had worked in Trump's 2016 campaign, which was being investigated. Trump never forgave Sessions for the recusal, arguing that Sessions should have kept control of the investigation and should have done everything he could to protect the president.

THE MUELLER PROBE officially started in May 2017, shortly after Trump became president, and lasted for more than 22 months. Trump regularly became rattled by the probe and the damage it might do to him. His resentment brought out his recklessness, his frustration with the legal and ethical limits on his power, his deceptiveness, and his desire for retribution against those he believed had wronged him. All this made matters worse by hardening the opposition and intensifying an atmosphere of rancor and hostility on all sides.

Mueller was an indefatigable, tough-minded prosecutor and he gradually amassed a record of guilty pleas and convictions of former and current Trump associates on a variety of offenses. Legal scholars speculated that Mueller might be closing in on members of Trump's family who had served as political advisers, and particularly daughter Ivanka Trump and her husband, Jared Kushner, who had moved into White House jobs. Such family prosecutions didn't happen, but the prospect deeply troubled the president for many months.

The Mueller investigation turned into the longest-running crisis of Trump's presidency, and one that he kept feeding through a campaign of sustained attacks, which were widely covered in the media. There were two Trump strategies—express vituperation in public to undermine Mueller, and attempt in private to prevent Mueller from interviewing Trump about alleged collusion and obstruction. Both strategies damaged the special counsel's investigation by raising doubts about its legitimacy, at least among Trump loyalists, and by limiting key information Mueller could obtain, especially in an interview with Trump.

Trump's two-pronged approach didn't advance principles of truth-telling or holding the nation's highest office-holders to account. But it was effective in protecting the president, which was the objective.[21]

Even though he was damaging Mueller's credibility with core Trump supporters, the president was on the wrong path with most Americans. Polls showed that a plurality of Americans believed Mueller more than Trump in late 2018 and early 2019, despite the president's sustained barrages against the special counsel. But the president, eager to shore up his base supporters and undermine the special counsel with such voters, continued his angry denials and vehement attacks on the investigation, which he repeatedly called a "witch hunt."

Typical of Trump's hyperbolic approach were his comments about Mueller in November 2018, the day after prosecutors said former Trump campaign chairman Paul Manafort had repeatedly lied to investigators and had violated the terms of a previous plea agreement with Mueller's office. Manafort had pleaded guilty in September 2018 to two counts of conspiracy related to his consulting work for Ukraine. But the special counsel said Manafort lied to prosecutors during his subsequent period of promised cooperation, and this violated Manafort's original agreement and opened him up to additional charges. By this point, several other former Trump campaign operatives had been charged with lying to federal investigators, including former senior campaign adviser and Trump's former White House national security adviser Michael Flynn, and campaign operatives Rick Gates and George Papadopoulos—a circumstance that continued to trouble the president.

On November 25, Trump resumed his barrage against Mueller and continued it for four straight days. "Did you ever see an investigation more in search of a crime?" Trump tweeted on November 28. He added that Mueller's investigation "has proven only one thing—there was NO collusion with Russia."[22]

Trump, again using Twitter, condemned Mueller's investigation as a "Phony Witch Hunt" conducted by a "conflicted prosecutor gone rogue" backed by a staff of "Angry Democrats."[23]

Trump also tweeted:

> The Fake News Media builds Bob Mueller up as a Saint, when in actuality he is the exact opposite. He is doing TREMENDOUS damage to our Criminal Justice System, where he is only looking at one side and not the other. Heroes will come of this, and it won't be Mueller and his . . . terrible Gang of Angry Democrats. Look at their past, and look where they come from. The now $30,000,000 Witch Hunt continues and they've got nothing but ruined lives.[24]

Mueller was an unusual opponent for Trump, unlike any other he had ever dealt with. The former FBI director wasn't interested in waging a public fight of dueling sound bites or tweets with Trump every day, sometimes every few hours. Instead, Mueller pursued his investigation privately and inexorably, and this rattled Trump because he couldn't do anything about it. Mueller also was very much unlike Trump in other ways: He wasn't interested in Trump's No. 1 life goal—making as much money as possible and using wealth as the main measurement of success and self-worth. And Mueller showed no interest in spewing insults and demeaning his adversaries, which Trump did with delight.

In a key legal move, Trump's lawyers, including Emmet Flood at the White House, wrote a memo explaining the legal arguments for protecting the president's executive privilege. These lawyers sent the document to the offices of Mueller and Rod Rosenstein, the senior Justice Department official who was overseeing the Mueller investigation, the *Post* reported.

Both sides agreed to a Trump interview with Mueller and it was scheduled for January 2018 but cancelled by John Dowd, then the president's lead attorney, fearing that Trump would make mistakes or lie. Mueller attempted repeatedly to reschedule the interview but the White House wouldn't agree.[25]

Trump's lawyers sent a large number of documents and channeled witnesses to the special counsel, attempting to make the case that no interview with the president was needed because whatever information he could provide was already under consideration.

At a meeting on March 5, 2018, at the special counsel's office in southwest Washington, Mueller raised the issue of a subpoena. And Trump's lawyers argued that the president had no obligation to talk to investigators. Mueller noted that he could issue a subpoena to force the president to appear before a grand jury. Dowd, the lead Trump lawyer, angrily replied, "You're screwing with the work of the president of the United States."[26] After that, the special counsel backed away from the subpoena idea and asked for a voluntary interview, which didn't happen.

Trump sent carefully prepared written answers to a list of questions from Mueller but declined to answer questions about his time in office, claiming executive privilege. And the president never did any kind of in-person interview with Mueller and his team. Trump's lawyers considered this a major victory since it spared Trump the possibility of committing perjury and didn't give Mueller ammunition directly from the president with which to embarrass or prosecute Trump.[27]

And the question of whether a president can be subpoenaed did not go to the Supreme Court, where the outcome would have been uncertain.

Trump's public attacks on Mueller again intensified. They were part of the now-familiar pattern of savaging his critics and often conveying false information.

This made matters worse for him by undermining his credibility, which was already in tatters for many Americans. The *Washington Post* found 6,420 cases in which Trump had made false or misleading statements of all kinds as of the autumn of 2018, less than two years into his presidency—an analysis that received wide circulation.[28] The *Post* also reported that most Americans no longer believed him, according to the newspaper's polls.[29] The numbers kept going up. By the end of 2018, the *Post* found that the president had spread 7,546 false or misleading statements during his first 700 days.[30] By June 2019, the number had gone up to more than 10,000 false or misleading statements by Trump.[31]

His use of false attacks and distortions were similar to the tactics used by Sen. Joe McCarthy (R-Wis.) in his anti-communist campaign of the 1950s. Speaking of McCarthy nearly 70 years ago, author Richard Rovere said the senator's spreading so many lies and unfounded charges made it difficult for anyone, including journalists, "to follow them all and easy for the average citizen to assume that below all the smoke there must be some fire," lending credence to his incendiary charges.[32] Trump had benefited from this dynamic for many years.

In late March 2019, after 22 months of investigation, Mueller sent his final report to the Justice Department, as required by law. He wasn't an independent counsel, but instead had the title of special counsel, so he couldn't release the report himself. Attorney General Barr reviewed the report for a few hours and rushed to release a summary of his own—saying Mueller concluded that Trump and his aides had not colluded with the Russian government even though the Kremlin meddled in the 2016 presidential election. This much was true. But Barr also reported: "[T]he evidence developed by the Special Counsel is not sufficient to establish that the President committed an obstruction-of-justice offense."[33]

This ran counter to Mueller's actual findings that Trump did attempt on multiple occasions to limit or shut down the investigation. Mueller said Trump's attempts to do this:

> were often carried out through one-on-one meetings in which the President sought to use his official power outside of official channels . . . The President's efforts to influence the investigation were mostly unsuccessful, but that is largely because the persons who surrounded the President declined to carry out orders or accede to his requests.[34]

Mueller actually drew no conclusions about whether Trump illegally obstructed justice, leaving the question for Congress to decide.

Trump was ready with a victory statement. "It was a complete and total exoneration," Trump told reporters, stretching the truth and attempting to portray a partial victory as complete vindication. "It's a shame that our country had to go through this. To be honest, it's a shame that your president had to go through this . . . This was an illegal takedown that failed."[35] Trump used the report to continue his story line of personal grievance, billing himself as the victim of a political establishment that deeply resented his challenges to the status quo.

Even after the investigation ended, Trump wouldn't let go. He insisted the probe was designed as the basis for a coup d'état to bring him down, and he pushed his Justice Department to investigate the investigators. He wanted to punish the government lawyers who had started the probe. "It was something like a vendetta," said political scientist Ross Baker.[36] No one could say where this investigation of the investigators would lead.

By refusing to move on, as other presidents would have surely done, he intensified the crisis atmosphere.

Leaders of the Democrat-controlled House of Representatives and several 2020 Democratic presidential candidates found plenty to criticize in Barr's summary of the report, adding to the polarization.

Rep. Jerry Nadler, D-N.Y., chairman of the House Judiciary Committee, wrote on Twitter that he would summon Attorney General Barr to testify about what Nadler called "very concerning discrepancies and final decision making at the Justice Department"—a reference to Barr's conclusion based on the Mueller report that Trump did not obstruct justice.[37] Barr declined to testify.

Mueller's team had by this point obtained indictments or convictions of a half-dozen former Trump aides in connection with the investigation. Most of these legal violations were for conspiracy or lying to investigators. Two dozen Russian intelligence operatives and other Russians had been charged in connection with election meddling.

Congressional investigators and media analysts, once they had a chance to read the Mueller report for themselves, discovered that the special counsel had produced a report that was very damning of Trump in many ways.

Mueller suggested that Trump had been eager to stop or limit the investigation but was blocked by advisers who felt his moves were potentially illegal, unwise or unethical. In the process, the advisers saved Trump from himself, according to the report.

A *New York Times* summary noted:

> The White House that emerges from more than 400 pages of Mr. Mueller's report is a hotbed of conflict infused by a culture of dishonesty—defined by a president who lies to the public and his own staff, then tries to get his aides to lie for him. Mr. Trump repeatedly threatened to fire lieutenants who did not carry out his wishes while they repeatedly threatened to resign rather than cross lines of propriety or law.
>
> At one juncture after another, Mr. Trump made his troubles worse, giving in to anger and grievance and lashing out in ways that turned advisers into witnesses against him. He was saved from an accusation of obstruction of justice, the report makes clear, in part because aides saw danger and stopped him from following his own instincts. Based on contemporaneous notes, emails, texts and F.B.I. interviews, the report draws out scene after scene of a White House on the edge.[38]

In one particularly vivid passage, the Mueller report noted that when then-Attorney General Sessions would not control or limit the jurisdiction of the special counsel, Trump decided to replace Mueller, which could be interpreted as an attempt to obstruct justice. On June 17, the president phoned White House counsel Donald F. McGahn II from Camp David and told him to have Deputy Attorney General Rosenstein fire Mueller because of what Trump called conflicts of interest, the Mueller report said.

McGahn wasn't buying it. He told the president that the supposed conflicts were "silly" and "not real" and they ended the conversation. But Trump, seething, called back and declared, "Mueller has to go. Call me back when you do it."[39]

McGahn decided he had to resign and drove to the White House to collect his belongings and submit his resignation. He told then-White House Chief of Staff Reince Priebus and senior Trump adviser Steve Bannon of his intentions and they urged him to stay on. McGahn changed his mind and remained for a while longer but it soon became clear to him that his rift with Trump couldn't be repaired.

Faced with this resistance from McGahn, according to the Mueller report, Trump told his former campaign manager Corey Lewandowski to give a message to Sessions ordering him to limit the scope of Mueller's investigation by focusing only on Russian interference in the 2016 election—a move designed to stop the probe into obstruction during the time Trump was president. Trump later denied this. The report said Lewandowski apparently didn't deliver the message because he never came face to face with Sessions. But Trump ratcheted up the pressure by criticizing his attorney general in an interview with the *New York Times*. At the end of 2018, as noted, he forced Sessions to resign and replaced him with Barr.

But the damage had been done. Trump found himself immersed in a crisis of confidence largely of his own making. He continued to label Mueller's probe a witch hunt and also refused to admit any mistakes, even though many of them, such as his frequent efforts to limit the investigation and his attempts to influence its outcome, were clearly spelled out by Mueller and in separate media accounts.

And the legal process would not end. Various federal, state and congressional investigations of Trump, his campaign and his business dealings continued. And Trump reacted in Nixonian fashion, stonewalling the release of information and declaring war on his political adversaries, especially majority Democrats in the House of Representatives who were ramping up several investigations of their own.

The comparisons with Watergate were stark. Law Professor Andrew Coan of the University of Arizona writes that Nixon's obstruction of justice was similar to Trump's behavior in trying to protect himself in the collusion-and-obstruction investigation by Special Counsel Mueller. "Nixon was not actually worried about national security or foreign relations as he claimed," Coan argued. "He was simply trying to protect his closest aides from criminal investigation and himself from untold political damage."[40]

When Nixon was pressured by Congress into releasing a transcript on August 5, 1974 of his damning conversation with key aide H.R. Haldeman, this became known as the "smoking gun" that proved obstruction of justice. Nixon resigned three days later rather than face impeachment. (See Nixon chapter.)

As Coan points out:

> A very similar case can be sketched [against President Trump]. Trump asked FBI Director James B. Comey to end the investigation of national security adviser Michael Flynn. Trump then fired Comey and applied unrelenting pressure on Attorney General Jeff Sessions to end the Mueller investigation. When Sessions wouldn't budge, Trump replaced him with an acting attorney general whose main qualification for office was his personal loyalty to the president. Finally, Trump nominated [William] Barr, a public—and it now turns out, an even fiercer private—critic of the Mueller investigation.[41]

There were other Nixon comparisons. "Some of Nixon's close aides thought that he was several people: polite and generous; thoughtful and impetuous; capable of exercising some progressive instincts; a hating, vindictive, crude man," wrote journalist Elizabeth Drew in a description that would apply equally to Trump.

> He needed, and sought, a great deal of flattery; his rages caused his aides to cower and hope that they would blow over. If a staff member did try to challenge his prejudices or dark side, Nixon would cut that person off.[42]

Both Nixon and Trump loved to embarrass their adversaries and saw enemies around every corner. They hated the mainstream news media and conducted or authorized aggressive campaigns to shatter the media's credibility. They considered themselves their own press agents and revolutionized presidential communication. Nixon pioneered the concept of controlling the White House's message, speaking to the country unfiltered by the media, and using pithy language and memorable visuals. These are the same techniques Trump is using today, updated by his constant use of Twitter and other social media and his preoccupation with communicating through the Trump-boosting conservative television network of Fox News.

Despite the Mueller furor, Trump was not paralyzed. In fact, he became an agent of change. On domestic issues, Trump mostly hewed to conservative policies and had some success working with a Congress controlled for his first two years by Republicans. During this period, the GOP enacted massive tax cuts, mostly for the wealthy and big corporations, and the Trump administration through executive action reduced federal regulations on businesses and imposed tariffs on some foreign countries' goods. The deficit burgeoned, but the stock market boomed and unemployment declined. Yet millions of workers complained that their incomes were stagnating because wages weren't keeping up with inflation and because of less demand for their skills. Many said they had to work two jobs to make the same money they used to make with one.

ON FOREIGN POLICY, the pattern was the same as on domestic issues. Trump was a disrupter who made a habit of creating a crisis and then using bluffs, bluster and bullying in order to get his way, with very mixed results.

In some ways, he broke with conservative orthodoxy and the conventional views of presidents and the major parties. Trump questioned the value of international agreements and organizations, including NATO, the alliance between the United States and European countries that had kept the peace with the Soviet Union since the end of World War II. He imposed a variety of tariffs on China, Mexico and other countries, adopting the kind of protectionist stance that his predecessors since World War II had rejected. He cozied up to dictators and authoritarian leaders including Vladimir Putin of Russia, Kim Jong Un of North Korea, and Xi Jinping of China.

He defied the conventional wisdom on how to deal with other countries by resorting to threats and brinkmanship instead of emphasizing cooperation and finding common ground.

Trump wasn't generating many international deals on peace, arms control, nuclear weapons or trade as he said he would. He was avoiding military confrontation but his critics said his bullying, bluster and brinkmanship would inevitably lead to a dangerous military encounter somewhere in the world. He rarely devised or revealed an exit strategy when he began a confrontation, so no one could be sure what he would settle for in resolving a particular crisis. The lack of clear goals from Trump made diplomacy more difficult.

Iran was a case in point. In May 2018, Trump removed the United States from a 2015 deal negotiated under President Barack Obama. Under the pact, Iran agreed to limit its nuclear program, which the United States said had been heading toward construction of nuclear weapons, in exchange for the U.S. lifting strong economic sanctions against the Tehran regime. Trump said it was a bad deal for the United States and gave up too much to Iran. Trump proceeded to reimpose sanctions, including restrictions aimed at stopping Iranian oil exports, and the Iranian economy deteriorated. Tensions between the two countries escalated.

In June 2019, Iran shot down an unmanned U.S. spy drone, which the Tehran regime said was in Iranian air space. The Americans said the drone was in international air space. Trump ordered retaliatory attacks on Iran but cancelled the strikes at the last minute. He explained that he learned that 150 people would have been killed, and this likely death toll seemed to be a disproportionate response to the downing of an unmanned drone.

Even some of his critics praised Trump for reversing course and stepping away from violence, even though he did it very late in the decision-making process. Others said he should have been more cautious from the start and seemed in a rush toward conflict before he considered all the facts, including the prospective death toll.

This was his pattern as president, which he used time and again: Rattle the saber and make threats, then back off at the last minute. It was a novel approach to crisis management but fraught with dangers, including the perception that Trump lacked the resolve to follow through and was bluffing.

Yet there could be positive results. Early in his presidency, Trump got into a harsh war of words with North Korean ruler Kim Jong Un over Pyongyang's provocative anti-ballistic missile tests and refusal to denuclearize the Korean Peninsula, a long-standing U.S. goal, and North Korea's development of a missile program that could threaten its neighbors. Trump derided Kim, a brutal dictator who had long been hostile to the United States, as "little rocket man" and Kim mocked Trump as a "dotard." When Kim continued testing missiles and nuclear technology, Trump warned that if war came he would rain "fire and fury" on North Korea. Yet the two men stepped back from the brink and met twice to get to know each other and attempt to find a peaceful way of resolving their differences.

Talks between the two broke down in early 2019 but Trump revived them, apparently on the spur of the moment, while he was visiting Asia in June 2019. During the trip, Trump tweeted the idea that he hoped to meet Kim in the heavily fortified Demilitarized Zone between the two Koreas on June 30. Kim agreed, and it resulted in a handshake seen around the world. Trump became the first sitting U.S. president to set foot in North Korea. This set the stage for resumed negotiations, according to White House officials.

THERE WAS ALSO Trump's negative impact on American culture. Trump "unfortunately has played the role of divider in chief," columnist David Ignatius wrote in the *Washington Post* just after the 2018 midterm election.[43]

> He tends to see himself as the victim in every drama, which makes it almost impossible to empathize with critics. When he sees a scab healing over a racial or ethnic wound, he often rips it off. He has turned resentment into a potent national movement.[44]

Trump's critics said this was no way to lead—or at least it wasn't the way America's most effective presidents had led in the past.

"There is an inherently parental role to being president of the United States," wrote Patti Davis, an author and daughter of Republican President Ronald Reagan and first lady Nancy Reagan.

> The person holding that office is supposed to know more than we do about dangers facing the country and the world, and is entrusted with making the appropriate decisions to keep us safe and secure. The president is supposed to keep us from falling. What happens when the president is the biggest child in the room—any room? It upends the natural order of things as surely as if a child's parents started throwing tantrums and talking like a second-grader.[45]

Patti Davis added:

> Children know how to scream and sulk; they don't know how to take control and restore order. They don't know how to plot out a responsible position and then act on it. A child occupies the White

House, and the world knows it. A friend's young son thought it was really funny when the president called someone "Horseface." He giggled when he saw the president on TV telling a reporter that her question was "stupid" and that all her questions are stupid. Nine-year-olds should be able to look up to the president of the United States, not feel that the president is one of them.[46]

As a crisis manager, "He's a bad planner but a good improviser," says political scientist Bill Galston, a former White House domestic-policy adviser to President Bill Clinton. " . . . He sheds strategies the way snakes shed skin. He is willing to say, 'What I said earlier doesn't hold up' So he changes and says what he said before doesn't matter. He is utterly unashamed to contradict himself." And his core supporters don't care as long as he moves toward the policy goals they want, such as lower taxes, less regulation and opposition to abortion.[47]

AS TRUMP BEGAN running for a second term, his path to re-election looked rocky. Only about 40 percent of the electorate was solidly committed to him. And he hadn't reached out effectively to other voters, such as the key voting blocs of suburban women, the college educated, African Americans and young people. All of them were turning against him.

In this difficult political environment, Trump managed to retain his hard-core supporters—nearly 90 percent of fellow Republicans approved of his job performance. They liked his attacks on the status quo and his handling of the economy. But he was derided by a similar percentage of Democrats and was increasingly seen by swing and independent voters as a narcissist with temperament problems whose approach and policies were too risky.

This dynamic showed that Americans eventually lose their fascination with even the most clever dramatic programming and the most compelling celebrities. Trump's White House reality show, which he created and produced and in which he starred, was becoming more than a bit tiresome.

Trump had violated some of the fundamental norms of leadership and crisis management that have applied to the American presidency since the founding of the Republic. Most of these traits were embodied by Abraham Lincoln, usually rated by historians as the best president. "What Lincoln had, it seems to me, was an extraordinary amount of emotional intelligence," historian Doris Kearns Goodwin has observed. "He was able to acknowledge his errors and learn from his mistakes to a remarkable degree. He was careful to put past hurts behind him and never allowed wounds to fester."[48]

This emotional intelligence is a quality that Donald Trump seems to lack. Certainly he has shown very little of it during his presidency, to the detriment of his leadership and to the consternation of most Americans.

Precis

Donald Trump tried to establish a new paradigm for presidential crisis management that in many ways undermined his leadership. He manufactured many crises, creating an atmosphere of constant turmoil and uncertainty from which, he argued, only he could extricate the nation. He specialized in excess, taking bold action but going too far, trying to adapt to changing circumstances but rarely setting forth clear policies or principles beyond a few slogans such as "Make America Great Again." He pointed to a strong economy as his main argument for reelection. He persevered in a handful of objectives and achieved a spotty record of success. At the same time, he undermined his own credibility. Everything, in the end, was about him.

Notes

1. Author's interview with Ross Baker, May 24, 2019.
2. Author's interview with Ross Baker, May 24, 2019.
3. Dan Mangan, "President Trump Told Lesley Stahl He Bashes Press 'To Demean You and Discredit You so . . . No One Will Believe' Negative Stories about Him," CNBC, May 22, 2018, cnbc.com/2018/05/22/trump-told-lesley-stahl-he-bashes-press-to-discredi-negative-stories.
4. Julian Zelizer, "Nancy Pelosi Is Making a Big Mistake on Impeachment," cnn.com, May 22, 2019, cnn.com/2019/05/22/opinions/nancy-pelosi-is-making-a-big-mistake-on-impeachment.
5. Zelizer, ibid.
6. Toluse Olorunnipa, "Policy Blitz Makes Border Key to Trump's 2020 bid," *Washington Post*, June 3, 2019, p. A2.
7. Ashley Parker and Robert Costa, "Trump's Big Role: Narrator in Chief," *Washington Post*, May 21, 2019, p. A1.
8. Richard Norton Smith, "Donald J. Trump," Interview Contained in Brian Lamb, Susan Swain and C-SPAN, *The Presidents: Noted Historians Rank America's Best—and Worst—Chief Executives*, New York: Public Affairs, 2019, p. 495.

9. Douglas Brinkley, "Donald J. Trump," Interview Contained in Brian Lamb, Susan Swain and C-SPAN, *The Presidents: Noted Historians Rank America's Best—and Worst—Chief Executives*, New York: Public Affairs, 2019, p. 488.
10. Philip Rucker and Josh Dawsey, "2 Years in, President Is at a Loss as Dealmaker," *Washington Post*, January 21, 2019, p. A1.
11. Perry Bacon, Jr. "Why Trump Blinked," FiveThirtyEight.com, January 25, 2019, fivethirtyeight.com/features/government-shutdown-ends.
12. Rucker and Dawsey, ibid.
13. Rucker and Dawsey, ibid.
14. James B. Stewart, "Why Trump's Unusual Leadership Style Isn't Working in the White House," *New York Times*, January 10, 2019, nytimes.com/2019/01/10/business/trump-staff-turnover-leadership.html.
15. Stewart, ibid.
16. Peter Baker, "Trump Declares a National Emergency, and Provokes a Constitutional Clash," *New York Times*, February 15, 2019, p. A1, https://www.nytimes.com/2019/02/15/us/politics/national-emergency-trump.html.
17. Michael Tackett, "Key Takeaways from Trump's Decision to Use a National Emergency to Build a Border Wall," *New York Times*, Feb. 15, 2019, nytimes.com/2019/02/15/us/politics/emergency-border-wall.html.
18. David Nakamura, "Courts Thwart Trump's Hard-line Border Agenda," *Washington Post*, January 16, 2019, p. A6.
19. Peter Baker and Maggie Haberman, "A Portrait of the White House and its Culture of Dishonesty," *New York Times*, p. 1, April 18, 2019, nytimes.com/2019/04/18/us/politics/white-house-mueller-report.html. Also see Matt Apuzzo and Adam Goldman, "The Mueller Report Is 448 Pages Long. You Need to Know These 7 Key Things." *New York Times*, April 19, 2019, p. A11, nytimes.com/2019/04/18/us/politics/mueller-report-pdf-takeaways-html.
20. Baker and Haberman, ibid. Also see John T. Bennett, "Trump Feared 'One of These Independent Counsels,' He Got Something Else," *Roll Call*, April 19, 2019, rollcall.com/news/trump-feared-one-independent-counsels-got-something-else.
21. Mark Mazzetti and Katie Benner, "Mueller Finds No Trump–Russia Conspiracy but Stops Short of Exonerating President on Obstruction," *New York Times*, March 24, 2019, nytimes.com/2019/03/24/us/politics/mueller-report-summary.html.
22. John Wagner, "Trump Attacks Mueller Probe for Fourth Straight Morning, Asks if It Will 'Go on Forever.'" *Washington Post*, November 27, 2018, washingtonpost.com/politics/trump-attacks-mueller-probe-for-fourth-straight-morning.
23. Eileen Sullivan, "Trump Lobs Insults at Special Counsel One Day After Prosecutors Say Manafort Lied," *New York Times*, November 27, 2018, nytimes.com/2018/11/27/us/politics/trump-mueller-manafort.html.
24. Sullivan, ibid.
25. Rucker and Dawsey ibid.
26. Rucker and Dawsey, ibid.

27. Rucker and Dawsey, ibid.
28. Glenn Kessler, Salvador Rizzo and Meg Kelly, "President Trump Has Made 6,420 False or Misleading Claims over 649 Days," *Washington Post*, November 2, 2018, washingtonpost.com/politics/2018/11/02/president-trump-has-made-false-or-misleading-claims-over-days/?utm_term=.a03e0ae0950e.
29. Kessler, Rizzo, and Kelly, ibid.
30. Kessler, Rizzo, and Kelly, ibid.
31. Paul Farhi, "Lies? The News Media Is Starting to describe Trump's 'falsehoods' that Way." *Washington Post*, June 6, 2019, Page C3.
32. Alonzo Hamby, *Man of the People: A Life of Harry S. Truman*, New York: Oxford University Press, 1995, p. 566.
33. Baker and Haberman, ibid.
34. Baker and Haberman, ibid.
35. Baker and Haberman, ibid.
36. "It Was Something": Author's interview with Ross Baker, May 25, 2019.
37. Kenneth T. Walsh, "Judiciary Committee Chair Wants Attorney General William Barr to Testify," U.S. News & World Report, March 25, 2019, https://www.usnews.com/news/national-news/articles/2019-03-25/judiciary-committee-chair-wants-attorney-general-william-barr-to-testify.
38. Baker and Haberman, ibid.
39. Baker and Haberman, ibid. Also see Will Rahn, "10 Times Trump May Have Obstructed Justice, According to Mueller," CBS News, July 23, 2019, cbsnews.com/news/obstruction-of-justice-10-times-trump-may–have obstructed-justice.
40. Andrew Coan, "William Barr's Memo on the Mueller Probe is Baseless and Dangerous," *Washington Post*, Dec. 20, 2018, https://www.washingtonpost.com/opinions/why-william-barr-is-wrong-on-the-mueller-probe/2018/12/20/a6d57a20-049f-11e9-b5df-5d3874f1ac36_story.html.
41. Coan, ibid.
42. Elizabeth Drew, *Richard M. Nixon*, New York: Times Books, 2007, p. 29.
43. David Ignatius, "What Would the Ghosts of 1918 Tell us Today?" *Washington Post*, November 9, 2018, p. A25.
44. Ignatius, ibid.
45. Patti Davis, "The Child in the White House," *Washington Post*, December 18, 2018, p. A19.
46. Davis, ibid.
47. Author's interview with Bill Galston, May 7, 2019.
48. Diane Coutu, "Leadership Lessons from Abraham Lincoln," *Harvard Business Review*, April 2009, hbr.org/2009/04/leadership-lessons-from-abraham-lincoln.

EPILOGUE

History shows that every president must deal with a crisis at some point. This premise holds true not only in cases of war and peace, such as George H.W. Bush's Persian Gulf War and George W. Bush's response to the terrorist attacks of 9/11, but also in other types of crisis. These include Franklin Roosevelt's initial decisions aimed at pulling the nation out of the Depression and Richard Nixon attempting to survive the Watergate scandal. They include Ronald Reagan's near-death experience when he was shot and Donald Trump's efforts to defeat an investigation into possible collusion with Russia during the 2016 campaign and attempts to impeach him.

Americans want their presidents to keep their campaign promises. But Americans also understand that when the promises are overtaken by reality, and when intended solutions don't work, it's time for a correction. Just as important, crises regularly erupt that are wholly unanticipated, and they require a president to use good judgment in adjusting to the new conditions. The best modern presidents, such as Franklin Roosevelt, Harry Truman, John F. Kennedy, Ronald Reagan and George H.W. Bush, did this well. Those who stuck to bad decisions, weren't flexible and refused to change, such as Lyndon Johnson, Richard Nixon and Jimmy Carter, by and large failed in crisis management.

There is a lesson here for Donald Trump in his presidency of perpetual crisis. He must decide whether some of his more polarizing policies should be modified, such as his obsession with a border wall between the

United States and Mexico. This has angered and upset many immigrants and lifelong citizens who want the nation to welcome the downtrodden, the persecuted and the poor. He might also consider modifying his commitment to raising tariffs, which has alienated many U.S. allies, and his brand of nasty, attack politics that is widening the nation's schisms and adding to our culture of contempt for people who act, look and think differently.

Nixon vs. Clinton

One particularly important historical theme stands out today in assessing presidents in crisis—the question of impeachment. In modern times, Richard Nixon and Bill Clinton were forced to deal with the serious possibility of impeachment and removal from office, as Andrew Johnson had to do in a much different time, after the Civil War in the 1860s. Donald Trump also has been facing the specter of impeachment.

Each president handled his particular impeachment crisis differently. Nixon resigned rather than face impeachment. Johnson, Clinton and Trump were impeached by the House of Representatives but managed to stay in office. The experiences of Nixon and Clinton are instructive today.

Why did Nixon exit in disgrace in 1974, while Clinton soldiered on in 1998 and 1999 in the thick of his own scandal? "One of the most important realities of our history is that Watergate came on the heels of the Vietnam War," says Lara Brown, director of the Graduate School of Political Management at George Washington University.

> The difficulty of war—the large loss of life combined with the sense that there was no way to win—and the release of the Pentagon Papers—in which many in the public realized they had been "lied to" about the war—contributed to the decline of trust in government which had begun in the latter half of the 1960s and it is evident in the polling.[1]

This distrust made it very difficult, perhaps impossible, for Nixon to hold onto his job. He seemed to embody the reality of the credibility gap.

Clinton, accused of obstruction of justice and perjury for testifying falsely about his affair with former White House intern Monica Lewinsky, fought impeachment all the way and, although the House did impeach him in 1998, the Senate acquitted him of all charges in 1999.

Under Clinton, trust in government was increasing, at least for a while—and this made a crucial difference. "Some of this rise in trust was about the productivity of the working relationship between the Republicans in Congress and the Clinton White House," says Lara Brown. "In essence, people were pleased that legislation was passing and compromises were agreed to across the aisle, from balancing the budget to welfare reform."[2] Americans concluded that the system was working well enough under Clinton that they should keep him in office, and the Senate agreed.

Political scientist Brandon Rottinghaus points out that the Watergate scandal, specifically, intensified the rising mistrust in government that was already there because of the lies and deceptions surrounding the Vietnam war and the overreach of Lyndon Johnson's Great Society in attempting to remake America through federal intervention. "So, the outcome of the resignation of the president [Nixon] was surprising but not shocking," he says.

In addition, Rottinghaus notes:

> The economy was a strong factor in the survival of Bill Clinton. With the U.S. economy booming, voters were reluctant to turn an incumbent president out of office. Party unity was another factor in the survival of Clinton. Nixon gradually lost the support of his Republican allies while Clinton maintained relatively strong support from his Democratic allies in Congress.[3]

Nixon's case was based on the abuse of political power while Clinton's was based on personal immorality. Americans saw a big difference, and most didn't think a presidential sin rose to the level of a serious political trespass or act of corruption that justified removal from office. Clinton's job approval rating, in fact, was 66 percent when he left the White House, a testament to his superior political skills and the public's sense that his personal failings weren't enough to force him out. Nixon's approval rating was 24 percent, indicating that the country believed his political and legal transgressions were much more serious.

Finally, Clinton's sexual impropriety came to light prior to the emergence of the "Me Too" movement of 2018 and 2019—in which women rebelled against sexual harassment, sexual abuse and improper behavior by men. Today, women's allegations of such conduct are taken more seriously than in the past. It's unlikely that Clinton would have survived a Senate vote today.

In the 2016 election, the country chose Donald Trump as president despite being well aware of his distortions and falsehoods, his inexperience in government, his past adulteries, and his vindictive nature. It's a fact that Trump lost the popular vote to Hillary Clinton, but he did win a clear victory in the Electoral College, which is determinative. And it appears that his coalition, even though it is less than a majority, has been holding together.

As the 2020 campaign began, many Americans—about 40 percent of the electorate, according to the polls—remained loyal to Trump. They approved of how he handled the economy and liked the way he was shaking up Washington and representing the white middle class and working class, which were still feeling left out and ignored by Washington elites. His goal appeared to be to "incite, agitate and irritate" his adversaries, which in turn inspired his core constituents to defend him as strongly as ever, said political scientist Ross Baker.[4]

In dealing with the prospect of impeachment, as shown earlier in this book, Trump spent two years undermining special counsel Robert Mueller's investigation of corruption and branding it as a "witch hunt," and he succeeded in damaging Mueller's credibility with Trump's core supporters. But, as with Nixon in the end, the president's evasiveness and distortions in dealing with Mueller left an ugly blemish on his presidency and further alienated many Americans from politics and government.

"Trump has an extraordinarily grandiose sense of what his power is about," historian Julian Zelizer says.

> He does not feel constrained by the norms and traditions that have held other presidents in check. He has now brought on board an attorney general, William Barr, who for years has been a proponent of a muscular executive branch in which the President has few formal limits. The combination in the Oval Office has produced explosive results.[5]

DURING LATE SEPTEMBER 2019, a huge political bombshell shook Trump's White House. It was the revelation, exposed by a federal whistleblower who was publicly unidentified at that time, about a July 25, 2019 phone call between Trump and the newly elected Ukrainian President Volodymyr Zelensky. A transcript of this call, demanded by House Democrats and provided by the administration, showed that Trump asked Zelensky to do him a "favor" by conducting a corruption investigation of Joe Biden, then the leading Democratic candidate to challenge Trump in 2020, and his son Hunter Biden, who was involved in business activities in Ukraine.[6]

Congressional investigators pointed out that at the time of the call, the Trump administration had suddenly suspended a multi-million dollar military aid package to Ukraine that the new government in Kiev desperately needed to ward off a threat from Russia. This appeared to be a "quid pro quo"—what House Speaker Pelosi later called bribery, which majority Democrats in the House considered an impeachable offense. Trump's aides also dangled a high-visibility meeting between Trump and Zelensky in exchange for the Biden investigation, Democrats said, based on testimony from witnesses. Such exchanges were ways to pressure the Ukrainian government to order the Biden probe and thereby help Trump's reelection by tainting one of his chief rivals. Democrats charged that this amounted to Trump inviting a foreign country to interfere in a U.S. election.[7]

Trump argued, unconvincingly, that he withheld the aid in order to persuade America's European allies to come up with more assistance to Ukraine so the United States could contribute less. Critics also accused the Trump administration of conducting a cover-up of the phone call, triggering comparisons to Nixon and Watergate. Trump denied this and said he was the victim of another "witch hunt" such as the Robert Mueller investigation of alleged collusion between Russia and the Trump campaign during the 2016 election.[8]

The revelations were enough for Pelosi, in late September, to announce the start of an official impeachment investigation of the president, which she had up to then been unwilling to begin. But after the whistleblower's disclosures and related damaging revelations, Pelosi and other Democratic leaders who controlled the House pressed ahead to determine whether to impeach President Trump by charging him with grave misconduct which would meet the constitutional standard of "high crimes and misdemeanors."

The chairmen of three House committees quickly subpoenaed Secretary of State Mike Pompeo and other Trump officials to provide documents related to the congressional probes into whether Trump improperly pressured the Ukrainian president to investigate what Trump said were corrupt practices in Ukraine involving Joe Biden and Hunter Biden.

It was the start of an all-out war between the congressional Democrats and the White House, amounting to still another crisis and the most important defining moment for President Trump up to that point. This became a prime example of Trump's approach to crisis management in both its positive and negative aspects.

Pelosi warned that if the administration refused to honor the subpoenas or declined to allow witnesses to testify, it would amount to obstruction of justice, which would in itself be an impeachable offense. But on October 8, 2019, Trump served notice that he wouldn't cooperate. His White House counsel Pat Cipollone wrote an eight-page letter to Pelosi and other Democratic leaders condemning the impeachment inquiry as partisan and illegitimate. Pelosi replied that Trump was making things worse for himself by obstructing justice and vowed that the probe would proceed to its conclusion no matter how angry or offended the president seemed to be.[9]

The broader point was that Trump was precipitating a constitutional crisis by attempting to expand executive power across the board. And he was not respecting the authority of the legislative branch of government, which the Constitution says should be co-equal to the executive. Other presidents had greatly expanded executive power on rare occasions during wartime, as with Abraham Lincoln, or when there was a grave economic calamity, as with Franklin Roosevelt. But Trump had no such existential crisis to deal with, and he vastly overreached, intent on strengthening his personal authority as much as possible without a higher cause.

As of early October, polls showed that Americans were deeply and almost evenly divided on whether to impeach and remove Trump.

His reaction to the impeachment inquiry illustrated his overall strategy for dealing with a crisis and illustrated the worst aspects of his pugnacious approach. His harshness and vindictiveness reminded Trump critics of why they disliked him so much to begin with, and reinforced their opposition to him, energizing the Democratic base against him. As always when he was in political trouble, his reaction was to attack, deflect, fume, and attack again. He was defiant, exasperated and combative in the extreme, and he depicted himself as the victim of dark conspiracies.

Trump, aiming to stir up anger among his supporters and rally them to his side, condemned the leading impeachers in Congress as "savages," compared the whistleblower to a spy who was guilty of treason, and denounced the "fake" news media for attempting to force him from office. He also dismissed the investigation as a "witch hunt"—the same words he had used to describe the Mueller investigation. He demanded the resignation of Rep. Adam Schiff, D-Calif, chairman of the House Intelligence Committee, and he called Schiff "shifty" and a "lowlife" who committed treason by criticizing the president and, in Trump's view, distorting the president's version of events.

His two angry news conferences with the visiting president of Finland on October 2 showed a president who was off balance and full of grievances, alienating people and groups he would need to thwart impeachment. He lashed out repeatedly and furiously at his adversaries, including the "fake" and "corrupt" media and leaders of the House impeachment inquiry. His vitriol, his inability to control his temper, and his paranoia were stunning. His aides said privately that he was furious because he considered the impeachment effort a purely partisan move by Trump haters to unfairly remove him from office—a sort of coup d'etat.[10]

His unhinged performances at these two news conferences—typical of how he handled the impeachment crisis—reminded me of Captain Queeg as played by Humphrey Bogart in *The Caine Mutiny*. In this film, Queeg tried to explain to a Navy court why his officers removed him from command during a storm. Driven by the pressure of the moment and a deep sense of victimhood, he revealed an imbalanced and erratic nature during the climactic courtroom scene. The only thing missing in Trump's performances were the ball bearings that Queeg rolled obsessively in his right palm during his testimony.

Trump insisted that his senior White House advisers, members of the Cabinet, and friends and associates outside government all jump on his bandwagon of recrimination and rancor. Unquestioning support for Trump and a willingness to viciously attack his critics became loyalty tests for him. This scorched-earth approach further offended his opponents, unsettled some fellow Republicans who believed he was making their political lives immeasurably more difficult, and deepened the news media's hostility.

Trump's constant offensive differed markedly from the strategy of Bill Clinton when he faced his own impeachment crisis. Clinton, as noted previously in this book, at first lied but then admitted wrongdoing in his sexual relationship with Monica Lewinsky. And Clinton apologized profusely for it. During his impeachment crisis, he compartmentalized the government's response, insisting that his lawyers deal with impeachment while his other White House staffers and the rest of his administration proceeded with the business of government. In personal terms, Clinton insisted that he was being treated unfairly, but he was mostly cool and collected and never accused opponents of treason. He portrayed himself as still doing his job for the people even under the enormous pressure of impeachment. It worked. While Clinton was impeached by the Republican-led House in December 1998, he was acquitted by the Republican-controlled Senate in February 1999 and he remained in office. Clinton's approval rating eventually rebounded.

Trump's response to the threat of impeachment was closer to Richard Nixon's. As the *New York Times* pointed out in an editorial entitled "The Only Option" on September 29, 2019, Nixon's strategy was fundamentally flawed. He refused to admit wrongdoing even when the evidence mounted against him. He and his lawyers stonewalled Congress and refused to give up important documents and transcripts even when under congressional subpoena, until ordered to do so by the courts. Meanwhile, Nixon and his supporters regularly talked about Watergate and condemned his would-be impeachers, just as Trump and his supporters did in his own impeachment crisis 45 years later. In the end, Nixon's credibility and effectiveness were shattered and, as the House moved to impeach him, he resigned in August 1974.

Trump's Nixonian crisis management put him in dangerous political territory. His defiance, his ridicule of adversaries, his distortion of the facts, his lack of contrition, and his disdain for civility and the norms of Washington hurt him badly.

On the positive side, he attempted to portray himself as working for the American people despite the impeachment proceedings, as Clinton had done. Among his techniques were staging events at places where the economy was doing well to congratulate himself, visiting U.S. troops, and meeting with foreign leaders. "I'm working my ass off," Trump announced at a rally in Sunrise, Florida on November 26.[11]

Trump continued to shake up the status quo with his attacks on his adversaries, foreign and domestic. "He believes being the disruptor is the end reason he was elected and what he was sent to Washington to do—drain the swamp," said Republican pollster Bill McInturff.[12]

As the impeachment inquiry proceeded that fall in the House Intelligence Committee, more U.S. officials and former officials painted a picture of a rogue foreign policy being conducted by Trump surrogates such as former New York Mayor Rudy Giuliani. The goal was apparently to circumvent government employees and lifelong diplomats whom Trump felt were trying to undermine him. Perhaps if he had listened to the warnings from inside the government about mixing foreign policy with partisan maneuvering and political deal-making, he might have avoided at least some allegations that he abused the power of the presidency to enhance his reelection prospects.[13]

Political scientist William Galston, a former White House adviser to Bill Clinton, told me in late November 2019 after the Intelligence Committee's impeachment hearings had concluded, that Trump's "lack of understanding of the Constitution" made him "unfit to be president." This view was widely shared among Democrats. "He says being president means he can do anything he wants," Galston noted.[14]

"He could have restrained his itchy Twitter finger but that's to ask the impossible," Galston said when I asked him what Trump should have done differently.

Mike McCurry, a Democratic strategist who worked as President Bill Clinton's White House press secretary, told me, "There were umpteen numbers of things he could have done that would have slowed the process. But that's not what the guy is. Whatever a conventional politician would do, he would do the opposite."[15]

This harsh pugnacity may have increased the zeal of those who wanted him to disrupt the status quo but at the same time it intensified the outrage of his adversaries. The net result was to push congressional Democrats ever closer to impeaching him.

On December 3, 2019, the Democratic majority on the House Intelligence Committee voted along party lines to forward a scathing anti-Trump report to the House Judiciary Committee. This report accused Trump of abuse of power in his attempted coercion of the Ukrainian president to damage Joe Biden as a presidential rival, and obstruction of Congress in blocking testimony and cooperation from key administration officials. The report triggered a fierce partisan debate in the Judiciary Committee about whether to pass specific articles of impeachment.

The Judiciary panel, filled with Democrats who wanted to rein in Trump's excesses and punish him, settled on two articles of impeachment on December 10. One article declared that Trump "abused the powers of the Presidency" through his Ukrainian gambit, and the second article accused him of trying to cover up his transgressions by obstructing congressional investigations into his dealings with Ukraine. The committee's Democratic leaders, presenting the case for the articles, said Trump would "remain a threat to national security and the Constitution if allowed to remain in office."[16]

Trump continued to make things worse for himself by baiting his adversaries and hardening their feelings against him. After Trump repeatedly derided House Speaker Pelosi and what he called the "radical" Democrats in Congress, Pelosi abandoned her initially cautious approach and announced her opposition to the president. "Our democracy is what is at stake," she told reporters on December 5. "The president leaves us no choice but to act, because he is trying to corrupt, once again, the election for his own benefit."[17]

Constitutional law scholar Laurence H. Tribe wrote, "The impeachment and removal of this president are necessary because Trump has been revealed as a serial abuser of power, whose *pattern* of behavior . . . makes clear he will repeat the same sequence again and again."

> Today, it's soliciting the help of Ukraine (and China and, yet again, Russia), both behind the scenes and out in the open, to attack the integrity of the next presidential election. Tomorrow, it could be seeking the help of foreign hackers to wage cyberwar on election machinery.[18]

Tribe added:

> A president whose Justice Department says he cannot be indicted, whose White House counsel says he cannot even be investigated, and whose lawyers say he can block the executive branch from participating in the impeachment process is a president who has become a dictator. None of us can feel safe in such a regime.[19]

Tribe also wrote separately that Trump had become "a lawless president, one who treats the Constitution as no big deal, impeachment as illegitimate and the powers of the presidency as limitless."[20]

Public opinion remained deeply split. A CNN poll conducted by SSRS, released on November 26, 2019, found that half of Americans said Trump should be impeached and removed from office, the same number as in October prior to the hearings. Forty-three percent said he should not be impeached and removed from office, the same number as a month earlier. Fifty-four percent of Americans disapproved of the job Trump was doing and 42 percent approved, about the same as a month earlier. Half of Americans had concluded that Trump demeaned his office and damaged the presidency—a very negative historical legacy.[21]

On December 13, the Democrat-controlled House Judiciary Committee voted along party lines 23 to 17 to approve two articles of impeachment accusing Trump of abuse of power and obstruction of Congress. The charges stemmed from his phone conversation with the Ukrainian president in July.[22]

Trump ratcheted up his criticism to blistering levels, repeating the same charges being made against him but directing them at the Democrats. On the eve of the House vote, he publicly released a six-page letter to Pelosi in which he said his opponents were "interfering in America's elections," "subverting America's democracy," and "obstructing justice," and he said the impeachment was part of an "illegal, partisan attempted coup."[23]

This presidential diatribe caused Democrats to dig in deeper. The full House, also controlled by Democrats, approved the two Judiciary Committee impeachment articles the following week, on December 18, mostly along party lines, sending the matter to the Republican-controlled Senate for trial. The House vote was 230 to 197 to impeach Trump for abuse of power, and 229 to 198 to impeach him for obstruction of Congress.

With these votes, Trump became only the third president to be impeached, along with Andrew Johnson and Bill Clinton.

The battle over impeachment and removal illustrated the deep partisanship that was infecting American life. Trump added to it by ferociously attacking his critics, distorting the truth, stonewalling Congress by refusing to provide information and keeping his aides from testifying before various committees, rejecting compromise on many issues, and constantly expanding executive power in defiance of Congress. In short, his pugnacious and narcissistic management of the crisis was a failure.

Historian Joseph J. Ellis, wrote in December, as the House prepared to impeach Trump, that the president's transgressions went far behind the formal charges of abuse of power and obstruction of Congress.

"The real charge against Trump...is that his entire presidency has been conducted on the belief that he stands above the law, is an elected monarch," Ellis wrote. "At issue is nothing less than preservation of the republican framework of the Constitution."[24]

As the impeachment drama intensified, Trump reverted to form and generated another crisis. Without getting support from Congress or U.S. allies abroad, Trump ordered the killing of Iranian Maj. Gen. Qassim Suleimani, who was identified by U.S. intelligence officials as the coordinator of terrorist acts against the United States. The lethal mission, carried out on Jan. 3, 2020 by U.S. drones, triggered a January 8 retaliatory missile attack by Iran's government on bases housing U.S. soldiers in Iraq. In a stroke of luck for the Americans, the Iranian attack caused no U.S. deaths but the episode resulted in the further deterioration of relations between Washington and Tehran. Some critics suspected that Trump was using the Suleimani killing to divert attention from impeachment and rally support for himself as commander in chief. But the Suleimani strike actually heightened concerns about Trump's judgment, impulsiveness and belligerence.

As this book went to press, the Republican-controlled Senate was moving toward acquitting Trump of the House impeachment charges with highly contentious partisan votes. But it was clear that the president's political survival had come at enormous cost. The impeachment crisis had brought him disgrace and left an ugly stain on the Trump presidency that no one could erase.

Notes

1. Lara Brown as quoted in Lesley Kennedy, "Why Clinton Survived Impeachment While Nixon Resigned After Watergate," History.com, October 1, 2018, history.com/news/clinton-impeachment-lewinsky-scandal-nixon-resigned-watergate.
2. Lara Brown as quoted in Kennedy, ibid.
3. Brandon Rottinghaus as quoted in Kennedy, ibid.
4. Author's interview with Ross Baker, May 24 2019.
5. Julian Zelizer, "Trump-Congress Confrontation Goes to Defcon 1," CNN.com, May 8, 2019, cnn.com2019/05/08/opinions/trump-congress-goes-to-defcon-1.
6. Karoun Demirjian, Elise Viebeck, Rosalind S. Helderman and Matt Zapotosky, "Whirlwind Week of Gripping Testimony Wraps Up," *Washington Post*, November 22, 2019, Page A1.

7. Demirjian et al., ibid.
8. Demirjian at al.
9. Alana Abramson and Tessa Berenson, "Inside the White House's Struggle to Address Impeachment," *Time*, October 30, 2019, www.time.com/5713064/white-house-congress-impeachment.
10. John Wagner, Felicia Sonmez and Colby Itkowitz, "Trump Lashes Out at Impeachment Inquiry in Fiery News Conference," *Washington Post*, October 3, 2019, Page A1.
11. Philip Rucker, "Trump Borrows Clinton Playbook," *Washington Post*, November 30, 2019, Page A1.
12. Author's interview with Bill McInturff, December 23, 2019.
13. Michael Gerson, "Using Power to Keep Power," *Washington Post*, November 22, 2019, Page A19.
14. Author's interview with William Galston, November 2, 2019.
15. Author's interview with Mike McCurry, November 25, 2019.
16. Mike DeBonis, John Wagner, Rachel Bade and Toluse Olorunnipa, "House Introduces Two Articles of Impeachment: Charges of Abuse of Power, Obstruction," *Washington Post*, December 11, 2019, Page A1.
17. Quoted in Eugene Robinson, "Trump is Impeaching Himself," *Washington Post*, December 6, 2019, Page A23.
18. Laurence H. Tribe, "The Democrats' Dangerous False Choice," *Washington Post*, December 8, 2019, Page A25.
19. Tribe, ibid.
20. Laurence H. Tribe, "Don't Let McConnell Hold a Sham Trial," *Washington Post*, December 17, 2019, Page A19.
21. Jennifer Agiesta, "CNN Poll: No Change in Views on Impeachment After Public Hearings," www.cnn.com/2019/11/26/politics/cnn-poll-impeachment-views/index.html.
22. John Wagner and Colby Itkowitz, "Impeachment Live Updates: House Judiciary Panel Passes Two Articles of Impeachment Against Trump," December 13, 2019, www.washingtonpost.com/politics/trump-impeachment-live-updates-trump-praises-republican-defenders-as-warriors/2019/12/13.
23. Michael D. Shear, "Trump Diatribe Belittles Impeachment as 'Attempted Coup' on Eve of Votes," *New York Times*, December 17, 2019, Page A1.
24. Joseph J. Ellis: "Every President Since Washington has been Accused of Misconduct, but Trump's is Off the Charts," December 15, 2019, www.cnn.com/2019/12/14/opinions/trump-impeachment-in-historical-context-ellis.

Selected Readings

Arnold, James R., *Presidents Under Fire: Commanders in Chief in Victory and Defeat*. New York: Orion Books, 1994.

Atkins, Ollie, *The White House Years: Triumph and Tragedy*. Chicago: Playboy Press, 1977.

Bernanke, Ben S., Timothy F. Geithner and Henry M. Paulson, Jr., *Firefighting: The Financial Crisis and Its Lessons*. London: Profile Books, 2019.

Beschloss, Michael, *Presidential Courage: Brave Leaders and How They Changed America 1789-1989*. New York: Simon & Schuster, 2007.

Beschloss, Michael, *Presidents of War*. New York: Crown, 2018.

Blumenthal, Sidney, and Thomas Byrne Edsall, eds., *The Reagan Legacy*. New York: Pantheon Books, 1988.

Bohn, Michael K., *Presidents in Crisis: Tough Decisions Inside the White House from Truman to Obama*. New York: Arcade Publishing, 2015.

Brands, H.W., *The General vs. the President: MacArthur and Truman at the Brink of Nuclear War*. New York: Doubleday, 2016.

Brinkley, Douglas, ed., *The Reagan Diaries*. New York: HarperCollins, 2007.

Brinkley, Douglas, *The Unfinished Presidency: Jimmy Carter's Journey Beyond the White House*. New York: Viking, 1998.

Broder, David S., *Behind the Front Page*. New York: Simon & Schuster, 1987.

Bush, George, *All the Best, George Bush: My Life in Letters and Other Writings*. New York: Scribner, 1999.

Cannon, Lou, *President Reagan: The Role of a Lifetime*. New York, Public Affairs, 1991.

Caroli, Betty Boyd, *Lady Bird and Lyndon: The Hidden Story of a Marriage That Made a President*. New York: Simon & Schuster, 2015.

Carter, Jimmy, *Keeping Faith: Memoirs of a President*. Fayetteville: University of Arkansas Press, 1995.
Carter, Jimmy, *White House Diary*. New York: Farrar, Straus and Giroux, 2010.
Clarke, Richard, *Against All Enemies*. New York: Free Press, 2004.
Clinton, Bill, *My Life*. New York: Alfred A. Knopf, 2004.
Clinton, Hillary, *Hard Choices*. New York: Simon & Schuster, 2014.
Cronin, Thomas, *On the Presidency: Teacher, Soldier, Shaman, Pol*. Boulder, CO: Paradigm Publishers, 2009.
Dallek, Robert, *Flawed Giant: Lyndon Johnson and His Times, 1961-1973*. New York: Oxford University Press, 1998.
Dallek, Robert, *Franklin D. Roosevelt: A Political Life*. New York: Viking, 2017.
Dallek, Robert, *An Unfinished Life: John F. Kennedy, 1917-1963*. New York: Back Bay Books, 2004.
D'Antonio, Michael, *A Consequential President: The Legacy of Barack Obama*. New York: Thomas Dunne Books, 2016.
Deaver, Michael K., *Nancy: A Portrait of My Years with Nancy Reagan*. New York: William Morrow, 2004.
Drew, Elizabeth, *Richard M. Nixon*. New York: Times Books, 2007.
Dobbs, Michael, *One Minute to Midnight*. New York: Alfred Knopf, 2008.
Drury, Allen and Fred Maroon, *Courage and Hesitation: Notes and Photographs of the Nixon Administration*. Garden City, New York: Doubleday & Company, 1971.
Duffy, Michael, and Dan Goodgame, *Marching in Place: The Status Quo Presidency of George Bush*. New York: Simon & Schuster, 1992.
Edwards III, George C. and Stephen J. Wayne, *Presidential Leadership: Politics and Policy Making (Seventh Edition)*, Belmont, CA: Thomson Wadsworth, 2013.
Fitzwater, Marlin, *Call the Briefing! Reagan and Bush, Sam and Helen: A Decade with Presidents and the Press*. New York: Times Books, 1995.
Fleischer, Ari, *Taking Heat: The President, the Press, and My Years in the White House*. New York: William Morrow, 2005.
Garthoff, Raymond L., *Reflections on the Cuban Missile Crisis*. Washington, DC, Brookings Institution, 1989.
Gilbert, Robert E., *The Mortal Presidency: Illness and Anguish in the White House*. New York: Basic Books, 1992.
Goldman, Peter and Tom Mathews, *The Quest for the Presidency 1988*. New York: Simon & Schuster/Touchstone, 1989.
Goodwin, Doris Kearns, *Leadership in Turbulent Times*. New York: Simon & Schuster, 2018.
Goodwin, Doris Kearns, *No Ordinary Time: Franklin and Eleanor Roosevelt: The Home Front in World War II*. New York: Simon & Schuster, 1994.

Greenberg, David. *Republic of Spin: An Inside History of the American Presidency.* New York: W.W. Norton & Co., 2016.
Hamby, Alonzo L., *Man of Destiny: FDR and the Making of the American Century.* New York: Basic Books, 2015.
Hamby, Alonzo L., *Man of the People: A Life of Harry S. Truman.* New York: Oxford University Press, 1995.
Harris, John F., *The Survivor: Bill Clinton in the White House.* New York: Random House, 2005.
Hayes, Stephen, *Cheney.* New York: Harper Collins, 2007.
Heilemann, John and Mark Halperin, *Game Change: Obama and the Clintons, McCain and Palin, and the Race of a Lifetime.* New York: HarperCollins, 2010.
Hitchcock, William I., *The Age of Eisenhower: America and the World in the 1950s.* New York: Simon & Schuster, 2018.
Hundt, Reed, *A Crisis Wasted: Barack Obama's Defining Decisions.* New York: Rosetta Books, 2019.
Johnston, David Cay, *The Making of Donald Trump.* Brooklyn, NY: Melville House, 2016.
Jordan, Hamilton, *Crisis.* New York: G.P. Putnam's Sons, 1982.
Kennedy, Robert F., *Thirteen Days.* New York: W.W. Norton, 1971.
Kennerly, David Hume, *Extraordinary Circumstances: The Presidency of Gerald R. Ford.* Austin, Texas: Center for American History, 2007.
Kuhn, Jim, *Ronald Reagan in Private: A Memoir of My Years in the White House.* New York: Sentinel, 2004.
Lamb, Brian, Susan Swain and C-SPAN, *The Presidents: Noted Historians Rank America's Best—and Worst—Chief Executives.* New York: Public Affairs, 2019.
Learning, Barbara, *Jack Kennedy.* New York: W.W. Norton, 2006.
Theo Lippman, Jr., Theo, *The Squire of Warm Springs: FDR in Georgia 1924–1945.* Chicago: Playboy Press, 1977.
Luca, Trenta, *Risk and Presidential Decision-Making: The Emergence of Foreign Policy Crises (Routledge Studies in U.S. Foreign Policy).* New York: Routledge, 2016.
Lynes, Russell, *The Tastemakers: The Shaping of American Popular Taste.* New York: Dover Publications, Inc., 1980.
Maraniss, David, *First in His Class.* New York: Simon & Schuster, 1995.
Maroon, Fred J., with Tom Wicker, *The Nixon Years 1969–1974: White House to Watergate.* New York: Abbeville Press, 1999.
May, Ernest R. and Philip D. Zelikow, eds., *The Kennedy Tapes.* Cambridge, MA: Harvard University Press, 1997.
May, Nathaniel, ed., *Oval Office: Stories of Presidents in Crisis from Washington to Bush.* New York: Thunder's Mouth Press, 2002.

McChrystal, Stanley, Jeff Eggers and Jason Mangone, *Leaders: Myth and Reality*. New York: Portfolio/Penguin, 2018.
McCullough, David, *Truman*. New York: Simon & Schuster, 1992.
Meacham, Jon, *Destiny and Power: The American Odyssey of George Herbert Walker Bush*. New York: Random House, 2015.
Morris, Dick, *Behind the Oval Office: Winning the Presidency in the Nineties*. New York: Random House, 1997.
Mundy, Liza, *Michelle, A Biography*. New York: Simon & Schuster, 2008.
Nixon, Richard, *In the Arena: A Memoir of Victory, Defeat, and Renewal*. New York: Simon & Schuster, 1990.
O'Donnell, Kenneth P. and David F. Powers, with Joe McCarthy, *Johnny, We Hardly Knew Ye*. Boston: Little, Brown, 1972.
Perry, Barbara A., *Jacqueline Kennedy: First Lady of the New Frontier*. Lawrence, KS: University of Kansas Press, 2004.
Perlstein, Rick, *Nixonland: The Rise of a President and the Fracturing of America*. New York: Scribner, 2008.
Phillips, Kevin, *American Dynasty: Aristocracy, Fortune, and the Politics of Deceit in the House of Bush*. New York: Viking, 2004.
Popadiuk, Roman, *The Leadership of George Bush: An Insider's View of the Forty-First President*. College Station, Texas: Texas A&M University Press, 2009.
Reagan, Nancy with William Novak. *My Turn: The Memoirs of Nancy Reagan*. New York: Random House, 1989.
Reagan, Ronald, *Ronald Reagan: An American Life*. New York: Simon & Schuster, 1990.
Reedy, George E., *The Twilight of the Presidency*. Cleveland, Ohio and New York: New American Library/World Publishing Company, 1970.
Reeves, Richard, *Portrait of Camelot: A Thousand Days in the Kennedy White House*. New York: Abrams, 2010.
Reeves, Richard, *President Kennedy: Profile of Power*. New York: Touchstone/Simon & Schuster, 1993.
Sabato, Larry, *Feeding Frenzy: How Attack Journalism Has Transformed American Politics*. New York: Free Press/Macmillan, 1991.
Sammon, Bill, *Fighting Back*. Washington, DC: Regnery, 2002.
Schweizer, Peter and Rochelle Schweizer. *The Bushes: Portrait of a Dynasty*. New York: Doubleday, 2004.
Skinner, Kiron K., Annelise Anderson, and Martin Anderson, *Reagan: In His Own Hand*. New York: Free Press, 2001.
Sorensen, Theodore C., *Kennedy*. New York: Harper & Row, 1965.
Stephanopoulos, George, *All Too Human: A Political Education*. Boston: Little, Brown, 1999.

Stern, Sheldon M., *Averting 'The Final Failure.'* Stanford, CA: Stanford University Press, 2003.
Stoughton, Cecil and Clifton, Chester V. *The Memories: JFK, 1961–1963.* New York: W.W. Norton & Company, 1973.
Tames, George, *Eye on Washington: The Presidents Who've Known Me,* New York: HarperCollins Publishers, 1990.
Tribe, Laurence and Joshua Matz, *To End a Presidency: The Power of Impeachment.* New York: Basic Books, 2018.
Troy, Gil, *The Age of Clinton: America in the 1990s.* New York: Thomas Dunne Books, 2015.
Truman, Margaret, *Harry S. Truman.* New York: William Morrow & Company, 1973.
Updegrove, Mark K., *Baptism by Fire: Eight Presidents Who Took Office in Times of Crisis.* New York: Thomas Dunne Books, 2009.
Walsh, Kenneth T., *Celebrity in Chief: A History of the Presidents and the Culture of Stardom.* New York: Routledge, 2016.
Walsh, Kenneth T., *Family of Freedom: Presidents and African Americans in the White House,* New York: Routledge, 2011.
Walsh, Kenneth T., *Feeding the Beast: The White House Versus the Press.* New York: Random House, 1996.
Walsh, Kenneth T., *From Mount Vernon to Crawford: A History of the Presidents and Their Retreats.* New York: Hyperion, 2005.
Walsh, Kenneth T., *Prisoners of the White House: The Isolation of America's Presidents and the Crisis of Leadership.* Boulder CO: Paradigm, 2013; Routledge, 2016.
Walsh, Kenneth T., *Ronald Reagan: Biography.* New York: Park Lane Press, 1997.
Walsh, Kenneth T., *Ultimate Insiders: White House Photographers and How They Shape History.* New York: Routledge, 2017.
White, Theodore H., *Breach of Faith: The Fall of Richard Nixon.* New York: Atheneum Publishers, 1975.
Winfield, Betty Houchin, *FDR and the News Media.* New York: Columbia University Press, 1994.
Woodward, Bob, *Bush at War.* New York: Simon & Schuster, 2002.
Woodward, Bob, *Fear: Trump in the White House.* New York: Simon & Schuster, 2018.
Woodward, Bob, The Agenda. New York: Simon & Schuster, 1994.
Woodward, Bob, *The Choice.* New York: Simon & Schuster, 1996.
Zelizer, Julian E., *Jimmy Carter.* New York: Times Books, 2010.

INDEX

9/11 terrorist attacks 161–171

Afghanistan 112, 116, 156, 168–169, 170
African Americans 12, 82
agriculture 27, 29
Air Force One 164–165
al Qaeda 156, 166
Anderson, Rudolf 70, 71
Arnold, James R. 76–77, 143–144, 146
astrology 129–130
attorney generals 87, 90, 194, 195, 200, 207–208
auto industry 182–184

Bacon, Perry 196
banks 24–25, 27, 175–176; *see also* economy
Barr, William 195, 204, 205, 207–208
Bay of Pigs 60, 61, 94
Berlin, wall 61
Bernanke, Ben S. 176, 179–180
Bernstein, Carl 86
bin Laden, Osama 166, 170
Bohn, Michael K. 51, 57, 64, 67, 71–72, 116–117, 144, 170
border wall *see* Mexico
Bradley, Omar 42, 44
Brady, James 123, 131
Brands, H.W. 41, 44, 45
Brinkley, Douglas 32, 194

Brown, Harold 110, 111, 113–114
Brown, Lara 218–219
Brzezinski, Zbigniew 108, 109, 111
Burlingame, Michael 8–9, 12
Bush, George H.W. 169; and the Persian Gulf War 133–148; personal/leadership qualities 145–146; public opinion on 141, 144–145
Bush, George W.: and the 9/11 attacks 161–171; and the banking system 175–176; personal/leadership qualities 157, 162, 168, 170

Cannon, Lou 120
Card, Andy 162–163, 165
Caro, Robert 81
cars 182–184
Carter, Jimmy 105; and the Iranian hostage crisis 107–118; personal/leadership qualities 116–117; use of diplomacy and sanctions 110, 113
Castro, Fidel 61, 63, 94
Cermak, Anton 19, 122
Cheney, Dick 144, 163–164, 165, 166, 167, 169
China 37, 39–40, 209
CIA 51, 94, 100, 168
civil rights 81–82
Civil War, American 8–9, 11–13
Civil Works Administration 27

237

Civilian Conservation Corps (CCC) 30–31
climate change 194
Clinton, Bill: impeachment 86, 150–159, 218–219; personal/leadership qualities 150, 156–157; public opinion on 155, 157, 158
Clinton, Hillary 150, 158, 190
Coan, Andrew 94, 207–208
Cold War: end of 46; the U-2 spy-plane incident 50–58, 61; *see also* Cuba
communism, fear of: anti-communist witch hunts 39, 43, 204; *see also* Korean War; Vietnam War
Confederacy 10, 11
Congress 140, 168; economic and domestic legislation 25, 128, 176, 178, 184, 209; *see also* Constitution; federal government
Constitution 12, 22, 126, 198
Cox, Archibald 86–90, 91
Cuba 94; Cuban Missile Crisis 59–74

Dallek, Robert 4, 20, 21, 25, 37, 72, 80, 122
D'Antonio, Michael 174, 183
Davis, Patti 211–212
Dean, John 87, 92
Dillon, Douglas 52, 62
Doar, John 92–93
Dobrynin (Soviet Ambassador) 69, 71
Dulles, Allen 51, 52

economic sanctions 110, 113, 139, 140, 210
economy: 2008 crisis 13, 174–187; Great Depression 4, 18, 20, 21, 22–23, 25, 27; *see also* employment; taxation; unemployment
Eisenhower, Dwight D. (Ike): personal/leadership qualities 54, 57–58; and the U-2 spy-plane incident 49–58
electricity 19, 29–30
Emancipation Proclamation 12
Emanuel, Rahm 13, 176
employment 27–28, 30–31, 182–184, 209; *see also* unemployment
ExComm 64–66, 69–70

Fahd bin Abdulaziz Al Saud, King of Saudi Arabia 135, 138
farm mortgages 24, 27
FBI 69–70, 90, 94, 95, 100, 202–203
federal courts/law 12, 89; *see also* Supreme Court
federal government 27, 76; shutdown 2018–2019 195–198; *see also* Congress; Constitution
Federal Reserve 178–179
Felzenberg, Al 4
financial and mortgage lending industries 174–175
financial crisis, 2008 *see* economy
Fitzwater, Marlin 136, 138, 139, 141, 143
Fleischer, Ari 163, 165
Ford, Gerard R. 99–106; attempted assassination of 121; pardoning of Nixon 99–100, 103–105; personal/leadership qualities 101, 105
foreclosures 24, 29, 174–175

Galston, Bill 182, 183, 212
Garfield, James 121
Gaulle, Charles de 54, 55–56
Geithner, Timothy F. 176, 178, 179–180
Goldwater, Barry 95
Goodwin, Doris Kearns 4, 10, 13, 80, 82, 212–213
Gorbachev, Mikhail 129, 137
Gore, Al 157, 175
Grant, Ulysses S. 10, 11
Great Depression *see* economy
Greene, John Robert 140, 142
Greider, William 155
Ground Zero, New York 167–168

Haig, Alexander 88, 90, 95, 126
Haldeman, H.R. 90–91, 92, 94
Hamby, Alonzo 38, 43–44
health care reform 184
Herter, Christian 52–53
Hinckley, Jr., John 123, 130–131
Hitchcock, William I. 50, 53–54, 56
Hitler, Adolph 65
Hoover, Herbert 18, 23
housing 24, 29, 175
Humphrey, Hubert 78–79, 81

Index

Hussein, King of Jordan 136
Hussein, Saddam 134, 136, 137, 144, 145, 169, 170

immigrants 193, 198, 218
impeachment *see* Clinton, Bill; Nixon, Richard M.; Trump, Donald
international law 167
Iran 169, 194, 210
Iranian hostage crisis 107–118
Iraq: Gulf War (1991) 133–148; invasion of Iran 115; U.S./allied invasion/occupation of (2003–2011) 168, 169–170; Western coalition/sanctions against 137, 139

Jackson, Andrew 122
Japan 36, 38, 143
Jaworski, Leon 91, 92, 101–102
Johnson, Andrew 86
Johnson, Lady Bird 77, 78
Johnson, Lyndon B. (LBJ) 75–84; death 80; declines to run for re-election in 1968 76, 77, 79–80; personal/leadership qualities 76; public opinion on 77, 80, 81; social activism and legacy 76, 82
Joint Chiefs of Staff, White House 137–138, 167
Jones, James/Jim 78, 79–80
Jones, Paula 152, 157
Jordan, Hamilton 109, 111, 114

Kamps, Charles 114–115
Katz, Milton 30
Kennedy, Edward 105
Kennedy, John F. 77, 121
Kennedy, John F. (JFK) 27, 56; and the Cuban Missile Crisis 59–74; and the Joint Chiefs of Staff 64–66; personal/leadership qualities 67, 71–72
Kennedy, Robert 66, 67, 71
Khomeini, Ayatollah Ruhollah 108, 111, 115
Khrushchev, Nikita: and the Cuban Missile Crisis 60, 63–64, 67–71; and the U-2 spy-plane incident 49–51, 54–56, 57

Kim Jong Un *see* North Korea
King, Jr., Martin Luther 81–82
Klein, Joe 154–155
Korean War 36–46
Kurds 144
Kuwait 133–134; *see also* Persian Gulf War

Lee, Robert E. 11
LeMay, Curtis, Gen. 65–66
Leuchtenburg, William 23
Lewinsky, Monica 149–153, 154
Liddy, Gordon 94–95
Lincoln, Abraham 7–15; assassination of 13, 121; personal/leadership qualities 8–11, 13–14
Lincoln, Mary Todd 11
Lincoln, Willie 11
Lockhart, Joe 153
Los Angeles Times 79–80

MacArthur, Douglas 35–46
Mattis, James 199
Matz, Joshua 95, 100–101
Maxwell Taylor, Gen. 62, 64
McCarthy, Eugene 77, 81
McCarthy, Joseph 39, 43, 204
McClellan, George B. 7, 9
McGahn, Donald F. 206–207
McKinley, William 121
"MeToo" movement 151, 219–220
Mexico 193, 195, 198, 218
Miller, Merle 44–45
Miller Center 96
Moley, Raymond 20, 28
Mondale, Walter 111, 112
Mubarak, Hosni 136
Mueller, Robert 165, 167, 200–208, 220
Murphy, Mike 197

NASA 52
National Security Council 64, 110, 111, 137, 138, 165; *see also* ExComm; Joint Chiefs of Staff
NATO 61, 168, 170, 209
New Deal *see under* Roosevelt, Franklin D.
New Republic 143
New York Times 31–32, 53, 61, 68, 117, 191–192, 197, 206, 207

news media 11, 139, 191–192, 194; *see also* radio; social media; television; *individual names of newspapers*
Nixon, Richard M. 82; news media and 208; resignation and legacy 86, 95–96, 100; Watergate and impeachment 85–98, 101–102, 207–208, 218, 219
North Korea 36, 169, 209, 210–211; *see also* Korean War
North Vietnam *see* Vietnam War
Norton Smith, Richard 13–14, 194
nuclear weapons 36, 40–41, 61–62, 210; agreements/programs 129, 194; *see also* Cuba

Obama, Barack 170, 173–187, 210; economic crisis and recovery plans 173–187; personal/leadership qualities 174, 176, 182, 185
oil 134–135, 136, 144, 210
Operation Eagle Claw 114–115

Pahlavi, Mohammed Reza (Shah) 108–109, 115
Paris summit meeting, and the U-2 incident 54–56
Parr, Jerry 123
Paulson, Henry M. 179–180
Pelosi, Nancy 192, 196, 198
Penn, Mark 156
Perkins, Frances 26, 28, 31
Persian Gulf War, 1991 133–148; casualties 143
Powell, Colin 137–138, 166, 168
Powers, Francis Gary 51, 52, 56
prohibition, end to 22
public opinion: on Carter 116; on Clinton 157, 219; on Ford 104–105; on G.H.W. Bush 141; on G.W. Bush 167–168; on LBJ 77, 80, 81; on Truman 41, 43–44; on Trump 196
Putin, Vladimir 209

Quigley, Joan 129–130

radio 4, 10, 25–27, 40, 68
Reagan, Nancy 124, 127, 129–130

Reagan, Ronald 115, 116; attempted assassination of 120–132; and the Cold War 46, 129; personal/leadership qualities 4–5, 46, 120, 131
Rice, Condoleezza 165, 167
Richardson, Elliot 87, 90
Ridgway, Matthew 41, 42
Roosevelt, Eleanor 18, 19, 20
Roosevelt, Franklin D. (FDR) 17–34, 174; attempted assassination of 19–20, 122; New Deal reforms *17*, 20–21, 24–25, 27–31; personal/ leadership qualities 18–20, 21–23, 30–31, 180; radio "fireside chats" 4, 25–27
Roosevelt, Theodore 122
Rosenstein, Rod 200–201, 203, 206
Rottinghaus, Brandon 157, 219
Rovere, Richard 204
Rumsfeld, Donald 101–102, 104, 165–166, 167, 168, 169
Rural Electrification Administration 19, 29–30
Rusk, Dean (Secretary of State) 62, 63, 69
Russia: and Trump 200, 204, 207; *see also* Cold War; Soviet Union

Saudi Arabia 135, 136, 138, 144, 169
Schumer, Chuck 196, 198
Schwarzkopf, Jr., Norman 138
Scowcroft, Brent 135, 137, 144
Seoul, South Korea 37, 41
Sessions, Jeff 195, 200–201, 206, 207–208
sexual harassment 151, 152
Shah of Iran *see* Pahlavi, Mohammed Reza
Shelton, Hugh 167, 168–169
Shiites 144
Sirica, John J. 88, 89
slavery/slaves 9, 12
Smith, Jean Edward 9, 10
social media 10, 193–194, 202–203
social security/welfare 20, 21, 29
Sorensen, Ted 66, 67
South Vietnam 76
Soviet Union 41, 209; *see also* Cold War; Russia

Starr, Kenneth 150, 151, 155, 157;
    Clinton's fury with 153, 154;
    interrogation of Clinton 152
Stewart, James B. 197
Sudan 156
Summers, Larry 175, 176
Supreme Court 13, 91, 93, 103, 190, 199
Sussman, Barry 86–87, 89–90, 93, 95
Syria 199–200

Taiwan 39–40, 41
Taliban 168
Tanzania 156
taxation 185, 191, 209
television 10, 27, 40, 59, 68, 78–79; Bush and 9/11 164, 165; Clinton and the Lewinsky scandal 153, 155; the Iranian hostage crisis 111, 115; Nixon's resignation 95–96; Persian Gulf War 141; Trump and 192, 209
Tenet, George 165, 166, 168–169
Tet offensive, Vietnam War 76–77
Thatcher, Margaret 135, 136
Time (magazine) 104
Tribe, Laurence 95, 100–101
Troubled Asset Relief Program (TARP) 176
Truman, Harry 35–47; attempted assassination of 121; dismisses MacArthur from command 42–43, 44–45; favours limited war in Korea 37, 40; personal/leadership qualities 38, 44, 46; public opinion on 41, 43–44

Trump, Donald 3–4, 10, 189–215; domestic tax policies 191; foreign policy 191, 194, 199; impeachment 192–193, 218, 220–221; news media/social media and 191–192, 193, 194; personal/leadership qualities 76, 190–191, 193–194, 195, 197–198, 213, 221
Turkey, U.S. missiles in 69, 70, 71
Twitter 10, 193–194, 202–203

U-2 spy plane incident 50–58, 61
UN Security Council: endorses post 9/11 U.S./allied military action 168; resolutions, Persian Gulf War 137
unemployment 18, 20, 177, 178, 179, 185; *see also* employment
United Nations 36
U.S. Constitution *see* Constitution

Vance, Cyrus 108–109, 110, 113, 114
Vietnam War 139, 146; and LBJ 75–83; public opinion on 143–144, 218

Wall Street Crash 18
Washington Post 68, 69, 86, 192, 196–197, 211
Watergate scandal 85–98, 101–102, 219
White House, appointees' turnover rate 199
Woodward, Bob 86
World Trade Center attacks 161–171
World War II 36, 134, 143
Wright, Susan Webber 154, 157

Zelizer, Julian E. 4, 115, 192–193, 220

Taylor & Francis eBooks

www.taylorfrancis.com

A single destination for eBooks from Taylor & Francis with increased functionality and an improved user experience to meet the needs of our customers.

90,000+ eBooks of award-winning academic content in Humanities, Social Science, Science, Technology, Engineering, and Medical written by a global network of editors and authors.

TAYLOR & FRANCIS EBOOKS OFFERS:

- A streamlined experience for our library customers
- A single point of discovery for all of our eBook content
- Improved search and discovery of content at both book and chapter level

REQUEST A FREE TRIAL
support@taylorfrancis.com